Warren County Tennessee

WILLS AND SETTLEMENTS

Volume 3
1887–1910

ABSTRACTED AND COMPILED

BY

Betty Moore Majors

HERITAGE BOOKS
2024

HERITAGE BOOKS

AN IMPRINT OF HERITAGE BOOKS, INC.

Books, CDs, and more—Worldwide

For our listing of thousands of titles see our website
at
www.HeritageBooks.com

A Facsimile Reprint
Published 2024 by
HERITAGE BOOKS, INC.
Publishing Division
5810 Ruatan Street
Berwyn Heights, MD 20740

Originally published 1996

International Standard Book Number
Paperbound: 978-0-7884-8855-9

PREFACE

This is the third in a series of abstracts of the early records of Warren County, TN. As with the previous volumes, this volume deals with the will books of the county. It extends the years covered through 1911, and abstracts information from every page in the Will and Settlement Books 8 through 11 and the years 1900-1910 as found in Volume 1 of the later Will Book. Again, care is taken to retain the spelling of the surnames as found, even though this often varies within a document.

The Will Book, Volume 1 of this County was used to record only the wills, while the earlier Will and Settlement Books were used to record guardianships, appointment of administrators, assignment of dower, claims against the U.S. Government, estate settlements, inventories, and sales, as well as wills. Some of the wills in this later book were previously recorded and unfortunately do not always give date of probate.

DEDICATION

Dedicated to my dear grandchildren Andrew Jonathan Diehl, Benjamin Judson Majors, Christina DeVault Majors and Catherine Elizabeth Majors. "The promise of the past and the hope of the future."

WARREN COUNTY, TN WILLS and INVENTORIES
Book 8, 1887-1892

pg 1-2. 4 Oct 1887. Anderson Safley's Estate Settlement. In the hands of the administrators $474.17. Recipts given by each of the following for $44.60 each: Cynthia Patton, Nancy Green (jointly with J.T. Green), Ann Boulding, Laura Chisom, S. Safley, D.A. Safley and Marion Safley. Balance of moneys in estate paid to debtors and clerks.

pg 3. 27 Oct 1887. Second sale bill of the Jas. Allison estate held at the residence of the Widow of James Allison. Several lots of corn, oats and wheat sold by E.C. Pepper administrator.

pg 3-4. 24 Oct 1887. Inventory and sale bill of the personal property of S.E. Higginbothom. Property purchased by Henry Higginbothom, W.H. Higginbothom, Aaron Higginbothom, Drury Higginbothom, Mrs. S.K.W. Higginbothom, Miss A. Higginbothom and others.

pg 4-5. 18 Oct 1887. M.S. Brewer, administrator of Mrs. M.J. Pollard reports no personal estate of his intestate in this county.

pg 5. 17 Oct 1887. Inventory of the Daniel Miller estate made by David Miller administrator.

pg 6. 17 Oct 1887. Settlement of the estate of Daniel Miller. Receipts for $213.55 each given by the following: Esther Miller, Joseph Miller, Jemima Gribble and David Miller.

pg 7-9. 7 Nov 1887. Inventory and sale bill of the personal estate of Harrison Smith, deceased as returned to the County Court by the administrators A. Smith and W.H. Smith. Purchases made by Mrs. Pete Smith, Butler Smith, Mrs. O. Smith, H. Smith, Byron Smith and others.

pg 9-11. 11 Oct 1887. Inventory of the personal property found as possessed of E.C. Wilson, dec'd as reported by M.L. Sellers and E.P. Wilson, administrators.

pg 11-12. 4 Nov 1887. Final settlement of the estate of J.A. Biles reported by T.M. Carroll, administrator.

pg 13. 23 Oct 1887. **Will of Ed W. Munford.** The last will and testament of Edward W. Munford, revoking all other wills by me made. I hereby give my whole property of every character to my beloved and faithful wife Mary E. Munford.. "the same may be treated to own in her absolute right, she knowing my wishes in regard to the children of my beloved brother William." I appoint her executrix. Witnesses: Thomas Black and W.C. Womack. Probated 5 Dec 1887.

pg 14-15. 3 Dec 1887. Settlement made with W.L. Swann, administrator of Margarett Green's estate.

pg 15-17. 26 Nov 1887. Sale bill of the estate of S.G. Hankins, reported by T.J. Hankins, administrator. Purchases by P.H. Hankins and numerous others.

pg 18-20. 19 Nov 1887. List of the personal property of Robert Webb, dec'd sold by J.K.P. Webb, administrator. Purchasers were S.F. Webb, Sindrilla Webb, L.B. Webb and many others.

pg 21-22. 29 Nov 1887. Sale bill of the personal estate of E.C. Wilson, dec'd sold at public sale on 22 Oct 1887. Most purchases made by Mrs. E.C. Wilson.

pg 23-24. **Will of James P. Stipes.** "I bequeath my wife Cleasanda Stipes all the affects she brought hear with her. As I sold her cow she can take choice of what cows I have to supply the place of the one I sold" [Generous, wasn't he.] Second, I give her my gray mare. Third, I give my only son Avza Lansford Stipes $500.00 and the household furniture that my father gave me. My personal affects are to be sold and after payment of my debts the residue to be equally divided between my wife Clearissa and my son Avza L. Should my son die without issue before he comes in possession of the $500.00 that I gave him, then it is to go back to the one that gave it, to wit, my father or his legal representatives. I appoint Jacob Stipes my executor. Mentions "Day and date above written" but was not dated. Witnessed J.T. Green and W.R. Paine. Presented for probate 3 Jan 1888.

pg 24-26. 21 Dec 1887. George F. Pennebaker, executor of the will of Sam F. Pennebaker, dec'd submits the inventory of the personal property of said dec'd.

pg 26-27. 2 Jan 1888. List of notes found in the papers of Robert Webb, dec'd, reported by J.K.P. Webb, administrator.

pg 27-30. Reported 5 Jan 1888. "Faulkner Springs, March 24, 1884." Inventory and sale bill of the personal property of W.J. Mason, dec'd reported by W.A. Mason, administrator. Purchases by W.A. Mason, Miss Maggie J. Mason, Miss Amanda A. Mason, J.B. Mason, Miss Sallie M. Mason, W.L. Mason, and others.

pg 31. 3 Feb 1888. Inventory and sale bill of the estate of Isaac Rains reported by Jesse Kell and R.R. Rains, executors of Isaac Rains.

pg 32. 4 Feb 1888. Inventory of the personal effects of John Marbury, dec'd that has come to the hands of W.S. Lively, administrator.

pg 33-34. 14 Feb 1888. Settlement of the N.R. Taylor estate made with J.C. Biles, administrator. Receipts for a total of $259.71 given by each of the following heirs: John M. Taylor, H.A. Taylor and Mary Ramsey.

pg 35. 30 Jan 1888. Settlement of the estate of Matilda Smoot, dec'd made with J.C. Smoot, administrator. In the hands of the administrator per sale bill dated 23 Jan 1886, the sum of $316.60. The following vouchers allowed: W.H. Smoot, $50.00; Nannie P. and J.M. Roach, $50.00; J.M. Smoot, $50.00; Sophia Lannon, $50.00; T.J. Henegar, trustee of Jane Willie Henegar and others $37.50; J.B. Henegar, $6.25; Marietta Harrell and Isaac Harrell, $5.00; D.P. Smoot, $5.00; T.M. Smoot, $5.00; and others.

pg 36-38. 18 Feb 1888. Sale bill of the personal property of James Woodlee, dec'd, S.R. Safley, administrator. Most purchases made by Albert and Lela Woodlee, P.A. Hoodenpyle, and Martha and Sallie McGregor.

pg 38-40. 5 Mar 1888. Inventory and sale bill of James Stipes's property which was sold by Jacob Stipes, administrator.

pg 41-41. 23 Feb 1888. Inventory of property sold on 18 Nov 1882 by Wm. Sanders, administrator of James Sanders, dec'd. Purchases made by Flora Sanders, L.P. Sanders, Julia Sanders and others.

pg 42. 5 Mar 1888. List of personal estate of E.C.

Wilson, dec'd sold at public sale on 21 Jan 1888 reported by M.L. Sellars, administrator.

pg 43. 5 Mar 1888. Inventory of personal effects which came to the hands of the administrator of Flora V. Chapman, dec'd. Signed H.H. Faulkner, administrator.

pg 43-44. 5 Mar 1888. Settlement made with J.M. Lively, administrator of Jemima Temple, dec'd.

pg 44. 2 Apr 1888. "Received of Col. Shuke of Nashville, in cash $250.00. I, Houston Durley do solemnly swear that the foregoing is a true report of all the effects that has come into my hands as administrator of Furmon Durley, dec'd." Signed H.D. Durley.

pg 44-45. 2 Apr 1888. List of the personal property of Jesse Slawghter, dec'd reported by Sarah Slawghter and H. Slawghter, administrix and administrator.

pg 45. 27 Mar 1888. Sale bill of the estate of David Wagner, dec'd reported by Joseph Wagner, administrator. Sales made to Thos Wagner, Mrs E.Wagner, C.B. Scott and C.W. Mathews.

pg 46. 2 Apr 1888. Settlement made with R.R. Etter, administrator of G.G. Wagner, dec'd.

pg 47. 10 Mar 1888. Inventory of the personal effects of David Wagner reported by Joseph Wagner, administrator.

pg 47-48. 7 May 1888. Sale bill of the estate or Jessee Slawghter, sold on 14 Apr 1888. Purchasers: Bettie Slawghter, Jesse Slawghter, Hugh Slawghter and others.

pg 48-49. 7 May 1888. Settlement made with W.B. Bridges, administrator of Allen Wilson, Dec'd.

pg 49-50. 17 Mar 1888. Report and settlement made with J.R. Grove, administrator of Jesse D. Jennings, dec'd. First inventory was made 4 May 1884.

pg 51. 26 May 1888. Settlement made with Joseph Wagner, administrator of David Wagner, dec'd. "There are five heirs of David Wagner and from receipts presented by the administrator, F.T. and E. Ganaway,

Thos. Wagner and G.G. Wagner have received from their father David Wagner $115.00 each making a total of $345.00, the amount due Foster Wagner and Susan Wagner, the other two children of David Wagner, to make the equal with the first named heirs is more than the amount in the hands of the administrator. The administrator will therefore divide the amount in his hands (which is $141.60) equally between Foster and Susan Wagner which would give each the sum of $70.80." Receipts signed by S.B. Wagner and Elizabeth Wagner for $70.80 on 18 May 1888.

pg 52-54. 5 May 1888. Inventory and sale bill of the assets of W.T. Swann, dec'd. Notes, accounts and property sold.

pg 55-56. 11 Jun 1888. **Will of John Meggerson.** "I, John Meggerson being of sound mind and having the property exercise of my reasonal facilties and have a perfect wright to dispose of my property at will, I, this day make my last will and testament. I first will my soul to God." I then will to my wife A.M. Meggerson all my real estate (livestock, furniture, etc.) during her lifetime (or widowhood), after her death to be sold and the effects to be equally divided between my daughter Mary Jones and granddaughter Vila Martin. I will to my daughter Mary Jones a side saddle and to her husband John C. Jones my rifle and to my granddaughter Vila Martin $14.00. The stock of goods in the store my executor will invoice and sale to the best advantage. After all my debts are paid my wife is to have $200.00, the remainder to be divided between my wife, my daughter Mary Jones and my granddaughter Vila Martin. I appoint Monroe Redman guardian for my granddaughter and John L. Byars executor.Witnesses: John L. Byars and A.M. Womack. Presented for probate 2 Jul 1888.

pg 57-62. 2 Jul 1888. Settlement made with J.W. and Oliver Towles, administrators of Arthur Towles, dec'd. The amount of $13233.49 divided among the five original heirs, gives each share $2646.69: J.W. Towles, one share; J.D. Lewis, one share; A.T. Mitchell, one share; J.S. Towles, 1/2 share; Eliza Murphy, 1/2 share; J.H. Webb, 1/8 share; John T. Webb, 1/8 share; A.T. Webb, 1/8 share; Mary Couch, 1/8 share; Judith Yagar, 1/8 share; Alice Couch, 1/8 share; Sally Haynes, 1/8 share; and Nancy Earles, 1/8 share.

pg 62-66. 22 Jun 1888. H.R. Etter's estate settlement,

original settlement made 4 Jan 1884. Payments made to date to J.M. Jett and wife May R., F.S. Grizzle and wife Maggie L., J.J. Meadows and wife Emma J., C.M. Rutledge and wife Carrie, W.G. Etter (as assignee of C.H. Etter), E.B. Etter, E. and H.E. Martin, W.T. and E.J. Hill, J.P. Etter, E. and H. Martin.

pg 66. 14 Aug 1888. Final settlement made with Thomas S. Myers, executor of J.W. Hill, dec'd. Per Settlement made 26 Aug 1882, one note for $259.24 due Wm. O. Hill was to remain in said executor's hands until it could be invested in lands and said land be settled upon the dec'd's wife Eugena and children. This land has been bought (Deed Book 15, page 511) so Myers states he has fully complied with the will of J.W. Hill, dec'd.

pg 67. 22 Aug 1888. Inventory of the estate of the late James Elkins--list of notes due. J.D. Elkins, administrator.
Sales bill of the estate of James Elkins, dec'd with purchases made by John Elkins and others.

pg 69-70. 28 Aug 1888. In hands of the administrator of J.H. Roberson, dec'd as of 5 Sep 1885, $23.51. Payments made to estate $451.83 since last report. Receipts of P.A. Roberson, guardian, $61.50; W.T. Roberson, $12.30; C.F. Roberson, $12.30; G.W.D. Roberson, $12.30. W.L. Swann, administrator.

pg 70-72. 30 Aug 1888. Settlement made with R.C. Barnes, administrator of W.C. Barnes, dec'd. Voucher allowed for Elizabeth Barnes, $106.90.

pg 73. 17 Sep 1888. Settlement with E.C. Pepper, administrator of James Allison, dec'd. Vouchers allowed for $1.08 each to: Cyntha Pepper; A. Allison; J.F. Allison; J.W. Allison; J.C. and C. Tolly; B. Allison; R.L. and A.M. Tolly; and E.C. Pepper and wife.

pg 74-75. 21 Aug 1888. **Will of A.J. Curl.** I, A.J. Curl, being of sound mind and memory do make this my last will and testament. My body is to be decently intered according to my standing and condition in life. My executors are to pay off and discharge all my just debts. I will and bequeath to my beloved wife Minerva Curl the balance of my estate--"indeed every character of asset I may die seized and possessed of". I appoint my friend W.C. Womack my executor. Witnessed by Sam McRamsey and Jesse Hill. Offered for probate 5 Nov

1888.

pg 75-80. 5 Nov 1888. Inventory of the personal property and effects of Miles Bonner, dec'd, J.W. Cope and Miles Bonner, administrators of the estate. Sale bill of estate, sale held 13 Oct 1888. Purchases by Fannie Cope, Fannie Winton, Jack Bonner, Ann Scott, William Bonner, Alice Northcutt, Jennie Bonner, Mrs. William Bonner, Pope Bonner and others.

pg 80-91. 24 Aug 1888. Inventory of all the property or assets of Lod Rowland, dec'd which has come into the possession of J.T. Rowland, administrator, not exempt to his widow. Purchases made by L.K. Rowland, J.H. Rowland and many others. Numerous notes listed.

pg 92-94. 28 Jan 1888. **Will of W.E.B. Jones.** I, W.E.B. Jones do make and publish this, my will and Testament. First I will my soul to God my heavenly Father and I desire to be buried in the new Cemetery it the remains of my first wife can be removed, and if not, by her side and I desire my present wife, if she survives me to be buried on the other side of my body and a suitable monument worth $300.00 be erected over or by our graves with our names, ages, birthplace and dates of our birth and death inscribed thereon. If the remains of my first wife cannot be removed I desire to be buried by her side in the old cemetery and a monument erected there. The graves are to be enclosed by an iron railing fence. Second, I desire all my debts be paid. Third I will that my beloved wife Anne have during her natural life the houses and lot in McMinnville on which we now reside and all the household and kitchen furniture that is downstairs except one sewing machine and the piano, and that she to have one horse, buggy and cow. She is also to have a full child's share of my personal estate. Fourth, I will my law books and book cases to my son R.C. Jones if he elects to read law, the value of these to be deducted from his share of the estate. I will a good sewing machine to each of my daughters by my first wife, the value of same to be deducted from their shares and I will them all the household furniture upstairs in the room which they occupy for sleeping. Also to them I devise the town lots on Smithville or Chancery Street opposite my residence. I will the piano to my daughter Ideloi Crmine, the value of same to be deducted from her share of my estate. I will that all my other real estate be sold except the house and lot on which I now reside and

my lands in Dallas County, TX which I will to my son
William B. Jones and Mary Lucretia Jones equally at the
sum of $2000.00 each. My daughter Laura Jane is to
receive $500.00 more that the other legatees and she
shall be trustee for my daughter Emma Vistina. I
appoint my wife Anna L. and Laura J. Jones executrixes.
Codical: 2 Feb 1888. T.C. Lind, W.V. Whitson and Frank
Spurlock gave oath when will was presented for probate.
Date of probate not given.

pg 95-96. 3 Dec 1888. Inventory of the effects of M.F.
McCollock, dec'd presented by J.A. McCollock,
administrator. Sale of effects with purchases by J.M.
McCollock and others.
Sale was held at the residence of the deceased in Viola,
TN.

pg 97-98. 3 Dec 1888. Partial settlement of the estate
of Adam Nunley. Vouchers allowed (in total) to the
following: Mary Nunley, $156.02; T.J. Nunley, $171.05;
E.W. Nunley, $156.90; H.A. and Mary Moore, $155.00;
L.F. Patrick, $155.00; and Harrison Nunley, $186.80.

pg 99. 9 Nov 1888. **Will of Henry C. Brakeman.** First
and last will and testament of Henry C. Brakeman in
sound mind, makes this division of my property. I give
to my only son Stephen B. Brakeman all my property both
read and personal, as I have given to my daughter Flora
Alleman her portion (see deed from me to David and Flora
Alleman for one hald of 150 acres of land. Witnessed by
Thomas Mathews and T.J. Henegar.
Presented for probate 7 Jan 1889.

pg 100-101. 18 Oct 1886. **Will of Delilia Lewis.** I,
Delilia Lewis being of sound mind and memory do make and
publish this my last will and testament. First I give
to my son Sam H. Lewis and his heirs 137 1/2 acres of
land, being the place on which I now live provided he
cares of me during my natural life and settle my funeral
expenses after my death. Second I further bequeath that
the said Sam H. Lewis shall pay to my son J.K.P. Lewis
who now resides in Texas $100.00. Third, I further
bequeath that the said Sam H. Lewis shall pay my
daughter Delilia Rigsby of Warren County $50.00. I
appoint H.J. Christian the executor of this will.
Witnessed by P.G. Potter and Mal Potter. Presented for
porbate 7 Jan 1889.

pg 101-105. 4 Jan 1889. Report made by Mary Turpin,

administrix of L.C. Turpin, dec'd. Settlement of accounts against estate.

pg 106-108. 5 Jan 1889. Inventory of the assets of C.A. Brown, dec'd reported by L.B. Brown and sale of property.

pg 109. 8 Jan 1889. Settlement made with W.A. Mason, administrator of James Mason, dec'd estate. Vouchers allowed for $20.19 to each of the following: Amanda A. Mason, Maggie Mason, J.B. Mason, R.F. Mason, Sallie Mason, G.W. and Mattie Haynes, J.B. and Laura Mitchell and W.A. Mason.

pg 110. 9 Jan 1889. Settlement made this day with J.A. Gilley, administrator of A.Y. Gilley, dec'd. E.L. Smoot, formerly Gilly, voucher for $8.95 and administrators voucher for his share as an heir $8.95.

pg 111-112. 2 Jan 1889. Settlement with S.L. Cunningham, administrator ot Thomas Cunningham, dec'd. The amount of the debts of the estate ($15.75) remains after exhausting the balance of the personal assets in the hands of the administrator.

pg 112. 17 Jan 1889. **Will of Joseph Wagner.** "This is the last will and testament of Joseph Wagner, deceased, given in the presence of the undersigned witnesses 17 Jan 1889. First, I want my wife to have my Viola property and the gray mare and $2000.00 extra. Second, $100.00 to fence the graveyard. Third, each of my nephews and nieces except Oregon Shelton and Joseph Guest to have $100.00. Fourth, all of my sisters to have $100.00 each. Sister Lina Bryant [already] has $10.00 of hers. Fifth, I want $500.00 donated to the Gospel Advocate, the interest which to be used in sending the paper to poor persons who are not able to pay for it. Sixth, I want $500.00 to be used in building a church house in Viola. Seventh, the balance to be used in building up the cause of Christ in Hubbard and Fults Coves as the judgement of E.W. Smartt, John Rutledge and David Wooton may think best." Witnessed W.H. Moore, W.A. Sewell, John Rutledge and M.H. Gwyn. [See Minute Book 8, pages 165 and 166 for probate of this will.]

pg 113. 16 Jan 1889. Following is a settlement made with J.D. Elkins, administrator of James Elkins, dec'd.

pg 114-115. 4 Feb 1889. Inventory and sale bill of the personal property that came to the hands of J.C. Biles, administrator of B.C. Thomas, dec'd. Purchases made by Sam Thomas, Mrs P.E. Thomas and others.

pg 115-116. 12 Jan 1889. Inventory of the personal and real estate of the estate of H.C. Brakeman, dec'd reported by T.J. Henegar, administrator (with will annexed).

pg 116-117. 29 Oct 1888. Inventory of the personal property of the estate of Isaac Brooks, dec'd, reported by H.M. Finger, administrator. Received on 2 Nov 1885 of Matilda Brooks, former administrator, the sum of $66.73.

pg 117-118. 4 Feb 1889. Sale bill of the personal effects of Miles Bonner Sr. sold on 5 Dec 1888. Reported by John W. Cope and Miles Bonner.

pg 119-121. 1 Feb 1889. Settlement of the estate of H.B. Cope, dec'd. Inventory as of 5 Jul 1886 showed $3619.85, present balance $5393.11. Vouchers allowed for $745.00 to each of the following: J.L. and S.E. Comer; J.W.M. Cope [James]; Mary E. Morrow; A.T. Cope; H.J. and R.J. King; and J.W. Cope [John]. Reported by J.W. Cope, administrator.

pg 121-122. 21 Feb 1889. Inventory of the personal assets of the estate of Lucinda Jennings by O.B. Jennings,administrator. Vouchers allowing $16.50 to each of the following: J.E. and Elizabeth McGee; C. Tally; and J.D. Jennings. Vouchers for $8.25 each to H.C. Martin and W. Jennings.

pg 122-123. 4 Mar 1889. Inventory of the personal assets of A.J. Curl, dec'd which has come into the possession of W.C. Womack, executor of said A.J. Curl.

pg 123-124. 11 Feb 1889. Personal property of J. Meggerson, dec'd (notes and accounts). J.L. Byars, executor.

pg 124-129. 23 Feb 1889. Inventory of the personal effects of W.D. Smartt, dec'd reported by F.G. Smartt, administrator. Sale held 1 Feb 1889 with purchases made by Mrs. W.D. Smartt, Leucion Smartt, G.M. Smartt, J.P. Smartt, and others.

pg 129-130. 4 Mar 1889. Sale bill of the property of Jesse Slawghter, dec'd sold on 16 Feb 1889, by Hugh Slawghter, administrator.

pg 130. 22 Feb 1889. "To the Worshipful County Court of Warren County, the undersigned administrator would report that the following is an inventory and sale bill of the personal property of J.W.M. Cope, dec'd." Purchases made by: E.A. Cope [Elizabeth, the widow]; J.W. Cope [John, his brother]; and others. Reported by A.T. Cope [Adrian, another brother] the administrator.

pg 131-132. 3 Mar 1889. Inventory of the notes, accounts and other personal property of Joseph Wagoner, dec'd, reported by John Rutledge, one of the executors.

pg 132-133. 5 Mar 1889. Settlement made with J.J. Meadows, administrator of Harriett Moffitt, dec'd.

pg 133-145. 4 Mar 1889. Inventory of the personal estate (accounts, stock certificates and notes held) of W.E.B. Jones, dec'd, reported by the executixes of said estate, Mrs. Ann Jones and Miss Laura Jones.

pg 146. 5 March 1889. **Will of C. Coffee.** I, C. Coffee do make and publish this as my last will and testament revoking all other wills made. First, I direct that my debts be paid. Second, I have advanced my daughter Lela Lewis $1200.00. Third, I give to my daughters Halley and Jessee $1200.00 to make them equal with Lela. Fourth, I give to my wife Mary E. Coffee all the rest of my property both real and personal. Fifth, this gift to my daughters Hallie and Jessee are to them and their heirs. Sixth, at my wife's death, my property is to be divided between my three daughters. Seventh, I appoint my wife Mary E. Coffee my executor. Witnessed F.L. Leeper and Thomas Black. Presented for probate 1 Apr 1889.

pg 147-148. 1 Apr 1889. Inventory and sale bill of the personal property sold by J.T. Rowland, administrator of Lod Rowland, dec'd. Purchases made by Dick Rowland, Fulton Rowland, W.D. Rowland and others. One due bill on J.T. Rowland for $6.00 dated 7 Sep 1887.

pg 148-149. 17 Feb 1889. Sale bill and inventory of James Cunningham made by S.L. Cunningham, administrator. Purchasers Thomas Cunningham, William Cunningham, S.L. Cunningham and others.

Warren County, TN Will Book 8, Cont.

pg 149-150. 2 Apr 1889. A true and perfect list of personal property of Joseph Wagoner sold at public sale 23 Feb 1889 reported by John Rutledge.

pg 151. 30 Mar 1889. Settlement made with Houston Durley, administrator of Furman Durley, dec'd. Receipts for $22.86 given by Jinnie Durley and Charles Spurlock and Mollie Spurlock.

pg 152-153. 22 Apr 1889. Settlement made with P.G. Potter, executor of Zenos Sanders as required by law. Executor paid out $8.91 more than had come into his hands.

pg 153-155. 6 Apr 1889. Inventory of the personal estate of Leroy Hammons, dec'd by T.J. Henegar, administrator. Sale held 11 Apr 1889 lists purchases by Mrs. Hammons, T.F. Hammons, J.C. Hammons and others.

pg 156. 29 Apr 1889. Supplementary inventory of the F.M. McColloch estate made by J.A. McColloch, administrator.

pg 157. 29 Apr 1889. Settlement made with L.D. Mercer, administrator of John Fancher, dec'd. Voucher allowed for Mrs. Ann Fancher.

pg 158-159. 19 Apr 1889. Allen Wilson, dec'd estate settlement made with W.B. Bridges, administrator. In the hands of the administrator for settlement $1446.18 distributed thusly-- Vouchers for $103.14 each to: L.M. and R. Keaton; J.B. Wilson; Isaac L. Wilson; C.C. and Jas. Griffith; J.D. Wilson; W.B. and S.E. Burks; H.W. Wilson; Nancy Bridges; and M.J. and E. Butterbaugh. Vouchers for $51.57 each to: R.A. Craddock, J.T. Craddock, Samantha Hewit, Jeptha Wilson, Jasper L. Wilson, and T.N. Wilson. Vouchers for $34.38 each to: Thomas Wilson, John Love Wilson and Emsley D. Wilson. Voucher for $37.48 to D.W. Summers for J.P. Summers, N.J. Summers, D.W. Summers and J.W. Summers. Vouchers for $9.37 to: R.H. Summers; A.A. Summers; J.W. Summers; T.G. Summers; S.A and Jesse Cook; Elizabeth Dixon; and H.S. and N.L. Sauls.

pg 159. 2 May 1889. Settlement made with A.B. Webb, administrator of Anner Cantrell, dec'd. T.B. Cantrell, trustee for William and Della Cantrell.

pg 160. 3 Jun 1889. Inventory of goods on hand of the

John Meggerson estate reported by J.L. Byars.

pg 160-162. 29 Mar 1887. **Will of Martha Drake.** "By these presents <u>no</u> all men that I, Martha Drake do make this my last will and testament to the <u>airs</u> names in this will to wit: 1. John A. McGee, his airs four in number are to have his share. 2. Joseph E. McGee is to have his share while he lives after his death it is to go to his wife and children and is not to be squondered in any way. 3. Mary Ann Argo is to have 25 acres of land where she now lives including the buildings and spring. Some of the land to be timbered land after her death it is to return to her children if this 25 acres of land does not make Mary Ann Argo equal with the rest of the <u>ares</u> she is to be made equal out of the rest of estate. 4. Martin V. McGee is to have his proportional part with the rest of the children. 5. Archible McGee's porportional part is to be equally divided between his children six in number, each one of them that is of age I want them paid off their part all that are minors I [want] a guardian appointed for them. 6. James M. McGee his children is to have his portortional part they are five of his children all of them that are of age I want paid their part those that are minors I want a guardian appointed. 7. Martha C. McGee is to have $50.00 over and above her equal proportion and to be her own to hold and possess as her own while she lives and after her death to asend to her ares and my request is that she invest her part in land that she may have a home. 8. Rewben M. Drake my now living husband I want him to have a shear equal with the other airs. 9. I now state in this will that Joseph McGee has paid me all that he ever owed me and I have <u>bin</u> value compensated and I make his an equal <u>are</u> with the other ares. 10. All my personal property is to be sold and used to pay off my debts... 11. I now state if any of the above named airs are dissatisfied with this my will and bring suit or cause suit to be brought against the other airs such airs are to have nothing." Witnesses J.P. Quick and J.D. Jennings. Presented for probate 1 Jul 1889.

pg 162. 2 Jul 1889. Settlement made with Thomas S. Myers, special administrator of Jacob Akeman, dec'd.

pg 163-165. 25 Jun 1889. Inventory of the personal assets of the estate of E.J. Stubblefield, dec'd reported by Mrs. E. Stubblefield, executrix.

pg 165-168. 6 Jun 1889. Sale of property of William Collier held 18 Jan 1889 by John H. Collier administrator. Purchases made by Charley Collier, Jas. Collier, John Collier, Mrs. Nancy Collier, Cal Collier, Jessee Collier, W.P. Collier, Bud Collier, Nannie Collier, Widow Collier and others.

pg 169. 9 Nov 1886. **Will of Elizabeth Savage.** I, Elizabeth Savage do make and publish this as my last will and testament. First I direct that funeral expenses and debts be paid. First, I give and bequeath to my son John H. Savage and my daughter Elizabeth Davis all my money and property of any kind and appoint them my executors. I direct my executors to place over me and my husband George Savage such a monument as they think proper. I have heretofore given John H. Savage my lame mare. Witnessed by W.L. Sleakley Sr. and N.A. Roach. Presented for probate 5 Aug 1889.

pg 170. 21 Jun 1889. Settlement made with W.L. Swan, administrator of Margarett Green, dec'd. Vouchers for $69.35 each allowed for: Lucinda Lawson; Irene Baird; W.R. and J.S. Lowry; E.H. Green; Cindrilla Smith; Mauray and Whitson, assignee of Sam Green. Vouchers for $34.68 allowed for both E.R. Romans and J.B. Boren.

pg 171. 20 Jul 1889. Settlement made with L.D. Mercer, administrator of John Fancher, dec'd. Vouchers for $36.18 allowed for: Emily Joynes[?]; J.M. Fancher; Ann Fancher; W.and S. Barker; and W.and M. Fairchild. The administrator is credited for the share of Charles S. Fancher as he is indebted to the estate for $42.13.

pg 172-173. 3 Aug 1889. Sale bill of the estate of Rachel Green, dec'd by J.M. Smith, administrator.

pg 174-175. 16 Jul 1889. Inventory of the notes and accounts due the estate of William Collier, dec'd reported by John H. Collier, administrator. Notes of James and Jerome Collier, W.P.Collier, and J.T. Collier, as well as others. Accounts on W.P.Collier, C.M. Collier and others.

pg 176-178. 5 Aug 1889. List of property sold by O.D. Denton, administrator of Isaac Denton, dec'd on 7 Mar 1889. Purchasers J.M. Denton, Widow Denton, Sarah Denton, Green Denton, Isaac Denton, Octa Denton, Della Denton, Nancy Webb, Ella York, and others.

pg 178-180. 5 Aug 1889. Inventory of the estate of Jno W. Towles, dec'd. John H. Towles and Oliver Towles administrators.

pg 181-182. 1 May 1889. Settlement made with W. Smith, executor of W.O. Smith, dec'd. Voucher for $600.00 for W. Smith's share as devised by will.

pg 183. 30 Aug 1889. Supplementary inventory and sale bill of the personal estate of Miles Bonner, dec'd made by John W. Cope and Miles Bonner, administrators.

pg 184. 2 Sep 1889. Inventory of the property of Z.R. Smith, dec'd reported by G.W. Smith, administrator.

pg 185. 17 Aug 1889. List of property sold of Oliver Brewer, dec'd. Purchases by P. Brewer, T.H. Brewer, Phebe Brewer, E.B. Brewer, Elizabeth and Thomas Belcher. John R. Belcher, administrator.

pg 186. 26 Aug 1889. Sale of the Charity Barnes, dec'd property on 24 Aug 1889 reported by Isaac Barnes.

pg 187-188. 18 Sep 1889. **Will of E.R.P. Reynolds.** I, E.R.P. Reynolds, being of sound mind and memory, do make and publish this as my last will and testament. Item 1. All of my just debts to be paid. Item 2. I will to my beloved wife Susan Ann Reynolds all the balance of my effects both real and personal, including my Viola property for her life or widowhood. In the event of her marriage I want my remaining estate sold and equally divided between her and my ten children namely: Elizabeth H. Morgan, Allie C. Reynolds, Martha B. Etter, George Francis Reynolds, Edna S. Reynolds, Sarah J. Reynolds, Jesse E. Reynolds, Dillard G. Reynolds, Charles H. Reynolds and Mamie Reynolds. I appoint my brother H. James Morrow and my friend P.H. Winton my executors. Witnesses J.L. Thaxton and W.E. Garner. Presented for probate 7 Oct 1889.

pg 188-189. 2 Sep 1889. **Will of Robert McCorkle.** I, Robert McCorkle, Sr. of Warren County do hereby make this my last will and testament. First, I wish that all my debts and burial expences be paid. Second, I leave to my wife all my personal property of every kind except 100 acres which I leave to my niece Martha Poe. Fourth, Martha Poe to have 100 acres of land adjoining to her place including the improvement where Sims Vickers once lived and adjoining T.S. Myers land. Fifth, I leave my other lands to Effa Turner, and all the other lands not named above, including my lands in Vanburen County, to my nephews and nieces and heirs, brothers and sisters children, to be divided equally between them. Sixth, I appoint my wife Elizabeth my executor. Witnessed by Thomas S. Myers, Andrew M. Savage and Hallie G. Savage. Presented for probate 8 Oct 1889.

pg 189-190. 2 Oct 1889. Settlement made with T.S. Myers, administrator of Jacob Akeman, dec'd. Vouchers allowed for $11.00 each to the following: M.D.L. and J.A. Boyd; May J. Boyd and Vesta Turner; Martha Cantrell, Mary Savage and S.S. Akeman; John L. and D.T. Hays; and L.P. and J.F. Akeman.

pg 190-192. 2 Oct 1889. Settlement made with G.M Fults, administrator of David Fults, dec'd. Receipts for $13.12 from the following: G.W. Fults, James Hobbs, J.B. Tipton, A.J. Fults, Albert Crouch, Nathan Crouch, C.M. Northcut, W.E. Northcutt, and L.F. Fults.

pg 192-193. 11 Sep 1889. Settlement made with Jesse Hill and R.R. Rains, executors of Isaac Rains, dec'd.

pg 193-194. 4 Oct 1889. Settlement made with W.E. Nunley, administrator of Adam Nunley, dec'd. Vouchers allowed for $63.08 each to: L.P. Patrick, Sarah F. Nunley, T.J. Nunley, Harrison Nunley and H.A. Moore. Other vouchers allowed to: Harrison Nunley, $40.00; H. Patrick, $11.00; L.F. Patrick, $40.00; E.W. Nunley by H.B. Northcutt, $9.75; E.W. Nunley, $60.00; T.J. Nunley, $50.00. Previous report 14 Feb 1887.

pg 195-196. 14 Sep 1889. Sale bill of the personal property of the estate of Anderson Jourdon, dec'd held 14 Sep 1889.

pg 197-200. 4 Nov 1889. Settlement made with F.M. Moffitt, executor of the will of W.C. Hill, dec'd. "I give the executor F.M. Moffitt credit as an heir of said W.C. Hill, his share $1219.75."

pg 200-201. 4 Nov 1889. Settlement made with Sterling Savage, administrator of Elizabeth Savage, dec'd.

pg 201-202. 2 Nov 1889. Inventory and sale bill of the personal property of E.R.P. Reynolds sold on 17 Oct 1889 reported by H.J. Morrow, one of the administrators.

Warren County, TN Will Book 8, Cont.

pg 203-204. 18 May 1888. **Will of Mary D. Campbell.** I, Mary D. Campbell do make my will leaving my sister Blanch L. Lewis my now four living children Clarene Campbell, Connelly Trigg Campbell, Lureta Campbell, Eugena Campbell. The aforesaid Blanch L. Lewis taking full control of the estate as executor and having an equal share with my aforesaid children in the estate. To my eldest child Clarene Cambpell I bequeath my diamond ring and the watch given me by cousin Louise Jones. To Connelly Trigg Campbell his father's watch. To Lureta Campbell my watch and a chain given me by my dear husband. To Eugenie Campbell my set of Comes Jewelry. All other personal effects to be divided as described in a private letter to the aforesaid Blanch L. Lewis. Signed Mary D. Campbell at Nashville, TN. Witnessed by J.W. Turner, Louella Turner and E.C. Lewis. Presented for probate 7 Sep 1889.

pg 204-205. 29 Oct 1888. **Will of Nancy Brewer.** I, Nancy Brewer being of sound mind and desposing memory do make and publish this as my last will and testament. First, I desire that after death that my body be decently buried. Second, I desire that my funeral expenses and debts by paid. Third, It is my will that my husband Soloman Brewer shall have the tract of land on which we now reside. Said lands are bounded on the north by the Hopkins heirs, on the east by Elisha Bates, on the south by lands of Dyers heirs and on the west by Carr's land, containing 102 acres. Witnessed by J.A Lance and R.C. Barnes Presented for probate 2 Dec 1889.

pg 205-206. 3 Nov 1889. Second sale bill of the estate of Leroy Hammons, reported by T.J. Henegar, administrator.

pg 207. 2 Dec 1889. Settlement made with S.H.W. Higginbothom, administrator of S.E. Higginbothom, dec'd.

pg 208. 20 Nov 1889. Settlement made with Samuel Garmon, administrator of Mary Smith, dec'd. Vouchers allowed for $10.44 each to Jo Baldin, Donie Garmon, J.B. Garmon, Peter Garmon and Andrew and Eliza Grubbs. S. Garmon's share and that of Paralee Hammons given as $52.20.

pg 209. 20 Nov 1889. Settlement made with J.C. Biles, administrator of B.C. Thomas, dec'd.

pg 209-211. 4 Nov 1889. Inventory of notes, accounts, etc that came to the hands of the administrator which was possessed of Samuel Fuston, dec'd. Signed by W.J. Fuston, administrator.

pg 212-213. 8 Nov 1889. Settlement with R.H. Mason, administrator of Sam Black, dec'd.

pg 213-214. 28 Nov 1889. Settlement made with John Scott and Arch Scott, executors of Cooper Scott, dec'd.

pg 215-216. 7 Jan 1890. Supplementary sale bill of the estate of Miles Bonner, dec'd, sale held 30 Sep 1889 by J.W. Cope and Miles Bonner.

pg 216. 4 Jan 1890. Inventory and sale bill of the estate of Rachel Green, dec'd by J.M. Smith administrator.

pg 217. 13 Jan 1890. Report of E.C. Crane administrator of E.C. Jennings, dec'd.

pg 217. 30 Jan 1890. Settlement with S.E. Bratcher, administrix of W. Bratcher, dec'd. She is entitled to the balance in the estate of said W. Bratcher since he had no living children.

pg 217-218. 25 Jan 1890. Sale bill of the personal property of Isaac Denton, dec'd sold by the administrator O.D. Denton.

pg 218-220. 31 Jan 1890. Sale bill of the estate of E.S. Dunlop, dec'd held 19 Oct 1889. Purchases made by J.L. Dunlop, D.S. Dunlop, D.C. Dunlop, David Dunlop, Jr., and others. Reported by J.L. Cummings, administrator.

pg 220-221. 3 Feb 1890. Settlement made with Jacob Stipes, administrator of James Stipes, dec'd. G.S. Stipes, guardian receipt for $882.85. Clarinda Stipes receipt for $322.85.

pg 221-225. 1 Feb 1890. Sale bill of the personal estate of Samuel Fuston, sold at public sale 23 Nov 1889. Purchases made by W.J. Fuston, the Widow Fuston, Willie Fuston, Sam Fuston, and others.

pg 226-227. 8 Feb 1890. Settlement made with J.W. Cope, one of the administrators of Miles Bonner, dec'd.

Receipts of the heirs: receipts for $10.00 each by Fannie F. Winton, Mattie Winton, A.C. and May Christian, Ed Winton and Mollie Winton; receipts for a total of $200.00 each by Miles Bonner, Polk Bonner, W.C. and Sara Lock, William Bonner, A.J. Bonner; receipt for $100.00 by Milton Bonner; receipt for $15.00 by J.L. Bell.

pg 227-229. 18 Jan 1890. Statement of sale of property of Joseph D. Walling, dec'd by Thomas Walling, administrator. Purchases by Mrs. Harriet Walling, Jesse Walling, Nee[?] Walling, and others. Thomas Walling was of Boyd County, Ky in Feb 1890.

pg 229-230. 26 Feb 1890. Supplementary sale bill and inventory of the estate of H. Smith, dec'd.

pg 230-231. 28 Apr 1882. **Will of J.P. Scott.** I, J.P. Scott of Warren County do make this my last will and testament. First I direct that my body be decently intered at Mt. Zion in said county in a manner suitable to my condition in life, and as to such worldly estate as it has pleased God to intrust me with I dispose of as follows: First, I direct that my debts and funeral expenses be paid. Secondly, I will to my two daughters Mary E. Scott and Emma G. Scott and my son Elemmons B. Scott all my estate, both real and personal after the said two have recieved a good horse apiece and Mary E. a saddle out of my estate. The above is on condition that the above named children provied for and take proper care of their mother Mary D.A. Scott and their sister Martha J. Scott til their death. Witnessed by J.A. Biles and C.W. Mathews. Codicil dated 10 May 1882: My son William Scott shall have one dollar only out of my estate. Presented for probate 7 Apr 1890.

pg 232. 31 Mar 1890. Jesse Walling, administrator of O.H. Argo, dec'd reports that he has received a total of $1598.30 in the estate.

pg 233. 24 Apr 1890. Settlement with L.D. Mercer, administrator of John Fancher, dec'd. Vouchers for $6.83 each allowed to the following: W.M. and M.L. Fancher, Susan W. Baker, E. and J. Joyes[?], J.W. Fancher and Ann Fancher.

pg 233-234. 16 Apr 1890. Inventory of the personal estate of Mary Douglas, dec'd reported by M.Y.Troglin.

pg 234-235. 8 Apr 1890. Settlement made with C.M.

Rutledge, administrator of J.A. Safley, dec'd. (Former administrator J.M. Cunningham.)

pg 235-236. 5 May 1890. List of personal property made by W. Coppinger which was sold at the sale of John Stoner, dec'd on 26 Apr 1890. All purchases made by Susan Stoner.

pg 236-238. 13 May 1883. **Will of L. Brown.** Know all men by these presents that I, L. Brown of Warren County, farmer, in bad health and of a sound and disposing mind and memory do make and publish this my last will and testament. First, my will is that all my just debts and funeral expences be paid. Item 1, I give to my beloved wife S. J. Brown all my household goods, the use and income of my dwelling house land in District 13 "so long as she wears or keeps my name". At her death I will that all the above named items be sold by my executor and that equal distribution be made to my lawful heirs to wit: J.D. Brown, N.L. Brown, M.E. Hopkins, E.W. Brown, L.J. Brown, M.F. Brown, H.L. Brown, and Lillie S. Brown. H.L. Brown is to be given one black mare and my above named eight heirs to share equal. My two sons N.L. and E.W. Brown to be executors. Witnesses Z. Edge and J.M. Sparkman. Presented for probate 2 Jun 1890.

pg 239. 20 May 1890. An inventory of the personal property and effects of the estate of Mary L. campbell, dec'd reported by her executrix Blanch L. Lewis.

pg 239-240. 19 May 1890. Inventory and sale bill of the personal estate of S.H. Lewis, dec'd made by Martha E. Lewis. Sale held on 19 Oct 1889 with purchases made by Russell Lewis, J.K.P. Lewis and others.

pg 240-241. 21 May 1890. Report of funds received by H.B. Higginbotham, administrator of C.B. Chastein, dec'd.

pg 241-242. 31 May 1890. Settlement made with H.B. Higginbotham, administrator of C.B. Chastein, dec'd.

pg 242-243. 2 Jun 1890. Settlement made with T.J. Henegar, administrator of H.C. Brakeman, dec'd.

pg 243-245. 31 May 1890. Report of E.P.Wilson, one of the administrators of E.C. Wilson, dec'd.

pg 245-248. 2 May 1890. List of accounts on the books

of E.H. Williams, dec'd for 1889 made by T.E. Mabry, administrator.

pg 248-251. 4 Jul 1890. A true and perfect inventory and report of the personal estate and sale of the personal property which was subject to sale of the estate of J.R.P. Goodson, dec'd reported by John Goodson, administrator. Purchases by Tempie Goodson, R.V. Goodson, and others.

pg 252-253. 7 Jul 1890. Inventory of the estate of J.B. Dulue. Sale of a small amount of personal property with most purchases made by Harriett Dulue.

pg 253. 20 Jun 1890. Settlement made with T.J. Henegar, administrator of H.C. Brakeman, dec'd.

pg 254-255. 11 Jun 1890. **Will of James Purser.** I, James Purser of Warren County do make and publish this as my last will and testament. First, I direct my funeral expences and just debts be paid. Second, I have given my wife Paralee Purser $437.00, for which I have her receipt in lieu of Dower as stated in the receipt. I now direct that my executors pay her $100.00 which is all that I desire her to have either of my real or personal estate. Third, I give my son Luke Purser my 50 acre tract of land known as the Hagan tract. Fourth, I direct my executors to sell my home place containing about 100 acres and pay the proceeds of sale as follows: John Purser, $100.00; Jim Purser, $125.00; the children of my daughter Malvina, dec'd, $50.00 each. If there should be any [money] left after paying the amounts specified, I want it to be equally divided between my wife Paralee and my children now living. I appoint my son John Purser and my son in law Joe G. Byars executors of this my last will and testament. Witnessed by J.F. Morford and J.L. Neal. **Codicil:** 11 Jun 1890. I give the unto the following named persons the personal property of my estate: to my son John Purser.... to my wife Paralee Purser....., to my two granddaughters Florence and Malvina Byars.... to my daughter Mary Byars.....to my son James Purser... to my daughter Jane Byars... to my son Luke Purser.... to my daughter in law Melvina Purser... to my son in law J.G. Byars... Witnessed J.L. Neal and A.J. Cantrell. Recorded 4 Aug 1890.

pg 256. 26 Jul 1890. Settlement made with B.W. Womack, administrator of Artomisa Bethel, dec'd. Report of three

Warren County, TN Will Book 8, Cont.

sale bills.

pg 257. 1 Jul 1890. Settlement made with Hugh Slawghter, one of the administrators of Jesse Slawghter. Mrs Sarah Slawghter allowed $150.00.

pg 257-258 26 Jul 1890. Inventory of the personal property of J.M. Clendenon, dec'd reported by A.J. Clendenon, administrator.

pg 258-261. 20 Jul 1890. Sale bill and inventory of the personal estate of Martha McGregor, dec'd. Purchases made by Sallie McGregor and many others.

pg 262. 1 Sep 1890. Settlement made with John Cope, one of the administrators of Miles Bonner, dec'd. Vouchers allowed for A.L. and L.M. Christian, Fannie Winton, W.F. and T.G. Winton, P.H. Winton (as guardian), and L.F. and J.W. Cope.

pg 263-264. 26 Aug 1890. Settlement made with Jesse Hill and Elizabeth Swann, administrators of W.T. Swann, dec'd.

pg 265-266. 11 Aug 1890. Settlement made with J.D. Elkins, administrator of James D. Elkins, dec'd. Vouchers allowed for $67.30 to each of the following: Mira Smith and H. Smith; J.T. Collier; S.A. Hamilton; R. and N.E. Duncan; J.H. Collier; and J.C. and M.M. Womack. Vouchers allowed of $66.66 each to: W.P. Collier; Jess Collier; and C.M. Collier. Vouchers for $600.00 each allowed J.D. Elkins, Myra Gribble, Susan Elkins, and Jane Elkins.

pg 266. 19 Aug 1890. Settlement made with J.W. Smith, administrator of Rachel Green, dec'd.

pg 267-268. 1 Sep 1890. Settlement made with Mrs. M.E. Winton administrix of Stephen Winton, dec'd. Vouchers allowed for $7.80 each to: Jinnie L. Bryant, S.L. Wooten, J.A. Bryant, and Mrs. Winton. H. Walling guardian's receipt for $17.60.

pg 269-270. 22 Aug 1890. Settlement made with W.H. Smith and A. Smith, administrators of Harrison Smith, dec'd.

pg 270-271. 1 Sep 1890. Supplementary inventory and sale bill of the estate of Jessee Slawghter, dec'd reported by Hugh Slawghter, administrator.

pg 271. 29 Aug 1890. Settlement made with W. Sanders, administrator of James Sanders, dec'd.

pg 272. 1 Sep 1890. Settlement made with J.R. Gardner, administrator of Mary McGregor, dec'd.

pg 272-274. 23 Aug 1890. Inventory and sale bill of the property belonging to the estate of W.M. Brixey, dec'd, A.G. Jones, administrator.

pg 275. 6 Sep 1890. Settlement made with Mrs. Gracy Rodgers (now Nowlin), guardian of George Rodgers.

pg 275-276. 6 Oct 1890. Partial inventory of the personal estate of Zebeda Edge, dec'd made by G.W. Newby and J.M. Sparkman, administrators.

pg 276-277. 3 Nov 1890. Inventory and sale bill of the estate of James C. Edwards, dec'd as reported by J.J. McAfee, administrator. Sale held on 29 Oct 1890 with purchases made by Martha C. Edwards, J.P. Edwards and others.

pg 278. 21 Oct 1890. Final settlement made with H.L. Walling, guardian of Henry Jones who is now 21 years of age.

pg 279. 20 Oct 1890. Settlement made with John Scott and Arch Scott, executors of Cooper Scott, dec'd.

pg 280-281. 23 Oct 1890. Inventory and settlement made with Mrs. Harriett A. Clark, administrator of Johnson P. Clark, dec'd.

pg 282-283. 20 Nov 1890. Settlement made with Jessie Hill and Elizabeth Swan, administrators of W.T. Swan, dec'd.

pg 284. 1 Dec 1890. Sale bill of the personal property sold 30 Aug 1890 belonging to the estate of Zebeda Edge, dec'd. Purchases made by Mary Ann Edge, J.B. Edge and others. Reported by J.M. Sparkman, one of the administrators.

pg 285. 10 Dec 1890. Settlement made with J.R. Edge, administrator of J.B. Dulee [Dulu?], dec'd. Receipts from M.H. Dulee the widow.

pg 286. 30 Sep 1890. **Will of Massis Gaffin.** I Massis Gaffin of Warren County, realizing the uncertainty of life and being in feeble health but of sound mind and memory and judgment do make this my last will and testament freely and voluntarily, having full confidence in the judgment and managing ability of my beloved wife Jennie C. Gaffin, I hereby give and bequeath unto her my entire estate and nominate her as sole executrix of this my last will and testament. Witnessed by W.G. Cummings and O.F. Bruster. No probate date given.

pg 287. 31 Dec 1890. **Will of Aaron Burleson.** I, Aaron Burleson, do make and publish this my last will and testament. First I will and bequeath to my daughter Caroline Watley and her heirs the portion of my lands south of a line at my corner in the old Tucker line, running East across the Shellsford Road to Cardwell's line, also the mountain side tract. All north of said line to be sold and divided as follows after my debts are paid: Henry Dodson to have $5.00; Jesse B. Dodson to have $10.00; Ellen Dodson to have $10.00; and Mary Crittenden, $20.00. The remainder to be equally divided between my other daughters to wit: Lucinda Molder, Maria Molder, and Mary Frost, her son David Ben to have 2/3 of her share.. I give to Lucinda Watley all of my household furniture and I give Logan Watley my silver watch. The remainder of my property to be sold and given to Caroline Watley and her children. I appoint Albert Martin my executor. Witnessed my W.M. Maxwell and W.M. Bost. No probate date given.

pg 288. 30 Dec 1890. Settlement made with E. Patrick, administrator of William Patrick, dec'd. M.A. Patrick, widow of William Patrick.

pg 289. 29 Dec 1890. Settlement made with J.C. Jourdan, administrator of Andrew Jourdan, dec'd.

pg 290-291. 2 Jan 1891. Settlement made with Miss Blanch L. Lewis, executrix of Mrs. Mary L. Campbell, dec'd. Under the will of Mrs. Mary L. Campbell, Miss Lewis is entitled as a legatee to 1/5 of the estate. The children of Mrs. Campbell: Clarrene Campbell, Cornelly Trigg Campbell, Lureta Campbell are her remaining legatees and are entitled to 4/5 of her estate.

pg 291. 12 Jan 1891. Settlement made with William Coppinger, administrator of John Stone, dec'd.

pg 292-294. 29 Dec 1890. Inventory and sale bill of the personal property of James Purser, dec'd. Purchases made by Luke Purser, James Purser, Mary Byars, the widow Parlee Purser, Elizabeth Cantrell, and others. Reported by John Purser, executor.

pg 295-296. 5 Jan 1891. Settlement made with S.R. Safley, administrator of James Woodlee, dec'd. M.D.L. Boyd guardian's receipt for $272.00.

pg 296-297. 12 Jan 1891. Settlement made with J.L. Byars, executor of John Meggerson, dec'd. Amount now in the hands of the guardian after paying expenses to be equally divided between A.M. Meggerson widow of dec'd, Mary Jones, and Vilia Martin $473.52.

pg 298. 26 Jan 1891. Settlement made with E.P. Willson, administrator of E.C. Willson, dec'd. In hands of the administrator per last settlement $1033.05 from which vouchers for $112.12 each are allowed to: J.M. Willson; Nora Willson and Bula Willson by their guardian A.P.Mason; W.G. Willson; J.H. Willson; A.P. and Mary Mason; John G. Willson and Kirk Willson by their guardian E.P. Willson; also one share in said estate to administrator, he being one of the heirs.

pg 299. 22 Dec 1877. **Will of Elizabeth B. Rust.** Elizabeth B. Rust, a citizen of Warren County, age about 63 years, being of sound mind and knowing the uncertainty of life and the certainty of death, make this my last will, disposing of my property. Furniture, cooking vessels and a note on Thomas B. Rust to go to my son John B. Rust. A trunk I give to my son Thomas B. Rust. The balance of my property to my daughter Mary E. Hamrick. I appoint my son Johm M. Rust my executor. **Codicil:** 3 Jun 1885. I have since making my will, collected the above named note and invested the money in 1/2 interest in the Tate place which is fully described in a deed from John M. Rust to me dated 12 Apr 1884. I give this half interest to my daughter Mary E. Hamrick. No witnesses or probate date given.

pg 300-301. 28 Feb 1891. Settlement made with W.S. Swann, executor of Vesta McGregor, dec'd. C.B. Swann's receipt for amount in full due her 27 Feb 1890, she having authorized the executor to pay the balance of her interest to her sister Opha Mitchell.

pg 301. March Term of Court 1891. Final settlement

made with S.M. Smith, administrator of Rachel Green, dec'd. Vouchers for $18.92 each allowed to: J. Stipes (guardian); J.M. and B.T. Taylor; Artildey Mayo; M.S. McCollum; Dan and Vinie Bride: J.F. Smith; W.S.Pain (guardian of Mary Pain's heirs); "I credit the administrator with the balance in his hands, he being one of the heirs at law of Rachel Green, dec'd." Willie Green gave a receipt to the administrator for $6.00.

pg 302. 14 Feb 1891. Settlement maed with A.T. Cope, administrator of J.W.M. Cope, dec'd. Receipt of Mrs. E.A. Cope, as per order of County Court, Jan Term 1891, receipts dated 5 Apr 1890 for $110.00 and 3 Feb 1891 for $29.99.

pg 303-309. 27 Feb 1891. Settlement made with J.T. Rowland, administrator of Lod Rowland, dec'd. The administrator is credited with the following amounts paid to the heirs of Lod Rowland, dec'd: D.W. Rowland $260.00; J.W. and S.A. Gribble $55.00; W.P. and M.J. Hennessee $252.50; and W.F. Cotton, administrator of Elizabeth Cotten, dec'd $103.38.

pg 309-310. 29 May 1890. **Will of Mariah Lou Settles.** I, Mariah Lou Settles of McMinnville, do make and publish this my last will and testament. First I direct that my burying expences and all my debts be paid. Second, I give to my niece Mrs. Sue Anderson, daughter of my sister Mildred Settles who married P.M. Wade, the said Sue now being the wife of John C. Anderson, all my property both real and personal free from the debts or rights of her present husband of any other husband that she may have in the future. Third, I request my executor to place a suitable monument to mark my grave. I nominate John H. Savage my executor. Witnessed by J.C. Biles and Jessie Walling on 31 May 1890.

pg 311-312. 2 Mar 1891. Inventory of the effects of Miss Louisa M. Settles. "Also found heir loom and paraphnalia and family relics in use by the deceased at the time of her death. Mrs. Sue Anderson devisee and legatee of Mrs. M.L. Settles took possession of the family relics"

pg 313-314. 6 Apr 1891. Report of the sale made by John H. Savage, executor of M.L. Settles dec'd on 4 May 1891. Sold was the house and lot on the south west corner of Main and Chancery Streets. Mrs. Lizzie Hoodenpyle and Miss Mittie Hopkins became purchasers for

Warren County, TN Will Book 8, Cont.

$1750.00.

pg 314. 10 Mar 1891. I, C. Arnold, administrator of George W. Sparkman, dec'd would respectifully report that there is no personal estate belonging to said dec'd.

pg 315. 21 Feb 1891. Inventory and sale bill of the estate of Miss Mai Comer, dec'd reported by Thomas C. Lind, administrator. Purchases made by George Comer and others.

pg 316-317. 28 Mar 1891. Inventory of the estate of Colman Green, dec'd which has come to the hands of Monroe Haley as administrator.

pg 317-319. 25 Jan 1891. Inventory and sale bill of the personal property of James Purcer, dec'd reported by J.G. Byars, executor.

pg 319-320. 28 Apr 1891. Final settlement of the estate of C.B. Chasteen made with H.B. Higginbotham, administrator.

pg 320. 16 May 1891. Settlement made with J.C. Jordan, administrator of Anderson Jordan, dec'd as required by law in such cases. Vouchers allowed for $2.49 each to the following: A.J. Jordon, Wm. R. Jordan, Lou Jordan, John and Margaret Ann Dye, Janre and Wm. T. Black, J.A. Jordan, Henry Jordan, Mary Nunley, J.C. Jordan and Davis Jordan.

pg 321-323. 4 May 1891. Inventory and sale bill of the personal property of the estate of P.M. Myers, dec'd reported by the administrator J.B. Myers. Purchases made by Ester Myers, P.A. Myers, B.N. Myers and others.

pg 324-325. 4 May 1891. Inventory of the personal estate of James H. Hughes, dec'd submitted by Frank Colville, administrator.

pg 325-326. 9 Mar 1891. Settlement made with S.L. Cunningham, adminstrator of James Cunningham, dec'd.

pg 326-328. 20 Mar 1891. Sale bill and inventory of the estate of Mrs. Josie Smartt, dec'd. Purchases made by Lucien Smartt, J.P. Smartt, W.C. Smartt, and others. One account against F.G. Samrtt for $21.25. Frank G. Smartt, administrator of Mrs. Josie Smartt.

pg 329.   27 Dec 1890. **Will of S.J. Walling.** I, S.J. Walling, Sr., do hereby make and publish this as my last will and testament. First to give my soul to God who gave it. Secondly I appoint my two sons H.L. Walling and Jessie Walling my executors.. to support their mother, and after their mother's death to divide said estate equally among all my children. Sarah Wood's part to be paid in $10 or $20 installments as they think her necessities may require. Witnesses Luther E. West and A.H. Gross. Presented for probate June Term 1891.

pg 329-330. 29 Apr 1880. **Will of Richard McGregor.** I, Richard McGregor do make and publish this day my last will and testament. First, I direct that my funeral expenses and just debts be paid. Secondly, I give and bequeath to my wife Elizabeth McGregor all my land on which I now live containing 139 acres, all household and kitchen furniture, and all other property that I may die possessed of, so long as she remains a widow or until after her death. At that time, all the effects that remain are to be used to raise all my children and give them some schooling that they read and write, until they come of age. Thirdly, after the children come to age 21 and the death or marriage of my wife, then I direct my land and all my property be sold and equally divided between all my heirs of my first and second wife. I appoint Hendison Countis (my wife's brother) my executor. Witnessed by Shadrack Green, T.J. Cantrell, H.M. Womack, and J.C.B. Green.   Presented for probate June Term 1891.

pg 330-331. 30 May 1891. Settlement made with O.D. Denton, administrator of Isaac Denton, dec'd.

pg 331-332. 1 Jun 1891. Settlement made with J.L. Byars, executor of John Meggerson, dec'd. Receipts of: M.J. Jones, one of the heirs $150.40; Watson Martin, guardian of Vila Martin $164.41; and A.M. Womack, the widow $150.41.

pg 332-333. 22 Jun 1891.   **Will of W.S. Massie.** I, W.S. Massie, being of sound mind and disposing memory, do make this as my last will and testament. 1st, I direct that all my just debts and funeral expenses be paid. 2nd, I will that all the property both real and personal that I die seized and possessed of be vested in my wife Fidelia Massie, and after her death what ever remains is to be equally divided among all my children or their legal heirs. 3rd, I hereby appoint my beloved wife Fidelia Massey my executrix. Witnessed W.L. Swann, J.B. Lusk and Wm. Biles. Presented for probate July Term 1891.

pg 333-334. 6 Jul 1891. Sale bill of the estate of James H. Hughes submitted by Frank Colville, administrator. All but two of the purchases made by Mrs. L.A. Hughes.

pg 335. 21 Jul 1891. Inventory of the personal property of E.B. Rust, dec'd, reported by J.M. Rust, executor.

pg 335-336. 10 Jun 1891. Sale bill and inventory of the personal effects of the estate of Thomas Comer, dec'd, presented by W.L. Swann, administrator.

pg 337-338. 6 Jul 1891. Settlement made with Hugh Slaughter, administrator of Jessie Slaughter, dec'd.

pg 338. July Term 1891. Settlement made with J.R. Belcher, administrator of Oliver Brewer, dec'd.

pg 339. 6 Jul 1891. Inventory of the personal estate of Calvin Smallman, dec'd submitted by Larkin Miller, administrator.

pg 340. 3 Aug 1891. Settlement made with A.G. Jones, administrator of William Brixey, dec'd.

pg 341-343. 3 Jul 1891. Inventory and sale bill of the personal property of W. R. Akers, reported by W.M. Akers, administrator. Purchases made by J.R. Akers and others.

pg 343-346. Aug Term 1891. List of the accounts on the books by 1889, personal property and notes of E.H. Williams, dec'd, reported by T.E. Mabry, administrator.

pg 347-350. 2 Mar 1882. **Will of W.H. Magness.** "I, W.H. Magness, being in good health and of sound mind and disposing memory and knowing the uncertainty of life and the certainty of death, do hereby make this my last will and testament. When I die I resign my soul and spirit to God who give it.." After my burial expences are paid, I desire that my just debts be paid. My desire is that my wife E.J. Magness have a homestead if she desires it, my home place at Smithville, as much of the household and kitchen furniture as she wants, my carriage, a gentle horse, one good cow and 1/5 of all my personal estate, after my two sons, Willie and Eddy Magness are educated. The estate to pay for their education. At the death of my wife, my estate is to be divided equally between my children then living or to my grandchildren that may be alive. My real estate--two houses and lots in DeKalb County, 2 houses and lots in McMinnville, a small tract of about 58 acres near Lebanon in Wilson County, and some equities and land near and in Lebanan belonging to the J.F. Coe estate and sold for my benefit--to be sold. I have advanced my oldest daughter C.A. Smallman, wife of M.D. Smallman at least $1500.00 in 3 acres of land at Smithville and cash as an advancement. My three other children, J.E. Magness, William Harrison Magness and Eddy E. Magness to have a bedstead and bed clothing and $1500.00 in cash out of my estate ot make them equal to Mrs. Smallman. My daughter J.E. Magness is single and her share is to be placed in trust for her. Should she marry, the property to remain as her estate, separate and apart from her husband, and on her death, should she die without children, the remaining portion revert to my estate. When my sons Willie and Eddy complete their education, they may have as much as $2000.00 apiece to commence business with. Witnesses state that the testor of the above did not sign the same in their presence, but they are satisfied that it is his signature. J.S. Harrison and Jesse Walling. Probate in Minute Book 9, page 62. Recorded Sept Term 1891.

pg 351. 22 Aug 1891. Settlement made with W.H. and A. Smith, administrators of Harrison Smith, dec'd.

pg 351. No date. Inventory of the estate of T.R. Jones, dec'd made by Mary E. Jones, widow and administratrix.

pg 352. 5 Oct 1891. Sale bill of the estate of Julia Darnell, dec'd reported by J.Z. Darnell, administrator.

pg 352-354. 1 Oct 1891. Settlement made with H.J. Morrow, one of the executors of E.K.P. Reynolds, dec'd.

pg 354-355. 14 Sep 1891. Settlement made with Jessie Hill and R.K. Rains, executors of Isaac Rains, dec'd. Receipts for $70.00 each given by the following: Delphia Akers and W.M. Akers; W.P. Rains; Ann Rains; R.K. Rains; J.W. West; and John Rains.

pg 356-360. 22 Sep 1891. Sale bill of the estate of Mary Nunley, reported by H.A. Moore, administrator. Purchases made by T.J. Nunley, S.F. Nunley and many others. Sale held 5 Sep 1890.

pg 361. 4 Sep 1888. **Will of James Sillaway.** I, James Sillaway, being in good health and of sound and disposing mind do make this my last will and testament. I bequeath and dispose of my worldly estate in the following manner (to wit): First, may will is that my just debts and funeral expenses be paid, and I give and bequeath to my beloved wife Suana Sillaway all my estate both real and personal. At my wife's death, what is remaining of my estate is to be divided equally between my two sons Harry Silaway and Myrun Sillway. Witnesses J.D. Lusk, C.R. Johnson and W.A. Johnson. Recorded Nov Term 1891.

pg 362-363. 31 Oct 1891. Settlement made with W.J. Fueston, administrator of Samuel Fueston, dec'd. Advancements to the heirs of Samuel Fueston, dec'd (to wit): Hixey A. Fueston; Parlee York; Nancy Carter; W.H. York, atty in fact for J.E. White, etal; W.H. York, atty in fact for S. Pressnell etal; and W.J. Fueston, admr, one of heirs.

pg 364. 23 Oct 1891. **Will of W.T. Hix.** In the name of God, Amen. Knowing the uncertainity of life and being of sound judgement and sane mind, I certify my will concerning my property. After all my just debts are paid I want my beloved wife to have the use of all my property both personal and real during her natural life then to her hears forever. Witnessed by W.S. Bullen and T.J. Stephens.

pg 364. 14 Nov 1891. Inventory and settlement mady with H.B. Patten, administrator of Samuel Romans, dec'd. Administrator reports that he has not received anything whatsoever from said estate.

pg 364-365. 7 Dec 1891. T.J. Wagner, administrator of T.J. Wagner begs leave to submit the following; the amount of $170.70 is the full amount that has ever come into his hands.

pg 365-366. 4 Dec 1891. Settlement made with G.R. Gardner, administrator of Martha McGregor, dec'd.

pg 366-368. 2 Nov 1891. Settlement made with H.M.

Finger, administrator of J.C. Edwards, dec'd. Advancements made to following heirs: Thomas H. Faulkner; Bettie Edwards; P.H. Faulkner, guardian of Lucy Edwards; James H. Edwards; William D. Edwards; John H. Edwards, B.R. Edwards and William Edwards.

pg 368-369. 23 Nov 1891. Settlement made with J.E. Jones, administrator de bonis non of Leroy Hammons, dec'd, (T.J. Heneger, former administrator).

pg 370-372. 31 Oct 1891. **Will of Thomas C. Smartt.** I, Thomas C. Smartt, being of sound mind and desposing memory do make and publish this my last will and testament. First, I appoint my trusted friend J.C. Biles my executor, without bond. Second, I wish my debts and funeral expenses be paid first. Third, I give to the three children of my deceased daughter Octavia Dickey, viz, Clara, Mary and Maude, $100.00 each. Fourth, I give the three children Jessee, Sallie and Cicera Spurlock of my daughter Josie Spurlock $100.00 each. Fifth, I give to the children of my daughter Mary Black, viz Charly, Sallie and Jodie Black $100.00 each, but as I hold Charly Black's note for $100.00, the executor will pay Charly Black no money, but give him his note in satisfaction of his part of the bequest. Sixth, I give to my daughter in law, the widow of my son D.C. Smartt, $100.00. Seventh, I give to Mary Black, all my household and kitchen furniture and one cow and calf. Sally Black to have a calf and Hervy Smartt to have my watch. Jodie Black to have my piano. Eighth, my real estate is to be sold at public or private sale, to satisfy the above special bequests. The remainder he will divide equally between Mary Black, my daughter and my two sons Hervy Smartt and Frank Smartt. Mary's share not to be subject to the control or debts of her husband C.G. Black. The share of Frank Smartt will be vested in his wife Lucy as trustee.
Witnesses Samuel L. Colville and W.C. Womack. Probated 4 Jan 1892.

pg 372-373. 31 Nov 1891. Jesse Walling, administrator of W.H. Argo, dec'd reports the cash and notes received. Advancements of $179.15 made to the following heirs: C.V. Argo, Mrs. Aura Howell, E.J. Argo, T.C. Argo, O.E. Argo, Mary L. Langdon, and Mrs. ___ Adkenson. Due William Argo $179.15.

pg 373-375. 4 Jan 1892. Report of Jesse Walling, guardian of O.L., J.G., R.C. and L.C. Turpin. Received

24 Aug 1886 $400.00 each, total $1600.00. Interest received $512.00, paid out for minors $516.55, balance due children $1595.45. Note: "This entry made by mistake, should have been guardian's record."

pg 375. 22 Dec 1891. Settlement made with Thomas S. Myers, administrator of James Z. Hill, dec'd. The amount due the minor heirs of Charlotte Etter, dec'd $168.05. W.G. Etter, guardian gives receipt for this amount.

pg 376-377. 4 Jan 1892. "J.E. Jones, administrator, having been appointed administrator of the estate of Thomas M. Biles, dec'd would report that on 28 Dec 1891 I visited the late residence of Thomas M. Biles and made an investigation of the effects belonging to the said T.M. Biles." Sale of the effects held 29 Dec 1891 with purchases made by W.H. Biles and the widow.

pg 378. 2 Jan 1892. Settlement made with W.H. and A. Smith, administrators of Harrison Smith, dec'd. Vouchers for $13.00 each allowed for: W.H. Smith; A. Smith; H.P. and G.A. Carr; J.A. McGee; C.M. Collier; and Nancy Jennings.

pg 379. 28 Dec 1891. Inventory and sale bill of the personal assets of the estate of M.D. Crawly, dec'd reported by E.D. Crawly, administrator. Purchases by Ella Crawly, W.R. Crawly, Sallie Crawly, J.D. Crawly and others.

pg 380. 29 Dec 1891. Inventory and sale bill of the personal property of the estate of John Owens, dec'd which have come to the hands of Edmon Seals, administrator.

pg 381-382. 13 Mar 1880. **Will of H.L.W. Hill.** I, H.L.W. Hill, do make and publish this as my last will and testament. "Believing as a general rule the laws of the state fairly and equinomically execute settle and wind up estates more equitably than wills usually do, I have concluded to permit my estate to be mainly settled by said laws without much interference by will. I have two sons married, Virgil Hill and Franklin Hill. I had one daughter Bertha who married Dr. Wm. C. Barnes who is now deceased, leaving several children. I had a daughter who is married to John C. Myers and has several children. The balance of my children, four daughters, viz: Eliza Hill, Arthelia Hill, Octa Hill and Mary Hill are unmarried and living with me and their mother Virginia A. Hill at home." I advanced my married children favors, i.e. Dr. Barnes and family, Virgil Hill, and Franklin Hill all had use of lands and houses without rent; and John C. Myers was lent money to buy a house in Pikeville and helped them when their house got burnt. Therefore I want each of my unmarried children allowed $300.00 before the division of my estate. I appoint my wife Virginia A. Hill my executrix. "This will was written, signed, sealed and deposited and kept among my valuable papers but not witnessed til today (May 11). I have requested the witnesses whose names are signed below to witness this will and 3 copies" /S/ H.L.W. Hill. Witnesses C. Coffee and Frank R. Colville. Recorded Feb Term 1892.

pg 383. 16 Sep 1891. **Will of Carroll Parks.** Know all men by these presents that this is my last will and testament. At my death, after all debts and funeral expenses are paid, the remainded is to be owned and controlled by my wife Hixey Parks. She is to have control and be the administratrix of all my business. After her death the estate is to be equally divided among my six children or their heirs. Witnessed by Arsey Womack and C.M. Rutledge.

pg 383-384. 8 Jan 1892. Sale bill of the effects of Aron Burlison, dec'd reported by R.A. Martin, executor.

pg 384-386. 13 Jan 1892. List of the property of J.P. Hill, dec'd reported by E.L. Hill, administrator. Purchasers George Hill, Isaac Hill, Linelo(?) Hill, Lee Hill and others.

pg 386-390. 30 Jan 1892. Sale bill and inventory of the personal assets of the estate of J.B. Cope, dec'd, reported by G.A. Cope, administrator. Purchases made by V. Cope, Elijah Cantrell, J.P. Cotton, G.P. Cope, Susan Cope, C.D. Cope, John Cotton, C.L. Cope, T.C. Cotton, J.N. Cope, G.A. Cope and others.

pg 390-391. 29 Jan 1892. Inventory and sale bill of the personal estate of James Pettit, dec'd, sold at public sale 12 Dec 1891 reported by J.C. Pettit, administrator.

pg 391-392. 23 Jan 1892. Inventory and sale bill of the personal estate of T.R. Jones, dec'd. Public sale held 17 Oct 1891 by Mary E. Jones, administratix.

pg 393-394. 5 May 1890. Inventory of the personal property of R.J. Parker, dec'd made 1 May 1890 and reported by Lovie Parker, administratrix. Sale of property of R.J. Parker held 3 May 1890, with purchases made by Lovie Parker, Mertal Parker, G.W. Parker, D.W. Parker, J.R. Parker and others.

pg 395-396. 12 Jan 1892. Settlement made with George F. Pennebaker, executor of the estate of S.F. Pennebaker, dec'd.

pg 396. 22 Jan 1892. Inventory of the estate of C.T. Clark, dec'd, J.B. Clark, administrator.

pg 396-397. 12 Jan 1892. Settlement made with W.H. Magness, administrator of Mrs. E.J. Magness, dec'd. Receipts for $13.93 for shares of estate given by J. Ella Magness, Edgar Magness, Cordelia A. Smallman, and W.H. Magness (admr.).

pg 397-398. 13 Jan 1892. Settlement made with W.D. Hughes, administrator of J.B. Hughes, dec'd. Credit of $267.00 each for their share allowed: J.N. Hughes, J.P. Hughes, T.H. Etter and wife Mollie Etter, J.C. Hughes and W.D. Hughes.

pg 398-399. 13 Jan 1892. Settlement made with J.J. Meadows, trustee of St. Mary's School Fund donated by Wm. C. Hill. F.M. Moffitt was former trustee. Credit by vouchers allowed, to wit: Minnie Lee Meadows and Myrtle Moffit.

pg 400. 13 Jan 1892. Settlement made with E.L. Hill, administrator of J.P. Hill, dec'd. Heirs receipts for $22.98 from: L.C. Hill, B.W.C. Hill, Sue Etter, Linda Hill, J.J. Hill, E.L. Hill, and J.J. Meadows, guardian for Lea Hill.

pg 401. Feb Term 1882. Final settlement of the estate of R. Webb, dec'd, reported by J.K.P. Webb, administrator. Balance due the heirs of the deceased $112.75. There being five heirs in all making $22.85 due each. The administrator credits the notes and advancements of the heirs of all (but Crockett Webb heirs) with their share of the estate and also with his own share. Cinderilla Webb given $72.00 for a year's support.

pg 402. 16 Jan 1869. Will of Elizabeth Suttles. I,

Elizabeth Suttles do make and publish this my last will and testament. First I direct that my funeral expenses and debts be paid. Second, I give and bequeath to my daughter Lusie Settle who has resided with me all her life my house and lot upon which I now live in the town of McMinnville and all my property of every kind. Third, I nominate and appoint Josiah F. Morford my executor. Witnessed by Sam L. Collville and Asa Faulkner on 16 Jan 1869. Recorded March Term 1892.

pg 402. 7 Mar 1892. Supplemental sale bill of the property of P.M. Myers, dec'd by J.B. Myers, administrator. 93 gallons of brandy to Northcutt & Co., and 38 Gallons to Kelley & Co.

pg 403. 12 Mar 1892. G.W. Smith, administrator of G.R. Smith, settlement credited by $326.87 received by each of the four heirs: Louisa Smith, Mattie Smith, Nannie Smith, and the administrator (he being an heir at law).

pg 404. 18 Feb 1892. Sale bill of the estate of James Purcer, dec'd reported by J.G. Byers and John Purser, executors. Purchases by Luke Purcer. Joseph Rowland became the purchaser of the home place for the sum of $700.00.

pg 405. 13 Feb 1892. Inventory of the personal estate of J.W. Dougherty, dec'd made by L.F. Dougherty, administrator.

pg 406-410. 2 Mar 1892. Sale bill of the real estate and personal property of Dr. F.C. Smartt, dec'd made by J.C. Biles, executor. Due bills and accounts, notes, etc listed and the notation "There is a large number of old notes out of date on insolvent parties that have long since been barred by the statutes of limitations, also a great many medical accounts on the book of Dr. Smartt, dec'd that are on insolvent persons and also barred by statutes. The executor does not consider that these notes and account are worth listing."

pg 411. 12 Mar 1892. Settlement made with Arch and John Scott, executors of Cooper Scott, dec'd. The executors have paid out $282.34 more that had come to their hands.

pg 412. 26 Mar 1892. Settlement made with O.D. Denton, administrator of Isaac Denton, dec'd. Vouchers allowed for $5.30 each to Daniel Dodson, Martha Glenn, Pheba

Glenn, W.C. Womack as assignee of J.D. Denton and Susan Cantrell, Isaac Denton, Nancy and R.D. Webb, J.M. Denton. Vouchers allowed for $2.65 each to Harrison Glenn and Levi Glenn. Vouchers allowed for $1.75 each to G.W. Mitchell, W.C. Womack as assignee of J.F. Webb, and J.L. and R.D. Webb.

pg 413. 21 Mar 1892. Settlement made with C.W. Nunley, administrator of Adam Nunley, dec'd. Vouchers for various amounts allowed: F.J. Nunley for E.W. Nunley; F.J. Nunley for H. Nunley; F.J. Nunley for self; Sarah F. Nunley; H.A. and Mary Moore; F.J. Nunley for J.F. and S.E. Patrick. The administrator is credited with one share of said estate.

pg 414. 2 Apr 1892. G.B. Marler, guardian of Pearl Marler reports receiving $121.00 from the administrator of James Stephens, dec'd.

pg 414. 4 Apr 1892. Inventory or sale bill of the personal property of W.T. Hix, dec'd, sold on 30 Dec 1891 by A.F. Stubblefield, administrator.

pg 415. 4 Apr 1892. Inventory of bill of sale of the estate of Elizabeth Moffitt, dec'd reported by W.W. Ware, administrator.

pg 416. 4 Apr 1892. Sale bill and inventory reported by J.B. Clark, administrator of A.J. Goodson, dec'd.

pg 417-418. 5 Apr 1892. Inventory and sale bill of W.L. Swann, administrator of Dorcus Jordon, dec'd. First sale on 19 Feb 1892, second sale 4 Apr 1892..

pg 419-421. 4 Apr 1892. Sale bill and inventory of the personal assets of the estate of J.N. Myers, dec'd made by N.B. Jones, administrator. Purchases made by E.J. Myers, A.C. Myers, and others.

pg 421. 4 Apr 1892. Sale bill of the estate of Jno. West, dec'd submitted by R.K. Rains, administrator.

pg 422. May Term 1892. **Will of Mrs. Caroline Richmond.** I, Caroline Richmond being of sound mind and memory and mindful of the uncertainties of human life, do make publish and declare this my last will and testament in manner following: I give and bequeath all my estate, both real and personal wheresover situated, to my husband Cyrus Richmond. In witness whereof I have hereunto set my hand and seal, this 26 Sep 1891. Witnesses Thompson P. Crowe and Walker Crowe.

pg 422-425. May Term 1892. Settlement made with Miss Blanche Lewis, guardian of the estate of Clarisse Connelly Trigg Lineta and Eugenia Campbell [as found] Amount remaining in the guardian's hands from last settlement plus amount received for the estate of Helen Louise Lewis, dec'd and rents, less taxes and amounts paid out by guardian for her wards shows balance of $9539.46. [Settlement not completed.]

pg 426-428. 2 May 1892. Inventory of the personal property of the estate of H.L.W. Hill, dec'd by Frank Colville, administrator. Sale bill of the personal estate of H.L.W. Hill, dec'd. Purchases by V.A. Hill, I.C. Hill, Virgil Hill, Frank Hill, and others. Also in inventory was 121 barrels of apple brandy and a still and fixtures which have not been sold. The still cannot be sold until after this year's apple crop is taken care of, the dec'd having had contracts for the still for the year.

pg 429. 1 Apr 1892. Settlement made with Jesse Walling, administrator of O.H. Argo, dec'd. Due William Argo as per settlement made 31 Oct 1891, $179.15. William L. Argo receipt 10 Apr 1892 for $179.15.

pg 430-431. May Term 1892. Settlement made with Mrs. Lovie Parker, administratrix of R.J. Parker, dec'd.

pg 431-432. 15 Apr 1892. Final settlement made with W.J. Fuston, administrator of Samuel Fuston, dec'd. Receipts received for $72.70 from: W.J. Fuston; Parlee York; W.H. York as atty in fact; C.L. Carter; and Hixa Fuston.

pg 433. 2 May 1892. Inventory of the personal estate of H.L. Hill, dec'd, submitted by Frank Colville, administrator.

pg 434-435. 2 May 1892. Bill of sale of personal estate of H.L.W. Hill, dec'd. Purchases by V.A. Hill, Frank Hill, Virgil Hill, I.C. Hill [This is a repeat of the settlement on pages 426-428.]

pg 436-438. 6 Jun 1892. Settlement made with J.H. Towles and Oliver Towles, administrators of John W. Towles, dec'd. $1242.14 being the amount of the estate after deducting all expenses, leaves to each of the three heirs to wit: John H. Towles, Bettie Towles and Oliver Towles $419.14 each.

pg 439. 6 Jun 1892. Inventory of the estate of A.D. Wheeler, dec'd reported by Jesse Hill.

pg 440-441. 20 Aug 1891. Settlement made with J.H. Collier, administrator of William Collier, dec'd. Note on James Collier and receipt of Nancy Collier.

pg 442. 6 Jun 1892. Settlement made with A.G. Jones, administrator of William Brixey, dec'd. Receipt of Elijah Anderson, guardian of William Brixey's heirs.

pg 443. 23 Jun 1892. Settlement made with H.A. Moore, administrator of Mary Nunnelley, dec'd. Receipts from S.E. and L.F. Patrick, E.W. Nunley, H. Nunley, W.E. Nunley, T.J. Nunley and Sarah F Nunley against the estate.

pg 444. 24 Jun 1892. Sale of the personal property of J.W. Dougherty, dec'd held on 22 Feb 1892 by L.T. Daugherty, administrator.

pg 445. 8 Jun 1892. Settlement made with T.M. Moffitt, executor of W.C. Hill, dec'd.

pg 446. 13 Jun 1892. Inventory of the personal property and estate of Mrs. Frankie Bess, dec'd. M.J. Phillips, administrator, reports that Mrs. Bess left no personal property.

pg 447. 8 Jun 1892. **Will of William Sparkman.** Know all men by these present that I, William Sparkman do make this my last will and testament. First, I direct that my body be buried beside my wife in the Webb Graveyard. Second, that all my debts and burial expenses by paid. Third, I direct that my son Nelson Sparkman and his wife have the brown mare. Fourth, that my granddaughters Presly Statton and Rachel Johnson each have a bed, pillow and 2 quilts. The remainder of my property be sold and suitable gravestones be erected at my grave and that of my wife. The remainder of my estate is to be divided thusly: one fourth to my son Nelson Sparkman, another fourth to my daughter Violet L. Parker, another fourth to my daughter Fannie Statton and the remainding fourth to the children of my dec'd daughter Nannie Johnson, having previously given my

other children and grandchildren all I intend for them
to have. I appoint Nelson Sparkman and W.W. Parker my
executors. Witnessed by T.P. Bonner and A.O Johnson.
Recorded July Term 1892.

pg 448-451. 4 Jul 1892. Settlement with W.C. Womack,
executor of A.J. Curl, dec'd. Numerous lawsuits
mentioned. "Paid Mrs. Minerva Curl, per receipt "
$600.00.

pg 452-453. 16 Jul 1892. Settlement of T.J. Walling,
administrator of J.D. Walling, dec'd. "Hariet Walling,
widow, receipt $193.50." Amount of estate due the heirs
after distribution of expences: Hariet Walling, S.J.
Walling, Thomas D. Walling, John H. Walling, Jessie P.
Walling, W.P. Walling, Clyde Walling, Ivan Walling,
Nannie B. Walling, Claud Walling, each due $7.50.
Administrator's allowance $14.77.

pg 454. 22 Jul 1892. Inventory of the personal
property of Nancy D. Peay, dec'd reported by Chas. S.
Ivie, administrator with will annexed. Land sold to
W.M. Ivie and Mrs. Eliqa Tilford.

pg 455-458. 22 Jul 1892. Settlement made with Chas S.
Ivie, administrator with will annexed of Nancy D. Peay,
dec'd.

pg 459-461. 26 Jul 1892. Sale bill of the estate of
L.O. Paty, dec'd reported by W.T. Paty, administrator.
Purchases made by Widow Paty and others.

pg 462-463. 12 Mar 1885. **Will of R.P. Womack.** "I,
R.P. Womac<u>h</u>, being of advanced age but sound in mind and
in reasonable health, and recognizing the uncertainity
of life and the certainity of death, and wishing to
settle my affairs while living and to avoid controversy
over my estate when gone, among my children and my
children's children, do declare and establish this to be
my last will and testament. First, it is my desire that
my body when dead shall be decently intered.." and my
debts and funeral expenses be paid. Second, I appoint
my two sons W.C. Womach and B.F. Womach my executors.
Third, I desire my executors collect what is due me when
I am dead and to sell such personal property as I may
then own. Fourth, the surplus of my personal effects,
realestate and other property I wish to be equally
divided between my sons W.C. Womach; B.F. Womach; G.W.
Womach; and R.B. Womach; my daughter Octavia Wilson,

wife of Levi Wilson; my granddaughter Martha Ramsey who is the sole child and heir of my dec'd daughter Mary I. Kent, nee Womach; and my grandson Frank Simpson, the only child and heir of my dec'd daughter Malvina Simpson, nee Womach. Sixth, my executors to act without charge and without bond. Witnessed by J.S. McGeehee, W.J. Fuston and U.Y. Troglesen. Registered Sept Term 1892.

pg 464-466. 27 May 1879. **Will of A.J. Brown.** "Being desirous to arrange my pecuniary affairs and being in feeble health but sound in mind and having neither wife or children, hereby make and write my last will and testament.." First, I will that my just debts be paid. Second, I will to Andy Brown, son of Henry Brown and his wife Bettie Brown my shot gun. Third, I will my executor to pay to C.P. and C.C. Brown, sons of my brother John Brown $500.00 each. Fourth, the residue of my estate both real and personal to be equally divided as follows: to the children of Henry Brown and his wife Bettie, one fourth of the above, and if any more children should be born to them, I want them to share equally with their seven present children. Fifth, I will to Ann Reynolds, wife of E.N.P. Reynolds and her children that are now living or my herafter be born in wedlock one fourth of the remainder of my estate. Sixth, I will to Elizabeth Mooney, wife of Waynefield Mooney and her children and if they should have any more children, I want them to share equally with those now living, one fourth of the residue of my estate. Seventh, I will to the children of Ann Winton, dec'd, wife of W.B. Winton, one fourth of the remainder of my estate. The above gifts to my neices and their children are to be free from the control of their husbands. I bought the Adam Custer farm and gave it to Henry Brown to pay him for my board. This is not to be included in my estate. Eighth, I want my farm in Coffee County containing 305 acres to be sold. Ninth, I appoint my old partner and friend S.L.Colville my executor. Witnessed by C. Coffee and W.C. Womack. **Codicil.** 8 May 1882. I will to the children of Henry Brown (now dec'd) and his wife Bettie the Sloan tract containing 36 acres puchased of Clay Faulkner administrator of William Sloan, dec'd. I give this much more that my other heirs as I have lived with Henry Brown a long time and am now living with his family. Witnessed W.C. Womack and C. Coffee. Recorded Sep Term 1892.

pg 466-467. 10 Sep 1892. Sale bill of the estate of

A.J. Goodson, dec'd, reported by J.B. Clark, administrator. Purchases made by A.J. Goodson [Jr.], Mrs. E. Goodson, Jack Goodson and others.

pg 467-468. 5 Sep 1892. Sale bill of the property of A.D. Wheeler, dec'd, submitted by Jesie Hill, administrator.

pg 469-470. 5 Sep 1892. Inventory and sale bill of the estate of Joseph Cummings, dec'd by Denny Cummings, administrator. Purchases made by Dan Cummings and others.

pg 471-472. 27 Aug 1892. A.R. Hammer, clerk of the County Court of Warren County do hereby take and state an account against J.M. Sparkman and G.W. Newby, administrators of Z. Edge, dec'd. "Paid Mrs. Mary A. Edge, widow of Z. Edge, dec'd, $36.15."

pg 473. 21 Sep 1892. Settlement made with J.H. Collier, administrator of William Collier, dec'd. Credits of $42.00 each paid to each of the following: R. and Nancy Duncan; C.M. Collier; S.A. Hambleton; W.P. Collier; M.A. Smith; J.T. Collier; June Collier; Mary Womack; W.C. Womack, guardian of Frank Collier; J.H. Collier's share in estate.

pg 474-475. 5 Oct 1892. Inventory and sale bill of the personal property that has come to the hands of J.C. Biles, administrator of H.B. Ramsey, dec'd. Purchases made by A.J. Ramsey, D.A. Ramsey, Joseph Ramsey, David Ramsey, Andrew Ramsey, and others.

pg 476-478. 4 Nov 1892. Inventory of the personal property that has come in the hands of J.C. Biles administrator with will annexed belonging to the estate of A.J. Brown, dec'd.

pg 479. 3 Oct 1892. Inventory of B.W. Snipes estate, Martha Snipes, administratrix. Sale Bill of estate.

pg 480-486. 7 Nov 1892. List of the property sold at the sale of Uriah Jaco, dec'd submitted by John L. Byars, administrator. Purchases made by the Widow Jaco, Jeremiah Jaco, L.A. Jaco, S.D. Jaco, Parlee Jaco, Josie Jaco, P.J. Jaco and others.

pg 487. 4 Nov 1892. Bill of sale of Thomas Davis, dec'd estate sold on 4 Nov 1892 by Mrs. Eliza Davis, administrator. Most of the purchases made by Mrs. Davis.

pg 488-490. 2 Nov 1892. Settlement made with L.B. Brown, administrator of C.A. Brown, dec'd. Mamie E. Brown, widow, given year's support from 1888 to 1892.

pg 491-492. 11 Oct 1892. Settlement made with T.E. Mabury, administrator of E.D. Williams, dec'd. The administrator has paid out $46.95 more that had come into his hand.

pg 493-495. 9 Nov 1892. Inventory and sale bill of the estate of H.B. Higgenbotham, dec'd. Purchases made by W. Higginbotham, A. Higginbotham, R.L. Higginbotham, James Higginbotham.

pg 496. 3 Dec 1892. Settlement made with F.G. Smartt, administrator of Mrs. Josie Smartt, dec'd. He shows that there is nothing left in the hands of the administrator.

pg 497. 4 Dec 1892. Inventory of the estate of P.A. Roberson, dec'd, reported by W.R. Davenport, administrator. Sale bill of the property shows purchases by G.W.D. Roberson, Miss Ida Roberson, Will Roberson and others.

pg 498. 22 Nov 1892. Sale bill of the estate of Jane Estes, dec'd submitted by W.H. Smartt, administrator. Purchases by W.B. Estes and others.

pg 499. 31 Dec 1892. Sale bill of the personal property of S.J. Gibbs, dec'd, sold on 20 Dec 1892 reported by M.B. Harwell, administrator. Purchases by Joe Gibbs and others.

pg 499-500. 23 Dec 1892. Settlement made with J.J. McAfee, administrator of J.C. Edwards, dec'd. Mrs. Martha C. Edwards allowed $56.88 as guardian and $110.00 in her own right.

pg 501-502. 12 Dec 1892. Settlement made with Monroe Haley, administrator of Coleman Green, dec'd.

pg 502. 2 Jan 1893. Inventory of the personal estate of H.H. Wood, dec'd reported by T.M. Frazzier administrator.

pg 503-505. Jan Term 1893. Second sale of the personal property of Uriah Jaco, dec'd submitted by J.L. Byars, administrator. Purchases made by the Widow Jaco, G.W. Jaco, G.D. Jaco, L.A. Jaco, S.D. Jaco, P.J. Jaco, J.P. Jaco, Jessee Jaco, E.J. Jaco, Josie Jaco and others.

pg 506-507. 9 Jan 1893. Settlement made with J.R. Edge, administrator of J.B. Dulue [Dulea]. Payments made to U. Vanhooser, guardian, and to M.H. Dulue. "There is one minor child of J.B. Dulue, dec'd and the widow, who each take one half of the estate" ($5.77 each).

pg 507-508. 28 Jan 1893. Second sale bill of the estate of P.A. Roberson made by W.R. Davenport, administrator.

pg 509-510. 24 Feb 1893. Settlement made with J.M. Sparkman and G.W. Newby, administrators of the estate of Z. Edge, dec'd. J.B. Edge, M.E. Edge, J.R. Edge, G.W. Edge, M.J. Sparkman, and M.A. Edge give receipts for one share in the estate ($79.75 each). Mary Ann Edge gives an additional receipt for $38.85.

pg 511. 2 Mar 1893. Final settlement of the estate of T.R Jones, dec'd, Mrs. Mary E. Jones administratrix.

pg 512. 14 Feb 1893. Second sale bill of the estate of A.J. Brown, dec'd, sold by J.C. Biles, administrator.

pg 512-513. 1 Jan 1893. **Will of Marlin M. Phelps.** I, Marlin M. Phelps, being of sound mind and disposing memory do make and publish this, my last will and testament. First, it is may will that my debts and burial expences be paid. Second, I leave to John Alexander, my oldest son, $5.00, also to Spencer L. the same amount and to my daughter U.C. Woodlee the same amount, also to my daughter Maggie L. Pearson the same amount. My daughter Ella M. I leave to be provided for by her mother. Third, I leave to my beloved wife Harriet Precilla all the balance of my property of every kind. Fourth, I appoint my wife Harriet Precilla my executrix, to serve without bond. Witnessed by Thomas S. Myers, W.W.Ware and David Fairbanks. Entered for probate 6 Mar 1893.

pg 514-517. 22 Aug 1874. **Will of George Etter.** I, George Etter, being now seventy nine years old and for more that fifty years a resident of Warren County, TN, do make and publish this my last will and testament. First, I direct that my funeral expenses and all my debts be paid. Second, I will that my lands be laid off into lots as follows. Lot 1, my mountain lands known as the Carson tract. Lot 2, the Cedar tract. Lot 3, my lands on the south side of Town Creek where my son George lately lived. Lots 4-9, the land on the north side of the Creek where I now live to be laid off into six lots of 100 acres each. Lot 10, containing less that 200 acres including the dwelling house, (except where my son Henry now lives). The first 9 lots to be sold. Fourth, I will that all my personal property except that portion hereafter bequeathed to my wife by sold. Fifth, I will that after all my expenses and debts are paid, my estate is to be distributed in equal shares as follows. To my sons Henry Etter, George H. Etter, Boysdon R. Etter, Charles M. Etter, Thomas H. Etter, Jesse C. Etter, one share each. To my daughter Nancy Hays, Lucy Etter and Margaret Etter, one share each. To my grandchildren Jane and Emer, daughters of my dec'd son Stokley Etter, one share. The children of my dec'd daughter Elizabeth, (namely James Moffitt, George Moffitt, and Harrel Moffitt), one share. To the children of my dec'd daughter Mary (namely Ada McKnight, Louisa Woodlee and Frank Woodlee) one share. Sixth, I will to my wife Harriet Rowan Etter Lot 10. Seventh, should any of my children of grandchildren bring suit to set aside this will, they shall have no part of my estate. Lastly, I nominate my brother Henry R. Etter and my son Boysdon R. Etter my executors. Witnessed by Elijah Martin and W.G. Etter. **Codicil.** 11 Oct 1880. I have "lotted" my lands myself, and sold various of them to my son J.E. Etter, to my daughter Nancy Hayes, to my son G.H. Etter, to my son R.R. Etter, to my son C.M. Etter, to my son Thomas H. Etter, and to my son Henry Etter. Lot 10 is to be sold after the death of my wife as directed in my will. Recorded April Term 1893.

The following entries were recorded
earlier in this book, and re-entered here.

---

pg 518. 23 Jun 1892. Settlement made with H.A. Moore, administrator of Mary Nunley, dec'd.

pg 519. 24 Jun 1892. Sale bill of the personal property of the estate of J.W. Dougherty, dec'd held on 22 Feb 1892, reported by L.T. Dougherty, administrator.

pg 520-521. 16 Jul 1892. Settlement made with Thomas D. Walling, administrator of J.D. Walling, dec'd. See pgs 452-453.

pg 521. 13 Jun 1892. Inventory of the personal estate of Mrs. Frankie Bess, dec'd. Administrator M.J. Phillips reports she left no personal property.

pg 522. 22 Jul 1892. Inventory of the estate of Nancy D. Peay, dec'd, reported by Chas S. Ivie, administrator.

pg 523-526. 4 Jul 1892. Settlement made with W.C. Womack, executor of the will of A.J. Curl, dec'd.

pg 527. 21 Apr 1892. Settlement made with Jessie Walling, administrator of O.H. Argo, dec'd.

pg 528. 8 Jun 1892. Settlement made with F.M. Moffitt, executor of W.C. Hill, dec'd.

pg 529-531. 26 Jul 1892. Sale bill of L.O. Paty, dec'd, submitted by W.T. Paty, administrator.

pg 532-534. Will of R.P. Womack re-entered, see pgs. 462-463.

pg 534-535. Will of Wm. Sparkman re-entered, see pg. 447.

pg 536-538. 22 Jul 1892. Settlement made with Chas. S. Ivie, administrator of N.D. Peay, dec'd. See pgs. 454-458.

pg 1-13. 28 Mar 1893. W.S. French, administrator of the estate of John H. French, dec'd submits the schedule of the assets of the estate of the dec'd. Sale of livestock and lumber, notes due the estate, personal property.

pg 14-15. 3 Apr 1893. List of the property sold at the sale of H.H. Wood, sold by T. M. Frazier, administrator. Sale held on 27 Jan 1893, with purchases made by O.H. Wood, A.J. Wood and others.

pg 15-16. 24 Mar 1893. Inventory of the estate of J.L. Sewell, dec'd reported by W.A. Sewell. Notes listed on L.R. Sewell, W.A. Sewell, W.Y. Sewell, C.M. Sewell, Sallie L. Sewell, J.R. Sewell, Tennie Sewell, C.W. Sewell, Adie Sewell, Maggie Lawson and Mrs. W.Y. Haggard. The estate is "scattered over Tennessee, Alabama, Texas and Missouri." Administrator will try to collect and make settlement within 12 months.

pg 16. 30 Mar 1893. Sale bill of the personal property of the estate of Frank Spears, dec'd, by H.Spears, administrator.

pg 17. 18 Apr 1893. List of the property sold at the sale of George Etter, dec'd on 15 Apr 1893. Purchases by Lucy Etter, Maggie Etter and Vol Walker.

pg 18. 25 Apr 1893. Settlement made with J.J. Meadows, trustee of the St. Mary School Fund. $25.00 paid for one month's services as teacher to William Hayes.

pg 19. 22 Apr 1893. Sale bill and inventory of some corn and wheat etc sold by G.A. Cope, administrator of J.B. Cope, dec'd on 26 Mar 1893. Purchases made by Jim Cope, Elijah Cantrell, G.P. Cope, G.A. Cope and others. Received in cash $22.25 of Susan Cope.

pg 20-21. 1 May 1893. Inventory and sale bill of the personal effects of Laura J. Jones, dec'd reported by Frank Colville, administrator. Purchases made by Miss Minnie Jones, Mrs. Ann L. Jones, and others.

pg 22-27. 1 May 1893. Inventory and sale bill of the personal estate of Mrs. L.A. Hughes, dec'd, reported by

Frank Colville, administrator of the estate. Purchases by J.R. Hughes, T.J. Hughes and many others. Sale held 21 Mar 1893.

pg 28-30. 30 May 1893. Inventory and sale bill of the personal assets of Ann P. Peppers, dec'd which have come to the hands of J.C. Rankin as administrator. [Names of purchasers not given.] List of notes due estate.

pg 31-32. 2 May 1893. Settlement made with George F. Pennebaker, executor of the will of Sam F. Pennebaker, dec'd. George F. Pennebaker is guardian of Edwin S. Pennebaker.

pg 33. 5 May 1893. Settlement made with H.A. Moore, administrator of Mary E. Nunnelly, dec'd. Vouchers allowed to E.W.Nunnelly, W.E. Nunnelly, S.F. Nunnelly, T.J. Nunnelly, H. Nunnelly and S.E. Patrick. "I give the administrator credit of one share in the said estate of his wife being one heir at law".

pg 34. 12 May 1893. Settlement made with R.K. Rains, administrator of John W. West, dec'd.

pg 35-37. 27 Jun 1893. Inventory and sale bill of the personal effects of R.P. Womack, dec'd reported by W.C. and B.F. Womack, executors. List of notes due estate.

pg 38. 29 Jun 1893. Inventory and sale bill of the personal assets of A.J. Goodson, dec'd, reported by N.A. Goodson, administratrix.

pg 39-41. 1 Jul 1893. Inventory of the property belonging to the estate of E.C. Dunlap sold 17 Jun 1893.

pg 41. 17 Jun 1893. List of notes received belonging to the estate of E.C. Dunlap, dec'd, reported by W.H. Simpson, administrator.

pg 42-45. 20 Jun 1893. Inventory of the personal estate of William Sparkman, dec'd which have come to the hands of his executors, W.W. Parker and Nelson Sparkman. Sale held 14 Jul 1892 with purchases made by Nelson Sparkman, Fannie Slatton, Charley Slatton, Margarette Sparkman and others.

pg 46. 8 Jul 1893. Settlement made with W.M. Akers, administrator of W.R. Akers, dec'd. J.P. and Eliza Cotton receipt for $11.35 and J.R. Akers receipt for

$11.35. "I give the administrator credit with $13.35 his prorated share in said estate, he being one of the heirs."

pg 47. 1 Aug 1893. Supplimentary inventory of the estate of James Pettit, dec'd reported by J.C. Pettit, administrator. Cash received on judgement rendered in Seth Wright vs Huse Witt.

pg 48-49. 14 Aug 1893. Settlement made with R.A. Martin, executor of Aaron Burlison, dec'd.

pg 50. 15 Aug 1893. Settlement made with J.U. Smith, guardian of Lucy and Ada Bozeman.

pg 51. 11 Feb 1882. **Will of Mary Caulson.** I, Mary Caulson, being of sound mind and memory, do make and publish this my last will and testament. 1. It is my will that my body be decently intered according to my standing and condition in life. 2. My just debts are to be paid. 3. I will to my husband B.M. Caulson all the land east of the cross fence running in a northwest direction from a point in the south boundary line of the tract upon which I now live about one rod east of the corner of an old field known as the Wiley Mathews field...to T.T. Peay's south boundary line. At his death I will the above land to my neice Cora Rogers and the heirs of her body. 4. It is my will that my husband B.M. Causlon have all my personal property during his natural life except one horse, bridle and saddle and one cow which I wish my niece Cora Rogers to have, and at his death, Cora Rogers is to have all the personal property that may be left. 5. My executor is to sale all the land not listed above and divide the proceeds equally between my four brothers and six sisters and their heirs, namely: William Hammons, Rubin Hammons, John Hammons, Leroy Hammons, Elizabeth Sullivan, Caroline Hoover, Manerva Ann McGee, Rebecka Jones, Martha Faulkner and Margaret Watts. I appoint my friend H.M. Finger my executor. Witnessed by S. McRamsey and T.T. Peay. [No probate date given, but recorded at Oct Term 1893.]

pg 52. 1 Oct 1893. Settlement made with W.H. Smith, special trustee for Shockley School Fund in the 11th Civil District of Warren County, TN.

pg 53. 16 Sep 1893. Settlement made with J.S. Denby, administrator of Eliza Hawkins, dec'd. There was in the hands of the administrator in Aug 1885, $126.05. Denby paid $100.00 for services rendered the deceased before her death for 5 years.

pg 54. 30 Oct 1893. Settlement made with N.A. Goodson, administratrix of A.J. Goodson, dec'd.

pg 55-56. 17 Oct 1893. Settlement made with Edmond Seals, administrator of John Owen, dec'd.

pg 57. 28 Oct 1893. Inventory of the property of Mary Colson [Caulson], dec'd. "One tract of land in the 8th District of Warren County of 133 1/2 acres and 15 poles." Land purchased by William Ramsey, H.B. Bonner and F. Mansfield for $307.00.

pg 58-59. 4 Nov 1893. Settlement made with John H. Savage, executor of M.L. Suttles, dec'd.

pg 60-62. 13 Nov 1893. Report of receipts and disbursments made by J.C. Biles as assignee of J.W. Gray.

pg 63-64. 10 Nov 1893. Final settlement made with E.D. Crawly, administrator of M. D. Crawly, dec'd.

pg 65-68. 4 Dec 1893. Settlement made with Frank Colville, administrator of James H. Hughes, dec'd. Amount to be distributed to heirs $3774.97. Receipts for equal amounts received from each of the following: Daisey E. Blackman, James R. Hughes, Mrs. O.P. Wilkerson [written later as Mrs. W.M. Wilkerson], Mrs. L.A. Hughes, T.J. Hughes and L. May Robinson.

pg 69-70. 29 Nov 1893. Statement of assets of estate made this day with W.L. Swann, administrator of Thomas Comer, dec'd. Total remaining in the hands of the administrator $1275.82.

pg 71. 29 Nov 1893. Settlement made with W.L. Swann, administrator of H.J. Roberson, dec'd. Credits: Receipt for $5.37 from George Roberson, W.T. Roberson and C.F. Roberson and a guardians receipt for $26.85 from George Robertson.

pg 72-73. 28 Nov 1893. Settlement made with T.C. Lind, admininstrator of Mai Comer, dec'd. Nothing remaining in his hands as of this date.

pg 74. 28 Nov 1893. Final settlement made with J.C. Pettitt, administrator of James Pettitt, dec'd.

pg 75. 20 Nov 1893. Settlement made with W.H. Smartt, administrator of Jane Estus, dec'd. Receipts for 1/3 interest ($33.31) given by W.W. Wallace, W.B. Estus and D.E. Moore.

pg 76-80. 5 Dec 1893. Inventory of the personal assets of John T. Potts, dec'd, reported of J.E. Jones, former administrator. Frank Colville to be new administrator.

pg 81. 4 Dec 1893. Settlement made with J.B. Myers, administrator of J.M. Myers, dec'd. Mrs. E.S. Myers, year's support $60.00. Remaining in the hands of said administrator, $540.90, as of this date.

pg 82-84. 1 Jan 1894. The undersigned administrators of J.W. Miller, dec'd, return the following inventory and sale bill of the personal estate of said dec'd. Purchases made by Mrs. E. Miller, Jennie Miller, J.L. Miller Jr., A.C. Miller, W.B. Miller, and the widow. Signed J.W. Miller and J.M. Gribble, administrators.

pg 85. 9 Dec 1893. Settlement made with N.B. Jones, administrator of J.N. Myers, dec'd. Jones has paid out $11.15 more than has come into his hands.

pg 86-87. 12 Dec 1893. Settlement made with T.J. Wagner, administrator of S.B. Wagner, dec'd. Receipts for $6.71 received from each of the following: D.F. Wagner, T.J. Wagner, E.H. Wagner, F.L.Ganaway. Receipts for $4.46 received from each of the following: E.T. Ganaway, E.H. Miller, D.F. Wagner and T.J. Wagner. Receipt for $160.00 received from Mrs. M.E. Wagner.

pg 88. 18 Dec 1893. Settlement made with J.T. Darnell, administrator of Julius Darnell, dec'd. Receipts for $20.00 received from J.A. Tate, J.A. Anderson, and B.R. Davis. Receipt for $17.00 from Martha Summers, for $38.10 from J.T. Darnell as guardian and from him for $19.05 for one share in said estate.

pg 89-92. 29 Mar 1888. **Will of G.P. Moffitt.** "I, G.P. Moffitt, do here in write down my last will or what disposition I wish made of all my effects or what I am possessed of at my death." First I want my debts paid with my $1000.00 insurance policy. What is left I want equally divided among my heirs and wife if she is living. My wife is to be well provided for and a guardian appointed for my minor heirs. At the death of my wife the home tract is to be divided into as many parts as there are heirs. The dwelling and out buildings to be included in two shares and Laury and Robert Moffitt to have them as their shares. Commissioners to be appointed to divide the land equally. The part that may be going to Maude Myers, daughter of Maud and Eb. Myers, I want my daughter Laury Moffitt to take charge of and I appoint her its guardian until Maude is 21. If Laury should die, my son Venus is appointed in her stead. I appoint my daughter Laury as guardian of Fransina Watson's children. If Laury should die then E.L. and A.B. Moffitt are to be her successors. I appoint my three sons Venus Moffitt, Aaron Moffitt and E.L. Moffitt and my ____ Celia as my Executors. My wife may close my store at my death to pay my debts. Witnessed by W.H. Meadows and E. Webb. Entered for probate 5 Feb 1894.

pg 93. 11 Jan 1894. Settlement made with W.E. Nunley, administrator of Am Nunley, dec'd. Receipts for $17.62 given by Mary L. Moon, L.F. Patrick, T.J. Nunley and H. Nunley. Receipt for $35.45 from W.E. Nunley and $3.28 from S.F. Nunley.

pg 94. 27 Jan 1894. List of the property sold by H.M. Hennessee administrator of the estate of A.W. Hennessee, dec'd. Sale on 27 Nov 1893.

pg 95. 12 Jan 1894. A final settlement made with H.A. Moore, administrator of the estate of Mary Nunley, dec'd. Receipts for $1.64 from each of the following to settle the estate: E.W. Nunley, S.F. Nunley, T.J. Nunley, S.E. Patrick, W.R. Nunley, H. Nunley, and Mary Moore.

pg 96. 19 Jan 1894. Settlement made with W.T. Paty, administrator of L.O. Paty, dec'd. There is $76.60 remaining in the hands of said administrator as of this date.

pg 97. 12 Jan 1894. Settlement made with A.F. Stubblefield, administrator of W.T. Hix, dec'd. Administrator has paid out $67.50 more than has come to his hands.

pg 98. 5 Feb 1894. Sale Bill of the personality of the estate of E.A. McGregor, dec'd reported by J.H.

Warren County, Tn Will Book 9, cont.

Whitlock, administrator.

pg 99-100. 22 Nov 1893. **Will of Hugh Wilson.** "I, Hugh Wilson, do make and publish this as my last will and testament" First, I desire that my debts and funeral expenses be paid. Second, I desire that my beloved wife Saphronia Wilson have use and control of all my personal property during her life time. At her death it is my will that my son Hugh Jackson Wilson shall have use of same, and at his death, the same to be sold and divided between my heirs. Third, my wife is to have use of all my real estate. Fourth, my son John R. Wilson shall have all the property that he now claims as his own (one gray horse, one cow and his clothing.) Fifth, my son Hugh J. Wilson is to remain on the farm with my wife during her lifetime and should he die without issue then the lands should go the the balance of my heirs. Sixth, my wife Sophronia shall be my executor. Witnessed by W.T. Holmes, W.P. Raines and J.W. McGowan. [No probate date given, but recorded at March term 1894, Warren County Court.]

pg 101-103. 4 Jul 1884. **Will of Nathan Byars.** "I, Nathan Byars, being a citizen of the county of Warren and the State of Tennessee, and being of sound mind and disposing memory and knowing the certainity of death, do make and publish this as my last will and testament.." After my death I desire that my just debts and funeral expenses be paid. Second, I give my beloved wife Nancy Byars and my daughter Jane Byars all my personal property, including furniture, stock and farming implements "for their sole use unmolested by any one during their natural lives", together with my home lands including my mansion and out houses. After their death my real estate and personal effects that may be left to be sold. Executor to make deed to all except the lands that I have sold and conveyed to my son T.P. Byars. I have a widowed daughter Mary Fuston who lives upon a part of my lands that I have given to my wife and daughter Jane and I desire that she have that part of said lands that she lives upon during her nautral life or widowhood. Upon her death or marriage that land to remain with the home lands. Should Mary out live her mother and sister, these lands are to be sold, along with the rest of my estate and equally divided between all my children or grand heirs namely: Martha Potter, Samuel H. Byars, Druselah H. Evans, Mattie Byars daughter of Harold Byars my son, Mary Fuston, Janes Byars, J.L. Byars, O.D. Byars, H.G. Byars and F.P.

Byars. I appoint my son O.D. Byars my executor. Witneses J.T. Trapp and Isaac J. Jones. [No probate date but recorded at March Term 1894, Warren County Court.]

pg 102. 28 Feb 1894. Inventory of the estate of L.S. Smartt, dec'd, made by W.C. Smartt.

pg 103. 2 Mar 1894. Settlement made with Mrs. Martha A. Snipes, administratrix of W.B. Snipes, dec'd. There is nothing in the hands of the administratrix as of this date.

pg 104-111. 21 Feb 1894. Report of the personal property of Jas. A. Wheeler, dec'd and sale of same reported by J.E. and A.C. Wheeler. Purchases made by Mrs. Van Wheeler, J.E. Wheeler, Will Wheeler, Della Wheeler, A.C. Wheeler, Mrs. Will Wheeler and others.

pg 112-116. 6 Mar 1894. Inventory of the personal property and notes of the estate of John F. Potts, dec'd reported by Frank Colville, admininstrator.

pg 117-118. 6 Mar 1894. Settlement made with Frank Colville and Virginia O. Hill, administrators with will annexed of H.L.W. Hill, dec'd. "Sale of 117 barrels of brandy--$7909.57" After deduction all indebtedness and expenses, the sum of $1998.63 to be equally divided between nine heirs [not named here], making the sum of $222.07 for each.

pg 119-120. 2 Apr 1894. Inventory and sale bill of the estate of C.B. Summar, dec'd. Purchases made by the widow, George Summars, J.J. Summar, and others.

pg 121-122. 23 Mar 1894. An account of sales made of the personal property of the estate of William Duncan, dec'd at his late residence in the 4th Civil District of Warren County on 17 Mar 1894. All purchases made by J.C. Pettit. W.M. Duncan, administrator.

pg 123-125. 14 Mar 1894. List of property sold at the sale of A.J. Gribble, dec'd on 9 Mar 1894 reported by C.C. Zurngle. Purchases made by Widow Gribble, T.A. Gribble, J.A. Gribble, T.M. Gribble, D.L. Gribble, A.J. Gribble, Jr., Sam Gribble, J.T. Gribble, and others.

pg 126. 7 Mar 1894. Settlement made with R.K. Rains, administrator of John W. West, dec'd.

pg 127. 5 Mar 1894. "It appearing to the County COurt now in session that William Duncan has died leaving no will and Wm. M. Duncan, son of the said Duncan, dec'd having appeared and moved the court to appoint him administrator of the said William Duncan, dec'd, and having given bond and qualified as such.. the court ordered that letters of administration be issued to the said William M. Duncan." Inventory of the assets of the estate.

pg 128. 18 Dec 1893. Inventory of the rents of H.H. Wood, dec'd's farm received and goods sold by T.M. Frazier, administrator.

pg 129. 20 Mar 1894. Settlement made with T.M. Frazier, administrator of the estate of H.H. Wood, dec'd. Estate insolvent.

pg 130. 9 Oct 1883. **Will of Jeremiah M. Wilbur.** Sharpesfield. "As it is appointed unto all men once to die and as no man knoweth how long it may please his creator to continue him in the State of existence and it is the duty of mortal creatures to be prepared to leave this world whenever it shall please the All Wise Disposer of Events to call them hence, and it being my opinion that the best time to arrange a man's temporal affairs is when he is in the enjoyment of health and in possession of all his facilities therefore I, Jeremiah M. Wilbur will and bequeath to my wife Estella F. Wilbur all my real and personal estate whatever." I will that my wife pay the sum of five dollars to my son Alden H. Wilbur and five dollars to my grandson Roy S. Wilbur. I appoint my wife Estella Wilbur my administrator. Witnessed L.L. Bennett, Ambrosia Jerome, N.E. Bennett. Presented for probate 7 Mar 1894.

pg 131. 8 Apr 1894. Report of Heloise Clenny, administratrix of S.M. Clenny, dec'd.

pg 132. 24 Apr 1894. Supplementary inventory and sale bill of the estate of William Duncan, dec'd, reported by W.M. Duncan.

pg 133. 9 Apr 1894. Settlement of the estate of Leroy Hammons reported by J.E. Jones, administrator. Receipts for $80.00 each given by D.L. Hammons, Mary Singleton, and J.O. Hammons. Receipt for $65.00 given by T.F. Hammons and for $115 given by "Mary Paris (widow)" pg 134-137. 30 Apr 1894. Inventory of the estate of G.P. Moffitt, dec'd reported by E.L. Moffitt, one of the executors of the estate. [List of the store accounts due the estate.]

pg 138. 24 May 1894. List of property in the hands of Mrs. E.F. Wilber, administratrix of J.M. Wilber, dec'd.

pg 139. 4 Jun 1894. Sale bill of the estate of John B. Paris, reported by J.R. Paris, administrator. Purchases made by J.R. Paris, Mrs. J.R. Paris, Claud Paris and others.

pg 140. 4 Jun 1894. Supplemental sale bill of the estate of C.B. Summar, dec'd reported by H.C. Summar, administrator.

pg 141. 30 Jul 1891. **Will of Joseph Miller.** "Unto all it may concern, by these presents, be it known that I, Joseph Miller, in view of the brevity of humaan life and the certainty of death, do this day make this my last will and testament". I will my body be given a decent Christian burial. Second, after my debts and funeral expenses are paid, I bequeath to my beloved wife E.W. Miller all my real estate situated in the 3rd District of Warren County and all my personal property during her natural life and at her death I direct that said property be sold and divided as follows: 2/3rds of said property to be divided equally between D.H. Miller and J.J. Miller, sons of my brother D.T. Miller. The remaining 1/3 t will to my namesake Joseph M. Gribble, son of T.R. and Jemina Gribble. I appoint my beloved wife E.W. Miller executrix and D.T. Miller executor. Witnessed by Elvin Sparkman and J.C.B. Gribble. Presented for probate 4 Jun 1894.

pg 142. 4 Jun 1894. Settlement made with G.A. Cope, administrator of J.B. Cope, dec'd. "Credit by each heir's receipt: G.P. Cope, J.N. Cope, B.F. Cope, G.A. Cope, J.R. Glenn, Venus Cope and M.J. Patterson." [Heirs had received various sums before settlement.]

pg 143-147. 4 Jun 1894. Inventory of the estate of Sallie Stoner, reported by William Coppinger, administrator. Purchases at sale made by G.M. Stoner, W.B. Stoner, S.M. Stoner, and others.

pg 148-149. 24 May 1894. **Will of I.C. Garretson.** "This is my last will and testament." I wish my property in Viola be sold and the proceeds to go to the payment of a note I owe John Custer. I want my wife Martha to have my farm in Grundy County and at her death to go to my three children Walter, Marion and Fannie. I hold a note on W. Garretson with a balance of about $50.00 which I wish given up to him. I wish my mountain land in Grundy County sold and the proceeds divided equally among all my children. Witnessed by M.H. Gwyn, J.S. Roberts, and A.J. Brewer. "Having dissignated on yesterday the disposition of my property both real and personal, I hereby choose D.B.Hoover and E.W. Smartt my executors. 25 May 1894." Witnessed P.H. Ashburn and John Rutledge. Probate in Minute Book 10, page 35, recorded July term 1894 of Warren County Court.

pg 150. 19 Jun 1894. Report of George F. Pennebaker, executor of the estate of Samuel F. Pennebaker, dec'd, El Paso County, TX. Balance turned over to guardian $295.68, on 8 Jun 1894.

pg 151-156. 14 Jun 1894. Sale bill of the estate of John O. Pope, dec'd, reported by J.R. Oliver, administrator. Purchases made by Laura Pope, Mat Pope, and others.

pg 157-158. 6 Aug 1894. Final settlement of H.M. Hennessee, administrator of the estate of A.W. Hennessee, dec'd. Nothing remains in the hand of the administrator for distribution.

pg 159-160. 6 Aug 1894. Settlement made with Denny Cummings, administrator of Joseph Cummings, dec'd. The administrator has paid out $1237.25 more than has come into his hands.

pg 161. 6 Aug 1894. Inventory of the personal property belonging to the estate of John O. Pope, dec'd as received by the administrator J.R. Oliver.

pg 162-168. 14 Jul 1894. Inventory of the estate of I.C. Garretson, dec'd. List of notes and accounts due estate. Report made by D.B. Hoover and E.W. Smartt, executors of I.C. Garretson's estate.

pg 169-171. 6 Aug 1894. Inventory of the estate of E.J. Wood, dec'd, including accounts and personal property, reported by James S. Doyle, administrator.

pg 172-173. 3 Sep 1894. Inventory of the estate of

C.B. Summar, dec'd, including accounts that were found on his book, reported by J.J. Summar.

pg 174. 3 Sep 1894. Inventory of the estate of Alex Gribble, dec'd, reported by Sam Gribble, administrator, including stock issued in the name of the administrator's son Alex.

pg 175. 17 Aug 1894. Settlement made with J.E. Jones, administrator of the estate of Thomas M. Biles, dec'd Receipt for $30.00 given by Sarilda Biles.

pg 176-177. 12 Sep 1894. Sale bill of the estate of Ed. J. Wood, dec'd, reported by J.S. Doyle, administrator. Purchases made by Mrs. Wood, J.H. Wood, Emma Wood and others.

pg 178-179. 19 Sep 1894. Sale of the personal property belonging to the estate of I.C. Garretson, dec'd at Viola, Tennessee, 11 Aug 1894. Purchases made by Mrs. Martha Garretson, W.H. Garretson and others. Reported by D.B. Hoover and E.W. Smartt.

pg 180. 10 Sep 1894. Settlement made with Sam Gribble, administrator of Alex Gribble, dec'd.

pg 181-187. 13 Oct 1894. Settlement of estate of T.C. Smartt, dec'd, made by J.C. Biles, executor. Vouchers for the following: To Mary M. Black, trustee for Sallie and Jodie $200.00; to Mary M. Black on legacy $1280.00; to Jesse Spurlock, her legacy $100.00; to Cicero Spurlock, his legacy, $100.00; to Sallie Spurlock, her legacy, $100.00; to C.G. Black, Jr, his legacy $100.00; to Lucy Smartt, trustee on legacy, $1280.00; to H.S.Dickey, guardian of his children $300.00; to Mrs. J.E. Smartt, legacy, $1100.00; to S.H. Smartt on legacy $1505.40. Executor given $400.00 for his services.

pg 188. 18 Nov 1894. Sale of real estate belonging to the estate of I.C. Garretson, consisting of houses and lots and vacant lots in Viola, TN, sold on 25 Oct 1894. reported by D.B. Hoover and E.W. Smartt, executors.

pg 189. Nov Term, 1894, Warren Couty Court. C.C. Zeingle, administrator of A.J.Gribble, dec'd makes supplementary sale bill.

pg 190-191. 25 oct 1894. Settlement made with J.G. Byoors and John Purser, executors of the estate of James

Purser, dec'd. Settlement made with each heir for his interest of $20.15: Mary Byars, Jane Byars, James Purcer, John Purcer and Luke Purcer.

pg 192-197. 5 Nov 1894. List of property sold at the sale of John Gribble, dec'd on 11 Oct 1894. Purchases made by T.M. Gribble, G.W. Gribble, Charles Gribble, C. Gribble, H.B. Gribble, J.T. Gribble, J.C. Gribble, Buck Gribble, S.W. Gribble, J.H. Gribble, Tilman Gribble, J.M. Gribble, Joe Gribble, D.C. Gribble, Gabe Gribble and others.

pg 198-199. 5 Oct 1894. Settlement made with J.B. Clark, administrator of A.J.Goodson, Sr., dec'd. Balance left after expenses, $174.01 dispersed as follows: E.E. and J.S. Reeder, $20.00, part of share; N.A. Goodson, administrator, $20.00, part of share; A.T. Goodson $15.00, part of share; W.M. Johnson, part of share $14.00; James Green, guardian, $25.00; J.B. Clark guardian of Milas Goodson, $25.00; Eliza Goodson receipt of $25.00; W.W. Johnson, receipt for $10.00; T.A. Goodson, receipts for $15.00 overdrawn.

pg 200-201. 23 Oct 1894. Settlement made with Mrs. Eliza Ann Davis, administratrix of Thomas Davis, dec'd. She has paid out $109.18 more than has come to her.

pg 202-203. 16 Oct 1894. Settlement made with W.L. Swann, administrator of Thomas Comer, dec'd. Receipt of J.C. Biles for amount of judgment obtained by Geo. L. Beech vs George P. Comer and is paid out of the estate due George P. Comer, $256.20. Receipts for $256.20 for their share in the estate given by Mariah Beech and George L. Beech "in full of share of Mariah Beech in estate" and F.A. Comer for his share. J.C.M. Ross and Son, Thurman Bros and Co., and Ritchey and Bostick each as per order for a part of the share of Sallie M. White, and receipt of Sallie M. White for the balance of her share ($21.35).

pg 204-207. 10 Oct 1894. Schedule of property found on hand belonging to Elizabeth Barnes, dec'd which was sold on 15 Sep 1894 by R.C. Barnes. Purchases made by Charley Barnes, J.W. Barnes, R.C. Barnes, C. Barnes, Tilda Barnes and others.

pg 208-209. 14 Sep 1881. **Will of Absalom Clark.** "I, Absalom Clark of the County of Warren and State of Tennessee do hereby make and publish this as my last will and testament..." First I direct that my body be decently buried in the family graveyard near my residence and that my debts and funeral expenses be paid. Second, I give my daughter Louise Lusk, wife of John D. Lusk, and the heirs of her body all my personal property and the tract of land on which I now live and all other lands of which I may die possessed of. In the event my wife Elmira Clark should survive me, my will is that she shall retain possession of the property as long as she may live, then it is to go to my said daughter. I appoint my neighbor Benjamin McCollum executor. Witnessed J.F. Worford and J.C. Biles. **Codicil**, 9 Mar 1893, I now appoint instead of Benjamin McCollum, James Webb, Jr. as my executor. Recorded Nov Term 1894, Warren County Court.

pg 210. 31 Oct 1894. Report of J.J. Meadows, trustee of St. Mary School Fund. Tuition paid for Carlie M. Etter.

pg 211-212. 21 Dec 1894. Settlement made with M. Sparkman and W.W. Parker, executors of William Sparkman, dec'd.

pg 213-214. 7 Jan <u>1894</u>. Settlement made with John L. Byars, administrator of Uriah Jaco, dec'd. Reports Priscilla Jaco year's support $50.00.

pg 215-216. 2 Jan 1895. Inventory of Mary J. Faulkner, administratrix of Thomas H. Faulkner, dec'd. "She will state that Thomas H. Faulkner was in partnership with Robert Cantrell and his whole estate, with a slight exception was merged in the partnership and he did not have as much property on the outside as the law allowed for his widow and nearly the whole of his debts were paid out of the partnership funds..." There is still in the hands of the surviving partner a large amount of insolvent debts.

pg 217-218. 5 Jan 1895. Settlement made with Isaac Barnes, administrator of Charity Barnes, dec'd.

pg 219. 29 Dec 1894. Settlement made with J.C. Biles, administrator of H.B. Ramsey, dec'd. Hattie Ramsey's years support.

pg 220. 2 Jan 1895. Settlement made with T.M. Frazier, administrator of H.H. Wood, dec'd.

pg 221. 2 Jan 1895. Settlement made with W.W. Ware,

Warren County, Tn Will Book 9, cont.

administrator of Elizabeth Moffitt, dec'd.

pg 222. 4 Jan 1895. Settlement of the Shockley School Fund made by W.H. Smith, trustee.

pg 223. 1 Jan 1895. The final settlement made with Harret P. Phelps [signed as Hattie P. Phelps], executrix of W.W. Phelps, dec'd. Distributed $116.25 to each of the following: J.A. Phelps, S. T. Phelps, Maggie L. Pearsall, and Zipporah Woodlee.

pg 224-225. 24 Dec 1894. Settlement made with C.S. Ivie, administrator of Nancy D. Peay (with will annexed). Guardian's report from T.B. Ivie. Payments to Mrs. Martha Lillard.

pg 226. 21 Dec 1894. Settlement made with Arch Scott and John Scott, executors of Cooper Scott, dec'd. Executors have overpaid the amount received by $23.79.

pg 227. 23 Dec 1894. Sale bill of the estate of C.M. Sullivan reported by J.F. Sullivan.

pg 228-229. 7 Jan 1895. The undersigned administrator of J.W. McMillin, dec'd makes the following settlement. There is nothing further coming to the estate. Signed A.R. Ramsey.

pg 230. 31 Dec 1894. Settlement made with M.B. Harwell, administrator of S.J. Gibbs, dec'd. Administrator has paid out $12.85 more than has come into his hands.

pg 231-232. 5 Jan 1895. Settlement made with W.L. Swan, administrator of H.B. Higginbotham, dec'd. Receipts for $80.00 each given by Fannie and Wm. Pennington, William Higginbotham, R.L.Higginbotham, Rebecca Higginbotham, and J.S. Harrison, guardian.

pg 233. 4 Jan 1895. Settlement made with W.L. Swan, administrator of Dorcas Jordan, dec'd.

pg 234. 7 Jan 1895. Settlement made with William M. Akers, administrator of W.R. Akers, dec'd.

pg 235-236. 5 Jan 1895. Inventory and sale bill of the estate of M.A. Doty reported by E.T. McGee.

pg 237. 7 Jan 1895. Settlement made with W.M. Martin,

administrator of Thomas Witt, dec'd. Credits to William Witt and Sherman Witt for $10.00 each.

pg 238. 7 Jan 1895. Settlement made with J.B. Myers, administrator of P.M. Myers, dec'd. Creditors paid 80%.

pg 239. 29 Jan 1895. W.C. Womack, administrator of J.W. Burk, dec'd submits the inventory.

pg 240. 3 Jan 1895. Sale bill of the estate of H.H. Wood, dec'd, sale held on 22 Dec 1894. Reported by T.M. Frazier, administrator.

pg 241. 21 Dec 1894. Inventory and sale bill of the estate of William Duncan, dec'd reported by W.M. Duncan, administrator.

pg 242. 24 Dec 1894. Sale bill of the estate of John O. Pope, dec'd reported by J.R. Oliver, administrator.

pg 243-245. 19 Jan 1895. Sale bill of the estate of Laura Kirby, dec'd. Purchases by J.B. Kirby, Bettie Kirby, J.C. Kirby, J.C. J. Kirby, Bill Kirby, H.C.Kirby, R.S. Kirby, Billie Kirby, B.L. Kirby, Rosa Kirby and others.

pg 246-248. 7 Jan 1895. Inventory and sale bill of the estate of John Gribble, dec'd reported by H.B. Gribble, administrator. Includes notes due estate.

pg 249. 4 Feb 1895. Settlement made with W.A. Sewell, administrator of J.L. Sewell, dec'd. There remains in the hands of said administrator the sum of $654.50.

pg 250. 29 Jan 1895. **Will of William Houchin.** "I, William Houchin, being of sound mind and disposing memory, do make and publish this as my last will and testament." First, I direct that my funeral expenses and just debts be paid. Second, I will unto my mother Caroline Houchin and my two sisters Josephine Houchin and Florence Houchin, all my property of every kind. Third I nominate my sister Josephine executrix of this will. Witnessed by J.C.M. Ross and W.F. Elkins. Recorded in Warren County Court Feb Term 1895..

pg 251-260. 18 Feb 1895. Inventory and sale bill of the estate of Mrs. Jane G. Brown, dec'd, reported by B.W. Sparks, administrator. Purchases made by W. Brown, Steve Brown, Frank Brown, Billoat[?] Brown, Bill O.

Brown, J.L. Brown, W.B. Brown and others.

pg 261-263. 3 Nov 1894.   **Will of Patrick H. Coffee.**   I give to my beloved neice Bettie Smithson three houses and lots on P Street, west Washington (or Georgetown), D.C., numbers 2522, 2524 and 2526.   Should Bettie Smithson die without children, the property described above to be equally divided between Leilia Lewis and Jessie Reams and their children.   I will to my beloved neices Hallie M. Coffee, Leila Lewis and Jessie Reams and their children house and lot No.1118 on 5th Street NE in Washington, D.C.   Should Hallie M. Coffee die leaving no children, her interest is to go to her two sisters Leila Lewis and Jessie Reams.   Houses 1220, Linden Place, 1317 Linden Street and one half in lot 204 east Capt. Street in Washington D.C. I wish sold to pay my indebitness on my real estate in Washington, D.C. I direct my executor to pay to my brother A.S. Coffee $150.00 each year if he needs it so long as he is acting as executor of my estate.   My executors are to place a new stone 2 feet square of Georgia marble in the same pattern of the one now standing in the Coffee lot in the new cemetery, and a wrought iron fence to be placed over the grave of my father, mother and two brothers and markers to be used if the graves can be identified. "After my debts have been paid and my will carried out so far as directed by me, I will to the following persons the amounts to me paid out of the rents and profits arising from my property.   The same to be used to pay the said following bequeaths for the term of seven and one half years from the time said payments begin.   Should said bequests not have been paid in full at the expiration of the said seven and one half years, the payments will cease and nothing more will be paid on the same: To James Fulton Colville of Atlanta, $2000.00; To the heirs of George W. Hanegar, dec'd $2000.00; To the heirs of R.P. Womack, dec'd $1500.00; To Mrs. Louisa Spurlock, widow of John L. Spurlock, dec'd $100.00;, To William I. Hill, $250.00; To William G. Etter, $250.00; To D.F. Wallace, $400.00; To J.C. Ramsey, $100.00; To Capt. Thomas B. Rust $500.00.   These bequeaths, beginning with J.F. Colville and ending with Thomas B. Rust are not to interfere with carrying out the previous bequest in my will.   I further will to Bettie Smithson house and lot No 1120 on 5th Street, NE in Washington, D.C.   I appoint R.M. Reams my executor. Witnesses: S.H. Smartt, W.H. York, M.E. Sparks and H.F. Harwell.   Probated in Minute Book 10, pages 130-131.

pg 264. 23 Feb 1895. Sale bill of the estate of J.W. Miller, dec'd as reported by J.M. Gribble, one of the administrators.

pg 265. 20 Feb 1895. Sale bill of the estate of A.C. Clark, dec'd submitted by James Webb.

pg 266. 2 Apr 1895. Report of notes and accounts belonging to the estate of Joseph Douglas now in the hands of H.B. Bonner, administrator for collection.

pg 267. 8 Mar 1895. Settlement made with R.R. Etter, executor of the estate of George Etter, dec'd.

pg 268-270. 5 May 1895. Report of R.H. Mason, guardian of C.W. Smith. The settlement of the guardianship is reported for the past years. "Wyatt Smith claims the upper place by contract. If I had this place it would add much to their support. It will take a lawsuit to recover it and I have been advised if I can support the old people on the $150.00 from S.L. Brown's notes to make the best of the other place."

pg 271. 6 May 1895. The following is a true and correct inventory of the personal effect of Patrick H. Coffee, dec'd, which have come into my hands up to this date as executor of same. Signed R.M. Reams.

pg 272-273. 8 Apr 1895. Settlement made with J.C. Rankin, administrator of the estate of Ann P. Pepper, dec'd. There is yet due the heirs of Ann P. Pepper the sum of $1066.85. The eight heirs of Ann P. Pepper [not here named] to receive $133.35 each.

pg 274. 30 Apr 1895. Settlement made with W.R. Deavenport, administrator of Mrs. P.A. Roberson, dec'd.

pg 275-277. 6 May 1895. Settlement made with Jesse Hill, administrator of A.D. Wheeler, dec'd. Mary M. Wheeler receipt for $37.00 included.

pg 278-279. 8 Sep 1894. **Will of Mrs Virginia H. Beech.** "I, Virginia H. Beech of McMinnville, TN realizing the uncertainty of life and desiring that my children shall have the fullest enjoyment of what property I may have at my death, do hereby make and publish this my last will and testament." First, I direct that my executor pay my funeral expenses and debts. Second, I give the contents of my cedar chest to my grandchildren Virginia,

Betana and Lawrence Beech. Third, I give my furniture in my room to Virginia D. Beech, my granddaughter. Fourth, I give my wearing apparel to my two daughters-in-law. Fifth, I give my stock in Firt National Bank of Tullahoma, TN, amounting to $2500.00 to my granddaughter Virginia D. Beech when she becomes 16 years of age. Sixth, my stock in the Elk National Bank of Fayetteville, TN to be held in trust for my sons John and George L. Beech during their lives and at their death to be paid to my grandchildren equally, except Virginia D. Beech who has herein above been provided for. J. Walling is to be trustee and to pay to each of my sons one half of the dividends of said stock. Seventh, the trustee shall have power to change the investment. Eighth, the remainder of my estate is to be divided between my two sons John and George L. Beech. Eighth, I appoint J. Walling my executor. Witnesses W.C. Womack and S.R. Bruster. Probated 11 May 1895.

pg 280. 3 Jun 1895. Sale bill of E.C. Dunlap's estate. "The undersigned administrator of W.H. Simpson, dec'd would report the following sale of the personal effects of E.C. Dunlap, dec'd." Signed M.C. Simpson, administrator of W.H. Simpson.

pg 280. 28 May 1895. Account of sales of real estate made by D.B. Hoover and E.W. Smartt, executors of I.C. Garrettson, dec'd, made at Viola at public sale on 23 May 1895. 100 acres purchased by W.A. Griswold and the balance (6089 acres) by J.T. Garretson.

pg 281. 3 Jun 1895. Inventory and sale bill of the personal estate of Clabe Grove, dec'd reported by W.L. Grove, administrator.

pg 282-285. 24 Jun 1895. Settlement made with E.L. Moffitt one of the executors of G.P. Moffitt, dec'd. Executors have paid out $7.33 more that they had reported as by them received.

pg 286. 26 Jun 1895. Settlement made with W.L. Swann, administrator of H.B. Higginbothom, dec'd. Credits by voucher for $162.77 issued to: William Higginbothom, R.L. Higginbothom, Mrs. Rebecca Higginbothom, Fannie and William Pennington, and J.S. Harrison (guardian). Also one for $242.77 issued to W.V. Whitson, guardian.

pg 287. 26 Jun 1895. Settlement made with W.L. Swann, administrator of Darcus Jorden, dec'd. Receipts for equal shares ($14.54) given by Henry Jorden, J.A. Jorden, J.C. Jorden, A.J. Jorden, Lue Jorden, William R. Jorden, Marguritte Dye, Mary Nunley, and Jessie Walling as attorney for J. Blylock.

pg 288-289. 25 Jun 1894. **Will of O.M. Thurman.** I, Oliver M. Thurman of Warren County, TN, being of sound and disposing mind and memory, do make and publish this my last will and testament.. I give to my dearly beloved wife Lou Thurman all my property of whatsoever nature during the time of her life or widowhood and for the support of my children who may be under age at the time of my death. They shall receive such educational advantages as shall place them upon an equality with my other children. Upon the death or marriage of said Lou Thurman, I wish my estate to be divided as would be law be done in case of my death intestate, except that any of my children that are minors should receive addition to their share for their support and education. I appoint my wife and my oldest son Isaac J. Thurman as executors. Witnesses W.S. Lively and J.M. Lively. Probate date not given but recorded at July Term 1895 of Warren County Court.

pg 290-291. 19 Jul 1895. Settlement made with C.C. Zwingle, administrator of A.J. Gribble, dec'd. Remaining in the hands of the administrator the sum of $1049.27.

pg 292. 17 Jul 1895. Supplemental sale bill of the estate of John Gribble, dec'd, reported by H.B. Gribble, administrator.

pg 293-295. 6 Aug 1895. Inventory of the estate of William Houchin, dec'd, including bank stock, notes due estate reported by Josephine Houchin, executrix.

pg 296. 7 Aug 1895. Inventory of the estate of Mrs. V.H. Beech, dec'd reported by Jesse Walling, executor.

pg 297-298. 15 Aug 1895. Settlement made with John L. Byars, administrator of Uriah Jaco, dec'd. Each of the heirs give receipts as follows: Jennie Jaco, $309.95; Parilee Jaco, $309.95; Sarah Jaco, $309.95; Josie Potter and Blue Potter, $309.95; A.M. Clark, $209.10; Lou York and E.B. York, $213.60; N.E. Cunningham's estate $309.95; M.J. and J.B. Cherry, $134.82.

pg 299. 5 Sep 1895. Settlement made with B.L. Kirby,

administrator of Laura Kirby, dec'd.

pg 300-301. 4 Sep 1895. List of personal property of W.J. Fuston, dec'd that has come to the hands of S.C. Fuston as administratrix.

pg 302-303. 4 Sep 1895. Sale of the personal property of W.J. Fuston, sold by the administratrix Sarah C. Fuston, on 29 Aug 1895. Purchases made by Mrs. Arthur Fuston, Myra Fuston, A.T. Fuston, William N. Fuston, Sarah C. Fuston, T.H. Fuston, Sam Fuston, A.E. Fuston, Forest Fuston, Colonel Fuston and others.

pg 304. 7 Oct 1895. Settlement in full of all claims against said estate made with T.J. Hankins, administrator of S.G. Hankins, dec'd.

pg 305. 28 Aug 1895. Report of George F. Pennebaker of Los Angeles County, California, executor of the estate of Samuel F. Pennebaker, dec'd.

pg 306. 8 Oct 1895. Sale of the property of W.H. Simpson, dec'd held 7 Sep 1895 reported by M.C. Simpson. Purchases by R.L. Simpson, J.C. Simpson, James C. Simpson, Maggie Simpson and others.

pg 307-308. 15 Jan 1892. **Will of T.T. Peay.** First it is my will that my body be decently interred according to my condition in life. Second, I will that all my just debts be paid. Third, I will to my daughter Maggie and her husband J.W. Sanders $1050.00, having heretofore given them $1750.00. Fourth, I will that my wife Mary Peay and my daughter Tommy Smith have the balance of my estate, both real and personal, said property to be managed and controlled by my executors for the sole benefit of my wife Mary Peay and my daughter Tommy Smith. The executors are to sell the farm on which I live and my store house now occupied by Paty Bros. The reason I have not mentioned my other children in this will is because I have given them already their equable part of my estate. I have given my daughter Martha W. Kelton $4510.00. I have given John Paty about $7800.00 and my son Alton the same. I appoint my son-in-law John Paty and my friend S. McRamsey as my executors. Witnesses W.H. Moore and W.T. Paty. **Codicil;** 13 Jul 1893, I have paid over to my daughter Maggie and her husband J.W. Sanders previous to this date $400.00, leaving a balance of $650.00 more to be paid. Probate date not given but in Oct Term 1895 of Warren County

Court.

pg 309. 21 Sep 1895. **Will of Jane Elkins.** "For and in consideration of the love and affection I have for my beloved daughter Laura C. Swindell and her heirs, I do this day of my own free will and accord, after paying all funeral expenses give grant and convey unto the said Laura C. Swindell all personal property of which I am possessed, consisting of notes and accounts, all stock including horses, cattle and hogs, all farming tools and implements, wagons and household and kitchen furniture, ... Also all crops. I furthermore name Charlie Hudgens as executor to this, my last will and testament." Witnesses J.D. Templeton and G.W. Whiteaker. Nov Term, 1895, Warren County Court.

pg 310-311. 1 nov 1895. Inventory of the personal property of T.T. Peay, dec'd reported by J.W. Paty, executor.

pg 312-313. 20 May 1893. **Will of Daniel Osborn.** I, Daniel Osborn, being of sound and disposing mind and memory, and being desirous to settle my worldly affairs while I have strength to do so, do make this my last will and testament. First, I desire that my body be buried in a decent and Christian like manner. Second, I direct that my debts be paid. Third, I give to my dear wife Mary E. Osborn my brick house and land belonging to same in McMinnville, known as "The Brick". Fifth, I bequeath to my dear wife all my personal property of every description. Sixth, I bequeath to my dear wife my homestead farm on which we now live and at her death the title to same to be vested in my dear son Daniel Osborn. Seventh, I will that the home farm be kept up in a like manner as I have heretofore managed it. Eighth, I will that my wife Mary E. Osborn be the guardian of my son Daniel and that he shall be educated and maintained until he is 21 years old. Ninth, I appoint my wife Mary E. Osborn executrix of this, my last will and testament. Witnessed by J.C. Heed and Lida Heed. Recorded at Nov Term 1895, Warren County Court.

pg 314-315. 12 Mar 1885. **Will of L.F. Jeanmaire.** I, L.F. Jeanmaire of Warren County do hereby make and publish this as my last will and testament. First, I direct my funeral expenses and just debts be paid. Second, I give to my wife Heloise Jeanmaire all te property of which I may died seized of, both real and personal. I appoint her the executrix of this will. Signed by the testator in our presence and witnessed at his request by J.F. Morford and C. Coffee. **Codicil.** 24 Feb 1887. Louis F. Jeanmaire and wife Heloise whose signatures is affixed to this make it a part of this will that at the death of the last one of the two parties, their daughter Hermainia Jeanmaire shall receive the sum of $1400.00 separate from her regular share in the estate. Our daughters Julia A. Maddux and Susie M. Black having received the same amount in full. Signed by L.F. Jeanmaire and Heloise Jeanmaire. Recorded at Dec Term, 1895, Warren County Court.

pg 316-317. 2 Dec 1895. Inventory of the estate of Jane Elkins, dec'd reported by Charles Hudgens, executor.

pg 318-319. 7 Dec 1895. Sale bill of the estate of J.A. Snipes, dec'd, submitted by Albert Snipes. Purchases made by R.W. Snipes, C.W. Snipes, Luther Snipes, L.B. Snipes, B.W. Snipes, George Snipes and others.

pg 320. 7 Dec 1895. Inventory of the real estate of William Houchin, dec'd situated in the first Civil District of Warren County, reported by Josephine Houchin, executrix.

pg 321. 2 Jan 1896. Settlement made with T.M. Frazier, administrator of H.H. Wood, dec'd who reports that there is nothing remaining in the hands of the administrator.

pg 322. 23 Dec 1895. The last settlement with W.H. Smith, trustee for Shockley School Fund.

pg 323. 6 Jan 1896. Inventory of the estate of O.D. Byars, dec'd reported by Josie Byars, administratrix.

pg 324. 7 Jan 1896. Settlement made with J.C. Rankin, administrator of Ann Pepper, dec'd. Receipts for: $66.67 given by W.J. Pepper; $133.35 by Johnnie and Solomon Craven; $133.35 given by W.C. Pepper; $22.22 each given by E.J. Morrison, T.C. Talley, W.W. Fairbanks atty for _____, J.H. Talley, Bettie Allison, W.W. Fairbanks atty for ____ Talley and _____ Talley, W.W. Fairbanks atty for ____ Morrison and ____ Morrison and A.M. Morrison. $33.33 receipts given by Peter Craven, guardian, E.C. Roach, W.W. Fairbanks, atty for E.C. Pepper, E.J. Roach, Mollie Roach, Margaret and A.J.

Mitchell, Dora and J.B. Myers and J.C. Rankin, trustee for his children. $3.70 receipts given by Thomas Smith, James Smith and Sarah Smith. $26.65 receipts given by Prudence Talley, J.C. Talley. $65.15 receipt given by J.B. Eshman, guardian for M.F. and H.C. Carter.

pg 325-327. 6 Jan 1896. Settlement made with J.W. Gribble and J.M. Gribble, administrators of J.W. Miller, dec'd.

pg 328. 6 Jan 1896. Sale bill of the estate of F.C. Christian, dec'd, reported by M. Barnes.

pg 329. 25 Jan 1896. Supplemental inventory and sale bill made by James Webb, executor of the estate of Absalom Clark, dec'd, sale held 15 Dec 1895.

pg 330-331. 20 Jan 1896. Settlememt made with R.R. Etter, executor of the estate of George H. Etter, dec'd. The executor reports having received from the various notes on the heirs of the dec'd to wit: on Lucy and Maggie Etter, $3000.00; on J.C. Etter, $2031.00; on R.R. Etter, $1377.00; on T.H. Etter, $1648.00; on C.M. Etter, $1959.00; on H.R. Etter, $1234.00; on George H. Etter, $1310.00; and on Nancy J. Hays, $879.00. Vouchers of the heirs [for various amounts]: Jane Burns[?], Emma Lock, Frank Woodlee, J.M. Moffitt, Hattie Moffitt, Jennie Moffitt and Nancy Jane Hays.

pg 332-333. 22 Jan 1896. Settlement made with L.F. Daugherty, administrator of J.W. Daugherty, dec'd.

pg 334-335. 13 Jan 1888. **Will of Mrs. Eliza J. Mitchell.** "Know all men by these presents that I, Eliza J. Mitchell of McMinnville, TN being of good bodily health and of sound and disposing mind and memory, do make this my last will and testament." I hereby bequeath my house and lot on Lyon Street, McMinnville to my step grandson Jodie M. Lively on condition of his paying to my brother Matthew Lyon and my nephew Adolphus B. Cates $100.00 each. I also leave my household furniture to said J.M. Lively. Witnessed by T.B. Burman and R.S. Mitchell. **Codicil.** 7 Mar 1892. I, Eliza J. Mitchell do make this as a codicil to my will. It is my will that J.M. Lively take the house and lot absolutely at my death upon the payment of the $100.00 each willed by me to M. Lyon and A.B. Cates. Witnessed J.C. Biles and W.S. Lively. Probated at the Feb Term of Warren County Court in the year 1896.

pg 336-339. 2 Mar 1896. Inventory of the estate of C.M. Sullivan, dec'd made 15 Sep 1893 by J.F. Sullivan, administrator. List of notes and accounts due deceased. Sale of the personal property held 28 Sep 1893. Purchases made by Lizzie Sullivan, Sam Sullivan and others.

pg 340. 2 Mar 1896. Inventory and list of all that has come into our hands as administrators of C.B. Summer, dec'd, signed by S.J. Summer.

pg 341. 6 Jan 1896. Report and settlement of the estate of Drucilla C. Ross, dec'd, made by W.S. Ross, administrator.

pg 342. 26 Feb 1896. Settlement made with L.F. Daugherty, administrator of J.W. Daugherty, dec'd.

pg 343. 1 Mar 1896. Inventory of the goods and chattels of the estate of James Rowland, dec'd which remained at the death of his wife Permelia Rowland, reported by Alex W. Rowland, executor of the estate of James Rowland, dec'd.

pg 344-346. 16 Jan 1896. Items of personalty sold 5 Dec 1895 by J.W. Paty of the estate of T.T. Peay, dec'd.

pg 347. 20 Feb 1896. Supplementary inventory and sale bill of W.M. Duncan, administrator of William Duncan, dec'd. Sale held 4 Jan 1896 and the late residence of the deceased in the 4th District of Warren County.

pg 348-349. 12 Feb 1896. List of the property sold at a sale by M.V. Earles, administrator of Tabitha Earles Jan 1896. Purchases by T. Earles, A.W. Earles, Tom Earles, Willie Earles and others.

pg 350-354. 18 Feb 1896. Settlement made with E. W. Smartt and D.B. Hoover, executors of I.C. Garretson, dec'd. $2412.80 remaining in the hands of the executors after winding up the estate.

pg 355. 12 Mar 1896. Settlement of the estate of T.C. Smartt, dec'd, reported by J.C. Biles, executor. Credits: Mrs. Mary Black $10.00; S.H. Smartt legacy, $10.00; and Lucy Smartt legacy $10.00.

pg 356-357. 9 Mar 1896. Settlement made with J.F. Sullivan, administrator of C.M. Sullivan, dec'd.

Warren County, Tn Will Book 9, cont.

Remaining in the hands of the administrator $111.00 due the heirs.

pg 358. 21 Mar 1896. R.C. Barnes report of the inventory and sale bill of the estate of J.M. Herndon, dec'd. Purchases made by Sarah Herndon, Jim Herndon, Mrs. Herndon and others.

pg 359. 5 Mar 1896. Sale bill of the estate of D.S. McAfee, dec'd [purchasers names not given] reported by T.H. McAfee.

pg 360. 13 Mar 1896. Second sale bill of the estate of W.J. Fuston, dec'd reported by S.C. Fuston, administrator. Purchases made by C.E. Fuston, Sam Fuston, W.W. Fuston, and others.

pg 361. 20 Mar 1896. Inventory and sale bill of the estate of C.H. Bishop, dec'd reported by J.W. Barnes. Most purchases made by W.N. Bishop.

pg 362. 14 Mar 1896. Settlement made with J.R. Oliver and J.P. Hardcastle, administrators of John O. Pope, dec'd. Nothing remaining in the hands of the administrators.

pg 363. 18 Mar 1896. Following property came to the hands of F.M. Smith, administrator of Lecil Smith, dec'd (list of notes and accounts due estate.)

pg 364-365. 23 Mar 1896. Settlement made with D.B. Hoover and E.W. Smartt, executors of I.C. Garrettson, dec'd.

pg 366. 26 Apr 1896. Settlement made with Arch Scott, executor of Cooper Scott, dec'd. Executor has paid out $132.63 more than has come into his hands.

pg 367. 4 May 1896. Settlement made with E. W. Miller and D.S. Miller, administrators of Joseph Miller, dec'd. Administrators have paid out $41.85 more than has come into their hands.

pg 368. 22 Apr 1896. Settlement made with J.H. Whitlock, administrator of the estate of E.A. McGregor, dec'd. Whitlock has paid out $0.97 more than has come into his hands.

pg 369-370. 25 May 1896. Settlement made with John L.

Warren County, Tn Will Book 9, cont.

Byars, administrator of Uriah Jaco, dec'd. Balance in estate of $3.65 to be equally divided between the seven heirs, to wit: Nancy Cunningham, Josie Patter [Potter?], Lue York, Alice Clark, Jennie Ann Jaco, Paralee Jaco, and Sarah D. Jaco, each receiving $0.52 1/7 each. Mary Cherry is listed among the heirs but is not shown as receiving any money.

pg 371. 27 Mar 1896. Settlement made with C.C. Zwingle, administrator of A.J. Gribble, dec'd. $557.33 remaining in the hands of the administrator.

pg 372. 8 Apr 1896. Second sale bill of the estate of Sallie Stoner, dec'd reported by William Coppinger.

pg 373. 1 Jun 1896. List of the property sold at the sale of Nathan Byars, dec'd reported by F.P. Byars, administrator. Purchases made by F.P. Byars, J.G. Byars and others.

pg 374. 28 Mar 1896. Account and report of the sale of the personal property of the estate of James Rowland, dec'd left after the life estate of his wife Permelia Rowland, dec'd, made by Alex Rowland, one of the executors. Purchases made by J.E. Rowland, J.H. Rowland, Jane Rowland, and others.

pg 375-376. 25 May 1896. Settlement made with J.R. Paris, administrator of J.B. Paris, dec'd. The $1.25 remaining in the hands of the administrator is allowed him for his trouble.

pg 377. 20 May 1896. The following account made and stated with R.R. Etter, executor of George Etter, dec'd. Receipts for the following given by: Frank Woodlee, guardian for Lue Woodlee ($719.18), Nancy Hayes ($949.01), J.M. Moffitt ($46.09), Hattie Moffitt ($47.09), Jennie Moffitt ($20.00), Emma Locke ($104.69), Jane Barnes [also written Burns] ($104.69), and Lucy Etter, Maggie Shevlin, J.C. Etter, George H. Etter and C.M. Etter for $1119.18 3/4 each.

pg 378-379. 16 June 1906. Settlement made with J.M. Gribble, administrator of J.W. Miller, dec'd. The total assets of the estate $6598.57 to be divided among the heirs of J.W. Miller, dec'd, to wit: J.L. Miller, Randy Sewell, Dolly Hash, Levisa Clark, Alex Miller, Julia L. Gribble, J.C. Miller, W.V. Miller, J.W. Miller, Jennie Moffitt, and J.E. Clark, atty in fact for Willy and

Horace Thurman to receive a total of $597.37 each.

pg 380. 10 Jul 1896. Settlement of the estate of L.S. Smartt, dec'd made by W.C. Smartt, administrator. Administrator has paid out $2.33 more than has come into his hands.

pg 381-382. 18 Jul 1896. Sale bill of the estate of A.E. Witty, dec'd reported by M.B. Roberson, administrator.

pg 383-384. 22 Jul 1896. Inventory of the goods and chattles of the estate of J.W. Woodlee, dec'd presented by F.E. Woodlee, administrator. J.W. Woodlee owned one half interest in the partnership of the firm of Woodlee and Meadows engaged in the manufacture of apple brandy.

pg 385-397. 3 Aug 1896. Inventory of the estate of J.P. Gartner, dec'd, presented by L.P. Gartner, administrator. Extensive list of notes and accounts due the deceased plus short list of personal property.

pg 398-400. 3 Aug 1896. Settlement made with John Goodson, administrator of J.R.P. Goodson, dec'd. The following received dispursements from the estate: John Goodson, I.J. Goodson, Sophia and C.W. Capshaw, Tennessee Goodson, C.C. Wright, A.W. Green and Liddie Green, A.J. Goodson, and R.V. Goodson.

pg 401-402. 27 Nov 1895. **Will of Sam L. Colville.** I, Sam L. Colville of McMinnville, being of sound mind and disposing memory, do make and publish this my last will and testament. First I direct that my just debts be paid. Second, I have heretofore advanced $5000.00 to my following children: to my daughters Mary Womack, Ida Lind, Ellen Bagley and to my sons Charles Colville, Frank Colville, and Warner E. Colville. I have advanced $12,000.00 to my son Sam L. Colville. In the distribution of my estate I wish each of my children to be charged with what I have advanced them, making them all equal with my son Sam L. Colville. I have a marriage contract with my beloved wife Bethiah L. Colville in which she will receive $400.00 per year. It is my will that the executor set apart sufficient sum to provide said $400.00 for her during her life. All property and effects which she brought to my house on or after our marriage belongs to her. The share of my daughter Mary Womack is to be held in trust for her separate use and at her death be equally divided among her children. As to my real estate, the children should divide among themselves, and if they cannot do so it is to be sold and the proceeds divided as herein directed.. I appoint my son Frank Colville executor of this my last will and testament. [No witnesses named]. Probated in County Court, Aug Term 1896.

pg 403. 22 Aug 1896. Settlement made with R.R. Etter, executor of George Etter, dec'd. Receipts for $1119.18 given by Thomas H. Etter and S.S. Patterson (Executor of H.R. Etter, dec'd) and receipts for $5.00 given by Emma Lock and Jane Burns.

pg 404. 10 Sep 1896. Inventory of notes belonging to the estate of M.J. Davis, dec'd coming into hands of D.H. Wooten and W.E. Smartt, administrators.

pg 405. 26 Aug 1896. Sale of part of the personal estate of J.W. Woodlee, dec'd made by F.E. Woodlee, administrator on 15 Aug 1896. Purchases made by F.E. Woodlee, D.H. Woodlee, D.W. Woodlee, J.C. Woodlee, Frank Woodlee and others.

pg 406. 10 Aug 1896. Sale bill of the estate of Alfred Elkins, dec'd reported by J.T. Hillis.

pg 407. 8 Sep 1896. Inventory of the personal estate of G.W. Wood, dec'd reported by J.I. Martin, administrator.

pg 408-410. Sep Term, 1896. Settlement made with W.C. Womack, atty in fact for R.B. Womack, administrator of R.R. Womack, dec'd. Settlement to pay $0.50 on all the claims filed against said estate.

pg 411. 9 Oct 1896. Settlement made with C.C. Zwingle, administrator of A.J. Gribble, dec'd.

pg 412-413. 5 Oct 1896. Inventory of the personal property belonging to the estate of C.K. Mauzy, dec'd, reported by Charles Mauzy, administrator of C.K. Mauzy, dec'd.

pg 414-415. 26 Sep 1896. Inventory and sale bill of the estate of F.L. Montandon, dec'd reported by Albert Montandon, administrator.

pg 416-420. 5 Oct 1896. Sale bill of the estate of William Womack, dec'd as reported by F.M. Womack, administrator. Purchases made by A.J. Womack, Mrs. M.A. Womack, Dr. Arsey Womack, J.M. Womack, Jr., F.G. Womack, Jno Womack, Jr., Bettie Womack, Abner Womack and others.

pg 421. 10 Oct 1896. Settlement with C.C. Zwingle, administrator of A.J. Gribble, dec'd. He has paid out $47.41 more than has come into his hands.

pg 422-424. 2 Oct 1896. List of the personal property sold by Charles Mauzy, administrator of C.K. Mauzy on 2 Oct 1896. Purchasers include Bill Mauzy and others.

pg 425. 6 Nov 1896. Settlement made with W.C. Womack, administrator of John W. Burks, dec'd. He has paid out $1.90 more than has come into his hands.

pg 426-427. 28 Aug 1896. **Will of J.W. Hash.** In the name of God, Amen, I, J.W. Hash of Warren County, TN, being of sound mind and memory and considering the undertainty of this frail and transitory life, do therefore make ordain, publish and declare this to be my last will and testament. First, after my debts are paid, the residue of my estate both real and personal I dispose of as follows: If my beloved wife should out live me I will to her one third of the 200 acres on which I live, bound by C. Arnold's land near Rock Island and the Caney Fork River, beginning at the mouth of the Collins River. At my death my son George W. Hash is to have one third of the whole tract. The other two thirds is to be divided equally between Henry Hash and J.M. Gribble. Witnessed W.S. Hash, John W. Hash and J.D. Hash. Probate Nov Term, 1896, Warren County Court.

pg 428. 6 Nov 1896. Settlement made with R.C. Barnes, administrator of Elizabeth Barnes, dec'd.

pg 429-430. 9 Nov 1896. Inventory of the estate of J.W. Hash, dec'd, reported by John W. Hash, administrator of J.W. Hash.

pg 431. 30 Mar 1895. **Will of James M. Holman.** Colorado Springs, Colorado. I, James M. Holman being of sound mind and disposing memory make this as my last will and testament. I give my wife Allie R. Holman all my property both real and personal and appoint her my executrix. Witnessed W.E. Bassett, H.S. Hawks and J.A. Sill. Probated Nov Term, 1896, Warren County, Court.

pg 432. 11 Nov 1896. Settlement made with W.M. Duncan,

administrator of William Duncan, dec'd.

pg 433. 21 May 1895. **Will of Jennie Moffitt.** I, Jennie Moffitt, being this day of sound mind and disposing memory and realizing man is of few days and must soon pass away, do hereby make and publish this my last will and testament. First I will that my body shall rest in a cement vault on top of the ground. I desire it to be constructed as to keep my coffin from off the ground. Although I have one brother James M. Moffitt and two half sisters, Mrs. R.S. Potter and Mrs. Frank Massie, it is my will to give all I may possess at my death to my oldest sister Harriett E. Moffitt who has taken care of me all my frail life. Therefore I will and bequesth to Harriett E. Moffitt all my estate, real, personal or mixed. I hereby appoint my sister Harriett E. Moffitt my executrix. No witnesses given. Probated Nov Term 1896, Warren County Court.

pg 434-435. 20 Nov 1896. Settlement made with Frank Colville, one of the executors of H.L.W. Hill, dec'd. Credits by voucher to Mrs. V.A. Hill, Virgil Hill, Frank Hill, Mary D. Hughes, Sue E. Myers, Eliza Deakins, Athelia Cain, and Octa Myers, each to receive one share ($230.71) from the estate. C.L. Barnes, Livey Barnes, L.H. Barnes, William Barnes, V.A. Coppinger, Charity Hall, Adelia Mowdy to receive $24.36 each from the estate and the _____ Barnes heirs to receive $60.40, (their division of one share of the estate).

pg 436-437. 20 Nov 1896. Settlement made with Frank Colville, administrator of Miss Laura J. Jones, dec'd. Credits by voucher to: C.T. Thurman (guardian), Mary Lou Brown, W.B. Jones, R. Ed Jones, Minnie Jones Tucker, each to receive $235.60 from the estate.

pg 438-443. 23 Nov 1896. Inventory and sale bill of the estate of S.H. Wheeler, dec'd, made by G.S. Shankle, administrator.

pg 444-446. 7 Nov 1896. List of the property sold by C.I.L. Barnes, administrator on Sat, 2 Nov 1896, it being part of the estate of C.M. Northcutt, dec'd. Purchases made by W.E. Northcut, J.J. Northcut, Mrs. A. Northcut and others.

pg 447. 23 Dec 1896. Settlement made with W.H. Smith, Trusteee of Shockley School Fund.

Warren County, Tn Will Book 9, cont.

pg 448-449. 11 Dec 1896. Settlement of the account of H.B. Gribble, administrator of the estate of John Gribble, dec'd.

pg 450. 26 Dec 1896. Final settlement made with William Duncan, administrator of William Duncan, dec'd.

pg 451. 17 Dec 1896. J.R. Paris, administrator of the estate of Joseph Milton, reports that the deceased left no personal property to be administered, that all the personal property left by him was exempt and in the hands of his widow.

pg 452. 11 Jan 1897. J.J. and A.C. Summar, administrators of C.B. Summar, dec'd report that they received from R.F. Jones, clerk of the County Court of Cannon County, TN in the case of A.C.and J.J. Summars vs Nancy Summars, et al, the sum of $220.00, it being balance of proceeds of lands sold in said cause.

pg 453. 28 Dec 1896. Inventory of notes, accounts and sale bill of the estate of C.M. Northcut, dec'd, reported by C.I.L. Barnes.

pg 454. 4 Feb 1897. Settlement made with E.W. Smartt, one of the executors of I.C. Garretson, dec'd.

pg 455. 6 Feb 1897. Sale bill of the estate of J.W. Woodlee, dec'd, reported by F.E. Woodlee.

pg 456-457. 6 Feb 1897. Sale bill of the estate of G.W. Wood, dec'd submitted by J.I. Martin. Purchases made by Ebby Wood, L.P. Wood, Jack Wood, Vick Wood, E.B. Wood, Rice Wood, J.T. Wood, E.E. Wood, and others.

pg 458. 27 Feb 1897. Settlement made with J.F. Sullivan, administrator of C.M. Sullivan, dec'd. Receipts for $12.00 given by each of the following heirs: C.M. Sullivan, Lizzie Sullivan, W.A. Sullivan, Dorah Sullivan, J.S. Sullivan, M.K. Green, G.W. Sullivan and J.F. Sullivan.

pg 459. 24 Feb 1897. Sale bill of the estate of W.J. Fuston, dec'd, reported by S.C. Fuston.

pg 460-461. 24 Feb 1897. Settlement made with Mrs. Sallie C. Fuston, administratrix of W.J. Fuston, dec'd.

pg 462-463. 19 Jul 1895. **Will of George M. McWhirter.**

Know all men by these presents that I, G.M. McWhirter of the 3rd Civil District of Warren County, considering the uncertainity of this life and being of sound mind and memory, do make declare and publish this my last will and testament. First, I give and bequeath to my daughter Sallie Catherine McWhirter 3 acres of land joining Jeremiah Jaco, east of the Bud Peay house. I give to my son John A. McWhirter, my daughters Sarah E. Cantrell and Ellen Payne, my son Sampson McWhirter, my daughter Martha E. Clark, L.C. Gibson's heirs and Margaret P. Perry, all that tract of land conveyed by James H. Rhodes to John Cunningham and by said Cunningham to G.M. McWhirter and wife, containing 124 acres, except the three acres described above. Third, I give to my daughter Sallie C. and my sons Newton C. and Wade H. McWhirter all the land conveyed by Mary Worthington, Wm. Renshaw and wife to George M. McWhirter containing 26 acres and a tract conveyed by J.E. Rawlings to G.M. McWhirter. Fourth, I want my sons Newton and Wade each to have a bed and bed clothes and Sallie to have her bed and her sewing maching. I want sufficient of my personal property sold to satisy my debts and the rest, including furniture, stock, farming implements, etc divided between Sallie, Newton and Wade McWhirter. I nominate O.T. Gibson my executor. Witnessed David S. Dunlop and P.M. Womack. Admitted to probate Mar Term, 1897.

pg 464. 1 Mar 1897. List of property sold at public sale on 28 Nov 1896 belonging to the estate of William Womack, dec'd, reported by F.M. Womack, administrator.

pg 465-466. 9 Mar 1897. Inventory and sale bill of the estate of John M. Jones, dec'd that has come into the possession of R. Ed Jones, administrator.

pg 467-468. 3 Dec 1894. Sale bill of the estate of A.J. Willis, dec'd sold 19 Nov 1894 reported by P.H. Winton and J.L. Thaxton, administrators.. Purchases by A.F. Willis, Sally Willis, and others.

[g 469-470. 22 Mar 1897. Settlement made with J.L. Thaxton and P.H. Winton, administrators of A.J. Willis, dec'd. $425.05 to Sallie Willis, Guardian, and an equal amount as her share in the estate, she being one of the heirs.

pg 471. 20 Mar 1897. Settlement made with M. Barnes, administrator of F.C. Christian, dec'd. Josie

Christian, widow given $25.00.

pg 472. 11 Oct 1895. **Will of Frank Mitchell.** I, Frank Mitchell of Warren County, being in feeble health of body, but in sound mind and disposing memory, aware of the uncertainty of life and certainty of death, do make and publish this my last will and testament. First I direct that my debts and funeral expenses by paid. Second, I give to my beloved friend Martha L. Earp and her heirs all the money and property of whatever descripton I may die seized of. Third, I nominate said Martha L. Earp sole executrix of this my last will and testament. Witnessed G.W. Ramsey and David H. Wooten. Entered to probate 2 Apr 1897.

pg 473. 6 Apr 1897. Settlement made with H.B. Bonner, administrator of Joseph Douglas, dec'd.

pg 474. 9 Apr 1897. Inventory of the estate of Frank Northcut, dec'd, submitted by Buck C. Cope, administrator.

pg 475-485. 12 Apr 1897. Inventory of the estate of E.T. Drake, dec'd, submitted by Laura Drake, administratrix of the estate, including accounts, notes, etc.

pg 486-487. 13 Apr 1897. Settlement made with J.J. and C.A. Summars, administrators of C.B. Summars, dec'd. M.A. Summar, widow [Name spelled both Summar and Summars throughout this settlement.]

pg 488-489. 23 Apr 1897. Settlement made with Frank Colville, administrator of Mrs. L.A. Hughes, dec'd. Vouchers for $223.52 issued to T.J. Hughes, J.R. Hughes, Mrs. Daisy E. Blackmore, Mrs. L.M. Robinson and Mrs. O.P. Wilkerson out of estate.

pg 490. 11 May 1897. Settlement made with J.J. Meadows, trustee of St. Mary School Fund. F.M. Moffitt, former trustee.

pg 491-492. 7 May 1897. Settlement made with Mrs. W.C. Simpson, administratrix of W.H. Simpson, dec'd.

pg 493-494. 3 May 1897. Settlement made with H.M. Finger, executor of the estate of Mary Colston, dec'd. The following credits given by the following for their share in the estate: James Hoover, D.B.Hoover, M.A.

Hoover, Mary J. Hector and Eliz. Holloway (joint receipt for one share); George Hammons, M.A. Smith, Martha Hoover, F.C. Hoover and P. Hoover (joint receipt for one share); J.C. Hammons, (receipt for his share in the estate); T.F. Hammons (receipt for his share in the estate); L.R. Hammons, (receipt for his share in the estate); Minerva McGee, (her receipt for her full share); Mary E. Singleton, (her receipt for her full share in said estate); Martha C. Faulkner, (her receipt for her share in said estate, being one share); Jane Miller, Ann Philps, S. Carter, J.B. Hammons (joint receipt in full for their share in said estate).

pg 495. 3 May 1897. List of personal property of C.K. Mauzy, dec'd sold by Charles Mauzy, administrator on 30 Mar 1879.

pg 496-499. 3 May 1897. Inventory of the personal effects of William Thaxton, dec'd reported by J.F. Thaxton.

pg 500. 24 Apr 1897. Report of the estate of Joseph L. Bryant, dec'd. "I have this day received as administrator for Jos. L. Bryant, $17.38, it being a part of his interest in J.P. Bryan_ estate." Signed R.J. Carden, administrator.

pg 501. 31 Mar 1897. Inventory and sale bill of the estate of G.M. McWhirter, dec'd, submitted by N.P. McWhirter.

pg 502. 14 May 1897. Sale bill of the estate of Absolum C. Clark, dec'd, submitted by James Webb, administrator.

pg 503-504. 11 May 1897. Property of W.A. Hancock, received by W.T. Outlaw, administrator, from the house at Jacksboro.

pg 505-508. 11 May 1897. Sale bill of the estate of W.A. Hancock, sold 8 May 1897, reported by W.T. Outlaw, administrator.

pg 509. 12 May 1897. Report of George F. Pennabaker of Los Angeles, California as executor of the estate of Sam F. Pennabaker.

pg 510. 24 May 1897. Sale of property of E. Bruce Etter, dec'd, sold 27 Apr 1897 reported by Livingston

Barnes, administrator. Purchases by W.G. Etter and Miss Bettie E. Etter and others.

pg 511-513. 22 May 1897. Inventory and sale bill of the estate of H.J. Cardwell, dec'd, submitted by W.J. Cardwell, administrator. Purchases made by F.M. Cardwell, Mrs. Louisa Cardwell and others.

pg 514. 31 May 1897. Settlement made with John Duncan, administrator of the estate of Nancy Duncan, dec'd.

pg 515. 3 Jun 1897. Additional inventory and sale bill of E. Bruce Etter, reported by Livingston Barnes, administrator.

pg 516. 9 Jun 1897. Report of the assets of the estate of J.R. Hayes, dec'd given by S.L. Cunningham, administrator.

pg 517. 7 Jun 1897. W.C. Crawford, administrator of the estate of C.C. Roberts, reports that no goods, monies or chattels have come into his hands as administrator, nor will there be any, the dec'd having disposed by will of all his property.

pg 518. 7 Jun 1897. Settlement made with J.B. Clark, administrator of C.T. Clark, dec'd. Administrator has paid out $45.00 more than has come into his hands.

pg 519. 7 Jun 1897. Settlement of the estate of Elsie Gribble, dec'd reported by Ed Sparkman, administrator.

pg 520. 3 Jun 1897. Sale bill of the estate of Frank Northcutt (col), dec'd at the residence of Edmon Cope in the 7th District of Warren County on 21 Apr and 14 May 1897. Reported by Buck Cope, administrator.

pg 521-523. 1 Jun 1897. Inventory of the estate of F.L. Montandon, dec'd reported by Albert Montandon.

pg 524. 26 Jun 1897. Inventory of the personal effects of S.M. Hennessee, dec'd, made by W.T.L. Hennessee, administrator.

pg 525. 21 Jun 1897. Sale bill of the estate of Ida E. Jones, dec'd, reported by R.E. Jones, administrator. Purchases by Lucy E. Jones and others.

pg 526-527. 26 Jun 1897. Settlement made with M.C.

Simpson, administratrix of W.H. Simpson, dec'd. Intestate was administrator of E.C. Dunlap, dec'd, which M.C. Simpson must account for.

pg 528. 7 Jul 1897. Settlement of the estate of Mrs. V.H. Beech, dec'd by Jesse Walling, executor. Paid out to John Beech, $4532.09, to George L. Beech, $4532.09, to J.W. Smith, trustee $5500.00.

pg 529. 12 Jun 1897. Inventory of all the property or assets of Thomas W. Wilson, dec'd, which has come into the possession of Eleatha Wilson, administratrix and Thomas W. Wilson, Administrator. All purchases made by Edward Wilson.

pg 530. 1 Jul 1897. Sale bill of the estate of J.H. Walker, dec'd, reported by J.H. Lorance, administrator.

pg 531. 4 Aug 1897. Sale bill of the estate of Mrs. L. Parker, dec'd reported by T.M. Carrol. Purchases made by Billy Parker, Clarance Parker and others.

pg 532. 20 Aug 1897. Settlement made with Mrs. Sallie Fuston, administrix of W.J. Fuston, dec'd.

pg 533-536. 28 May 1897. Sale bill of the estate of Mary A. Summar, dec'd by G.C. and J.J.Summar, administrator. Purchases by J.J. Summar, Henry Summar, G.C. Summan, A.L. Summar, C.F. Summar, J.D. Summar, C.B. Summar, C.A. Summar and others.

pg 537-538. 21 Aug 1897. Sale bill of the estate of Joe L. Blanton, dec'd reported by John Blanton, administrator. Purchases by James Blanton, John Blanton, Hanah Blanton and others.

pg 539. 4 Sep 1897. Inventory of the estate of Mrs. S.E. McClarty reported by A.B. McClarty, administrator.

pg 540. 18 Aug 1897. Sale bill of the estate of Haywood Turner, dec'd, by W.H. Turner, administrator.

pg 541. 3 Nov 1893. **Will of Martha Brown.** I, Martha Brown, being of sound mind and memory, do make and publish this, my last will and testament. First, it is my will that all my just debts be paid. Second, I will to my daughter Ann Reynolds and the heirs of her body all and every part of what I may die seized and possessed of. I appoint my brother P.H. Winton my executor. Witnessed S. McRamsey and P.H. Winton. Admitted for probate 5 Oct 1897.

pg 542. 1 Jul 1897. **Will of J.D. Campbell.** I, J.D. Campbell am lawfully seized and possessed of 80 acres out of a 124 acres tract of land conveyed to me by E.J. Wood in the 11th Civil District of Warren County on the head waters of Charley Creek. After my just debts are paid, I want my daughter Pearllee Bailey to have the remaining 70 acres while she lives and at her death her three youngest children Author Bailey, Dollie Bailey and Thomas Vince Bailey to have same. I also include Pearlee Bailey's other two children Allie D. Bailey and John A. Bailey and give them equal shares with the rest of their brothers and sisters. I want D. Bailey to wind up my business after my death. Witnessed by J.A. Lance and J.F. Wilson. Probated 5 Oct 1897.

pg 543. 6 Oct 1897. Settlement made with W.T. Paty, administrator of the estate of L.O. Paty, dec'd. Josie Paty's receipt for $74.00.

pg 544. 12 Oct 1897. Settlement with Mrs. Lillie Rice, administratrix of C.E. Rice, dec'd.

pg 545. 20 Oct 1897. Settlement made with J.J. and A.C. Summars, administrator of C.A. Summars, dec'd.

pg 546. 8 Nov 1897. Settlement made with A.B. McClarty, administrator of the estate of S.E. McClarty, dec'd. A.B. McClarty is credited with $1006.98 his share of this estate. A.B. McClarty as guardian of Norah McClarty for her share $1006.98. Mrs. Jessie Fisher credited for her share in the estate $1006.98.

pg 547. 23 Oct 1897. Settlement made with W.C. Pigg, administrator of the estate of Andrew Pigg, dec'd. Credit W.C. Pigg, heir with $12.50 and Caladoni and E.J. Glasebrooks, joint heirs, with $12.50.

pg 548. 8 Nov 1897. Settlement made with Mrs. M.C. Simpson, administratrix of W.H. Simpson, dec'd.

pg 549-555. 18 Nov 1897. Settlement made with Frank Colville, administrator of John T. Potts, dec'd. Receipts for $564.10 each given by: Amanda B. Ludwick, Nancy C. Gore, Lydia R. Fulton, and T.E. Potts. Receipts for $141.02 each given by: Amanda R. Gall, Ava M. Reed, Everet A. Taylor, Charles C. Taylor, Laura C. Purcell, and Jno R. Purcell. James F. Fulton as guardian gave receipt for $282.05.

pg 556-557. 1 Feb 1895. **Will of S. McRamsey.** I, S. McRamsey being of sound mind and memory do make and purlish this my last will and testament. First, I will that my just debts be paid. Second, I will to Mrs. Jessie Winton $200.00 as evidence of the very tender regard I have for her. Third, I will to my granddaughter Emma E. Winton $500.00. The reason that I give her no more is that I have given her through her father P.H. Winton the farm on which P.H. Winton now lives. Fourth, I will all the balance of my estate to my grandson McR. Winton. If he should die without issue then it is my will that my farm in the forks of Hickory Creek descend to his sister Emma E. Winton for the sole benefit of her and the heirs of her body. Witnessed by Jesse Hill and C.S. Cardwell. Codicil. [Not dated] I further direct that McR. Winton shall have the right to dispose of the above property at any time he sees fit. Admitted for probate 6 Dec 1897.

pg 558. 29 Nov 1897. Inventory of the estate of George R. Lock, dec'd, reported by W.T. Pollard, administrator.

pg 559. 7 Dec 1897. Inventory of the estate of Rachel Nunley, dec'd to be sold at public sale by J.N. Hughes, administrator.

pg 560-561. 6 Dec 1897. Sale bill of the estate of Bettie Mathey, dec'd submitted by J.H. Edwards, administrator.

pg 562. 7 Dec 1897. Settlement made with Josie Byars, administratrix of O.D. Byars, dec'd.

pg 563. 30 Aug 1894. **Will of Chaney Finger.** In the name of God, Amen, knowing the uncertainty of life and the certainty of death and having reached a ripe old age and being without child or children or any relative on earth that I know anything of, I do make and publish this, my last will and testament. First, I desire that my debts and funeral expenses be paid. Second, I desire that I be decently buried beside my husband at Bascomb Church graveyard. Third, I give to Josie Gribble, wife of Jeff Gribble all my real and personal property and my home place which my late husband and me purchased from John Brewer.. I make this bequeath to Josie Gribble because I raised her from a child and she has been kind

to me and cared for me.   I appoint Jeff Gribble my
executor.   Witnessed Geo. M. Whitson and W.R. Smith.
Probated 28 Dec 1897.

pg 564.   11 Dec 1897.   Additional settlement made with
J. Albert Snipes, administrator of J.A. Snipes, dec'd.
Robert W. Snipes, L.B. Snipes, Arthur Snipes and
J.Albert Snipes receive their share in the estate.

pg 565-566.   21 Dec 1897.   Settlement made with C.S.
Ivie,   administrator   of   Nancy   D.   Peay   (with   will
annexed).

pg 567-570.   9 Dec 1897.   Sale bill of the estate of
George R. Lock, dec'd, reported by W.T. Pollard.
Purchases made by J.T. Lock, J.L. Lock, Will Lock, Sam
Lock, and others.

pg 1. [Blank]

pg 2. 29 Nov 1897. **Will of Sallie Bowers.** For love and affection that I have for my sister Elizabeth Edge (col) and my friend Jessie Miller and wife, I will to them as follows: I give to my sister the house that I live in and all the land that is fenced for her lifetime, but with no right to sell it. At her death it shall belong to Jesse Miller. I give to Jesse Miller all the land that I own that is not fenced lying between my house and Charles Creek. Witnessed by E.M. Yager and David Miller. Probated 4 Jan 1898.

pg 3. 8 Jan 1898. Settlement made with T.M. Carroll, administrator of L. Parker, dec'd as required by law.

pg 4. 16 Feb 1898. Settlement made with M.B. Robinson, administrator of Mrs. A.E. Witty, dec'd, widow of E.L.C. Witty.

pg 5. 29 Dec 1897. Inventory of the estate of E. Inglis, dec'd made by C.W. Inglis, administrator.

pg 6. 5 Mar 1898. Supplementary inventory of the estate of Frank Northcut (col), dec'd, reported by Buck Cope.

pg 7. 5 Mar 1898. Settlement made with B.C. Cope, administrator of the estate of Frank Northcut (col), dec'd.

pg 8. 7 Mar 1898. Inventory of the estate of Mrs. Arminta Fults, dec'd reported by W.H. Bidingfield, administrator.

pg 9-10. 23 Apr 1898. Settlement made with J.W. Paty, executor of the will of T.T. Peay, dec'd. "Mrs. Mary Peay shows receipt for $260.00. This amount is willed to Mrs. Tomie Smith and the above executor is by the will of T.T. Peay, dec'd appointed guardian of the said Tomie Smith and she being deceased the same is to be paid to the guardian of his heirs which are J.W. Paty and J.P. Bostick." The heirs of Mrs.Tomie Smith are Vera and Laura Smith.

pg 11-12. 29 Mar 1898. Final settlement made with R.C. Barnes, administrator of J.M. Herndon, dec'd. Mrs. Sarah Herndon's receipt for $15.80 included.

pg 13. 29 Mar 1898. Settlement made with R.C. Barnes, administrator of Elizabeth Barnes, dec'd. Credits for their share in the estate given by J.W. Barnes, C.D. Barnes, A.M. Lance, W.H. Jacobs, E.L. Winnard and M.M. Lance. Each received $21.21.

pg 14. [Blank]

pg 15. 7 May 1898. Inventory of the property of William McKegg reported by John H. King.

pg 16. 30 Apr 1897. Inventory and sale bill of the estate of Samuel Harrison, dec'd reported by his widow Elizabeth Harrison, administrator. Confirmed May Term 1898.

pg 17-18. 3 May 1898. Inventory and sale bill of the estate of Robert Miller, dec'd, reported by George F. Wagoner [signed Wagner], administrator. Sale held 15 Jan 1898.

pg 19. 5 Mar 1892. **Will of Tennie Harris.** To all persons whom these writing may come know ye that I, Tennie Harris being of sound and good mind and knowing the uncertainty of life and the certainty of death do make this my last will and testament. After my death the vacant lot that I own in McMinnville is to be sold and the proceeds be given to Martha Scott, daughter of Henry Scott. I want Ada Brewster and little Martha Scott to have anything else I may own at my death. Witnesses A.H. Gross and T. Bolin Jennings. Probated 6 Apr 1898.

pg 20. 25 Apr 1898. Settlement made with J.W. Barnes, administrator of C.H. Bishop, dec'd.

pg 21. 3 Oct 1893. **Will of Nancy Wagoner.** I, Nancy Wagoner, being of sound mind and memory do make this my last will.. First, I will that my body be decently buried. Second, I will that my just debts be paid. Third, I will that all my property be equally divided between my brother John Ruthledge, Mary Logue and the heirs of my sister Elizabeth Bonner, each to receive 1/3rd. Witnessed by S. McRamsey and J.R. Ramsey. Probated 22 May 1898.

Warren County, Tn Will Book 10, cont.

pg 22-23. 9 May 1898. Settlement made with A.C. Summars, administrator of C.B. Summers, dec'd. There is nothing remaining in the hands of the administrator.

pg 24. 21 May 1898. Sale bill of the estate of William McKaige, dec'd by John H. King, administrator.

pg 25. [Blank]

pg 26. 17 Nov 1897. Sale bill of the estate of M.A. Summar, dec'd, sold by G.A. Summar, administrator of the estate.

pg 27. 6 Jun 1898. Settlement made with W.L. Grove, administrator of Clave Grove, dec'd. [Mentions Chancery Court suit recorded in Book 13 page 238.]

pg 28-29. 13 Jun 1898. Inventory of the estate of A.P. Seitz, dec'd made by Albert Seitz, administrator.

pg 30-33. 4 Jun 1898. Sale bill of the personal effects of Mrs. Amanda Fults, dec'd, made by W.H. Bedingfield on 19 Mar 1898.

pg 34. 6 Apr 1897. **Will of Isaiah Jones.** I, Isaiah Jones, being of sound mind and disposing memory do hereby make and publish this my last will and testament. After all my debts and funeral expenses are paid, I give to my beloved wife Minerva Jones all my property both real and personal. Witnessed by W.C. Womack and Frank Colville. Probated 6 Jun 1898.

pg 35. 31 Jul 1889. **Will of William Stubblefield.** I, William Stubblefield, being of sound mind and memory do make this my last Will and Testament... First, my body is to be decently interred according to my standing and condition in life. Second, It is my will that my debts be paid. Third, I will to my daughter M.E. Stubblefield $1000.00 and that she is to remain at the place where I am now living and that she be provided with comfortable lodging and board during her life by whomever may occupy my farm after my death. Fourth, I will to the heirs of my son E.J. Stubblefield all the balance of my property. I have not given my son William H.H. Stubblefield anything in this will, since I paid for him $3000.00 on the purchase of the farm on which he now lives. I appoint my two friends S. McRamsey and G.W. Ramsey my executors. Witnessed by G.W. Ramsey and S. McRamsey. Probated 6 Jun 1898.

Warren County, Tn Will Book 10, cont.

pg 36-37. 7 Mar 1898. List of the notes of the estate of Elijah Anderson, dec'd presented by J.C. Anderson, administrator.

pg 38. 4 June 1898. Sale Bill and Inventory of the personal property of the estate of Lon Roach, dec'd, submitted by Robert W. Smith.

pg 39-40. July Term, 1898. Settlement made with Estella Wilber, executor of J.M. Wilber, dec'd.

pg 41. 25 Jun 1898. Inventory of the estate of Nancy Wagner, dec'd, except the household property which by agreement has been divided between the legatees [not named]. John Rutledge, executor.

pg 42. 19 Jul 1898. Settlement made with James Webb, Jr., administrator of A.C. Clark, dec'd.

pg 43-44. 9 Jul 1898. Settlement made with H.B. Gribble, administrator of John Gribble, dec'd. Division among the heirs, each receiving $61.35, as follows: H.B. Gribble, D.C. Gribble, G.W. Gribble, J.M. Gribble, J.M. Gribble as assignee of J.S. Gribble, W.D. Durham, guardian, Ellie Sparkman, M.E. Webb, J.S. Miller and Louise (heir), J.S. Miller as Atty for Carroll Gribble, J.S. Miller as Atty for Caroline Jaco, Sam Gribble, and J.S. Miller as Atty for Thomas Gribble. An additional $92.35 to be equally divided between the heirs of Jno Gribble, dec'd listed as: H.B. Gribble, D.C. Gribble, J.S. Gribble, G.W. Gribble, Ellen Sparkman, Louisa Miller, W.D. Durham (guardian), J.L. Miller (atty for three of the heirs) M.E. Webb, Sam Gribble, and J.M. Gribble, each receiving $7.10.

pg 45. 2 Jul 1898. Inventory of the estate of William Stubblefield, dec'd reported by A.F. Stubblefield.

pg 46. 25 Jun 1898. Inventory of the personal property of Nancy Wagner, dec'd reported by John Rutledge, executor.

pg 47. 21 Jul 1898. Settlement made with Charles Hudgens, executor of the estate of Jane Elkins, dec'd reports that he has realized nothing from the estate.

pg 48. 26 Jul 1898. Settlement made with A.H. Faulkner, administrator with will annexed of Mrs. E.J. Mitchell, dec'd.

Warren County, Tn Will Book 10, cont.

pg 49-50. 22 Jul 1898. Settlement made with S.C. Fuston, administratrix of the estate of W.J. Fuston, dec'd. Administratrix credited by vouchers of $62.41 to the following: W.N. Fuston, A.T. Fuston, T.H. Fuston, S.M. Fuston, and Belldora and G.B. Mears.

pg 51. 2 Sep 1898. Settlement of the balance of the personal property of Laura Kirby, dec'd.

pg 52. 1 Sep 1898. Settlement made with J.J. Meadows, trustee of St. Mary School Fund. "Cost for recording the original will of W.C. Hill and entering decree, etc..$2.75".

pg 53. 1 Sep 1898. Settlement made with F.P. Byars, executor of Nathan Byars, dec'd.

pg 54. 29 Aug 1898. Settlement made with W.T.L. Hennessee, administrator of Sam Hennessee, dec'd.

pg 55. 15 Aug 1898. Inventory of the personal property that has come to the hands of the administrators of W.J. Bailey, dec'd, reported by P.D. and T.B. Bailey..

pg 56-57. 21 Aug 1898. Sale bill of the estate of William J. Bailey, dec'd. Purchases made by Mrs. Bailey, Miss Kate Bailey, T.B. Bailey, Joe Bailey and others.

pg 58. 1 Aug 1898. P.H. Winton, executor of the estate of Martha Brown, dec'd. Mentions judgment against Audy, Reding, and H.B. Bonner in Aug 1892.

pg 59. 2 Sep 1898. Settlement made with E.W. Smartt and D.H. Woodlee, administrators of Mrs. M.J. Davis, dec'd.

pg 60. 3 Sep 1898. Settlement made with S.L. Cunningham, administrator of J.R. Hayes, dec'd.

pg 61-62. 6 Aug 1898. Inventory and sale bill of the personal property that has some to the hands of J.C. Biles and W.L. Newby, administrators of Mary E. Newby, dec'd. Purchases made by J.M. Newby, Mrs. ____ Newby, Mrs. W.L. Newby, Mrs. J.M. Newby and others.

pg 63-65. 2 Sep 1898. Settlement made with L.P. Gartner, administrator of J.P. Gartner, dec'd. Mrs. M.P. Gartner's receipt for $258.85 included.

pg 66-69. 29 Aug 18<u>70</u>. **Will of W.C. Hill.** I, William C. Hill do make and publish this my last will and testament. First I direct that my funeral expenses and debts be paid. Second, I give to my sister Elenza G. Bess, wife of John Bess, Sr., $50.00. Third, I give to my brother Andrew J. Hill $100.00. Fourth I give to the living children of my sister Sallie Simms, dec'd 40 acres of land near the head of Trinity River, Texas to be equally divided between said children.. Patent for said land issued in the name of J.P.M. Smith and signed by the Governor of Texas J. Pinkney Henderson on 20 May 1846, the title to me recorded in Recorders Office, Robertson County, TX in Patent Book 4, ages 287-288. Fifth, I give to my sister Harriet Moffitt, wife of Aaron Moffitt, $1000.00 for looking after me during various spells of sickness. This $1000.00 to be her separate use, apart from her husband. Sixth, I give my nephew Francis Marion Moffitt $1000.00 for his attention to my business during my sickness. Seventh, if there remains after settling my estate and the above bequeats, I give $1000.00 to St Mary's school on Hill's Creek, with Francis Marion Moffitt as trustee. Eighth, should there be a balance in the estate then I direct that all bequeaths be doubled. I appoint Francis Marion Moffitt my executor. Witnessed by H.L.W. Hill and Aaron Moffitt. Recorded in Warren County Court at August Term 1898.

pg 70-73. 20 Oct 1898. Settlement reported by L.E. West, assignee of Thurman Bros. and Co, stock of dry goods, shoes, etc. "We, I.J. Thurman, C.T. Thurman, William Thurman and Mrs. Lou Thurman, executrix of S.M. Thurman, dec'd, members of Thurman Bros. and Co."

pg 74-79. 28 Oct 1898. Inventory of the personal property belonging to the estate of D.W. King, dec'd reported by J.C. Biles, administrator. Purchases made at sale held on 20 Sep 1898 by P.W. King, Mrs. Tennie King, Polk King, J.H. King, Philip King and others.

pg 80. 7 Nov 1898. Inventory of the effects of T.H. Etter, dec'd reported by J.P. Hughes, administrator.

pg 81-82. 18 Oct 1898. **Will of Samantha Cunningham.** I, Samantha Cunningham being of sound mind and disposing memory, do make and publish this my last will and testament. First, my funeral expenses are to be paid. Secondly, my just debts are to be paid. Third, I give to my beloved sister Sarah E. Gribble my buggy, sewing machine, rocking chair, trunk, saddle, cook stove and dishes. Fourthly, I give to Evaleaner Couch one bed stead, feather bed and bed clothes, my bureau, rocking chair, center table plus $350.00 to be paid to her guardian for her education and other benefit. Fifth, I am anxious to have the family graveyard on the farm of J.T. Gribble cleared up and a good fence put around it, and tombstone placed at my father's grave and that of my sister Lamendas. Sixth, The balance of my estate to be equally divided between my sister Sarah E. Gribble and my brothers G.W. Cunningham, F.P. Cunningham and J.M. Cunningham with exception of the $200.00 F.P. Cunningham owes me. (F.P. to receive $200 less that the other three siblings.) Seventh, I appoint James T. Gribble my executor. Witnessed by J.L. Miller and F.G. Couch. Probate date not given.

pg 83. 1 Nov 1898. **Will of W.M. Reeder.** "This is my deed of gift to my wife Martha Jane, I want the home place run out and to be hers her life time or widowhood. Also all my stock save three colts and farming implements, also my wagon and harness, also the products of said farm this year, also all my hogs. I want the fattening hogs killed and put in th smoke house to be disposed of at her will. I also want her to have all my household and kitchen furniture." Witnessed by M.C. Green, J.H. Green and J. Fuston.

pg 84-85. 29 Nov 1898. Settlement made with C.I.L. Barnes, administrator of C.M. Northcut, dec'd.

pg 86. 15 Dec 1898. Inventory of the notes of the estate of Samantha Cunningham, dec'd reported by J.T. Gribble, administrator of her estate.

pg 87. 20 Dec 1898. Inventory and sale bill of the estate of W.M. Reeder, dec'd, reported by N.A. Reeder, administrator. Mrs. M.J. Reeder purchased one gray horse for $16.00.

pg 88. 27 Dec 1898. Supplementary inventory and sale bill of the estate of George M. McWhirter, dec'd. Sale held 23 Oct 1897 by N.P. McWhirter administrator with will annexed.

pg 89. [No date.] Settlement made with N.P. McWhirter, administrator of G.M. McWhirter, dec'd.

pg 90-92. 28 dec 1898. Settlement made with C.S. Ivie, administrator of Nancy D. Peay, dec'd. Payment made for

Martha Lilliard's care and burial expenses. "I find that by the provisions of the will of Nancy D. Peay, [Book 7, pg 520] the assets of this estate were incumbered with the suport of Martha Lilliard during her life and that the will directs a distribution of the assets after the death of Martha Lilliard in equal proportions to Lou Tilford, Mattie Guffin [Griffin?], Willie Guffin, and Paty Guffin, neices and nephews of the testatrix. Willie Guffin had died intestate with his father surviving him, who lives in the state of Texas."

pg 93. 2 Jan 1899. Settlement of the estate of Elsie Gribble, dec'd, Ed Sparkman, administrator.

pg 94. 2 Jan 1899. Supplementary inventory and sale bill of the estate of Elijah Anderson, dec'd made by J.C. Anderson, administrator.

pg 95-97. 2 Jan 1899. List of articles sold at the sale of Rachel Nunley, dec'd by J.N. Hughes, administrator. Purchases made by M. Nunley, L.N. Nunley and others.

pg 98. 3 Jan 1899. Sale bill of the corn belonging to the estate of W.J. Bailey, dec'd submitted by J.D. Bailey and T.B. Bailey, administrators.

pg 99. 4 Jan 1899. Inventory of W.H. Bedingfield, guardian of the C.M. Northcut heirs. "My wards own a small tract of 10 acres in the 7th Civil District, but same is all poor and very mountainous and rough, except five acres."

pg 100. 8 Apr 1898. **Will of John A. Northcut.** I, John A. Northcutt of Smartts, Warren County, have made my last will and testament in writing, bearing the date 18 Apr 1898. "First, sell one mare and buggy, one cow and the amount of bacon on hand and two mules. This is to go to Fannie Thaxton if I don't get my government money. If I do get it, that money is to go to her and the two mules is to go to the three boys. Sell or do as you please with one reaper, one drill and all the farming tools. Take charge of the wheat crop, cut it, have it thrashed and sell the wheat and pay the fertilizer bill, then put up a tombstone to your ma's grave, and pay yourselves the amount that you have paid for me in the Knights of Honor to date and it anything is left it is to be divided equally between you three boys. Man I

Warren County, Tn Will Book 10, cont.

want you to attend to this." [Not witnessed.] Admitted
to probate 6 Jan 1899.

pg 101.   7 Jan 1899.   Settlement made with J.T. Hillis,
administrator of the estate of Alfred Elkins.

pg 102.   22 Jan 1899.   Settlement made with J.R. Paris,
administrator of Joseph Melton, dec'd.

pg 103.   24 Jan 1899.   Settlement made with F.E.
Woodlee, administrator of J.W. Woodlee, dec'd. Mrs.Emma
Woodlee received $30.00 for year's support.

pg 104-105.   21 Feb 1899.   Final settlement of the
estate of C.K. Mauzy, made with Charles Mauzy,
administrator.   There   is   no   balance   in   the
administrators hands.

pg 106.   4 Feb 1899.   Last settlement made with F.E.
Woodlee, administrator of J.W. Woodlee, dec'd. Pro rata
credits to Emma Woodlee, F.E. Woodlee and R.R. Etter.

pg 107-108.   10 Mar 1899.   Settlement made with E.W.
Smartt and D.H. Wooten, administrators of the estate of
Mrs. M.J. Davis, dec'd.   "Leaving in the hands of the
administrators the sum of $1122.06 to be pro rated among
the heirs at law of the deceased according to their
rights and interests therein, as follows: D.H. Wooten,
brother, 1/4 interest;   Sallie Wooten, sister, 1/4
interest; Nannie E. Smartt, niece, 1/8 interest; Annie
Cowart, grandniece 1/24 interest; George Davis,
grandnephew, 1/24 interest; James Davis, grandnephew,
1/24th interest; W.H. Wooten, nephew, 1/8 interest;
Sallie Chumbley, niece, 1/8 interest."

pg 109.   6 Mar 1899.   Inventory of the personal assets
of Mrs. Martha McDonough, made by F.M. McDonough,
administrator.

pg 110.   13 Mar 1899.   Settlement made with W.H. Smith,
trustee of Shockley School Funds.

pg 111-113.   14 Jun 1889.   **Will of George W. Mead.**   "I,
George W. Mead, knowing the uncertainities of life and
the certainty of death and having been blessed by
Providence with some estate but denied an offspring to
inherit it and wishing to dispose of my property and
effects in a way honoring to God, but not unmindful of
the duty I owe and the affections I feel for my wife who

has been my companion in life's journey, and other claims on my bounty I am unwilling to disregard, therefore influenced by these considerations and wishing to set my house in order ere I die, I do make and declare and establish this as my last will and testament." First I wish my debts and funeral expenses paid. Second, I give to my beloved wife Caroline R. Mead, all my estate, real, personal and mixed. Third, After her death I wish the following distribution be made: I give $1000.00 each to my neice Eliza Bell Potts of Kentucky, and to my nephews George Mead Smith and David Mead DeBard of Warren County, TN and George Green of Warren County, PA. The remainder of my estate I give to the Trustees and Board of Managers of the South Western Presbyterian University at Clarksville TN in trust to aid poor young men in its theological department. Fourth, "The legacies given my three nephews is on the express terms and conditions that they abstain from drunkeness and riotous living. I am not willing that the fruits of my toil be so wasted." Fifth, the legacy given my niece Eliza Bell Potts is to be for her sole and separate use free and apart from her husband. Sixth, I appoint my wife Caroline R. Mead sole executrix of this will. Witnessed by Jas. S. Barton and Thomas Black. Presented for probate 11 Mar 1899.

pg 114-115. 30 Jan 1899. **Will of Cyrus Richmond.** I, Cyrus Richmond of McMinnville, being of sound mind and memory do make this my last will and testament. My will is my funeral expenses shall by my executor hereinafter named be paid soon as convenient. First, I give to my brother in law J.H. Willey $600.00 and my two gold watches. Second, I give to my sister Elsie Campbell $500.00. Third, I give to my niece and nephew Eunice and George Lawton $400.00. Fourth, I give to my sister Elsie Campbell $500.00 and the balance of the estate. I nominate my brother in law John H. Willey to be my executor. Dr. J.A. Smith and M. W. Long. Admitted to probate 6 Mar 1899.

pg 116-117. 27 Mar 1899. **Will of James Newby.** I, James Newby, do make and publish this as my last will and testament.. First I direct my funeral expenses and debts be paid. Second, I give to my wife Sarah Newby during her narural life, all the land I am seized of, about 285 acres. Thirdly, I give to my wife Sarah Newby all my personal property. Fourthly, I give to my son W.L. Newby all the above land at the death of his mother. Fifthly, I give to my son W.L. Newby all the personal property which my wife Sarah may die possessed of. Lastly, I nominate W.L. Newby my executor. Witnessed D.C. Oliver, W.C. Herndon, Sam Bishop. Admitted to probate 5 Apr 1899.

pg 118. 7 Apr 1899. "No personal property has come into my hands nor do I know of any that will come into my hands as administrator belonging to H.R. Gribble, dec'd." Signed B.F. Smith.

pg 119-120. 4 Apr 1899. Inventory of the personal assets of the estate of Cyrus Richmond, dec'd reported by Foss H. Mercer, administrator with will annexed.

pg 121. 4 Apr 1899. Inventory of the estate of J.H. Willey, dec'd reported by Foss H. Mercer, administrator. This estate consists of nothing except the $600.00 and two gold watches willed to said Willey by Cyrus Richmond.

pg 122. 21 Jul 1898. **Will of William W. Reilly.** I, William W. Reilly, being of sound and disposing memory and being desirous of settling my worldly affairs while I have strength and capacity to do make and publish this my last will and testament. I commit my soul into the hands of my creator who gave it and my body to the earth from whence it came. First, I direct that my debts and funeral expenses be paid. Second, I give all the remainder of my estate to my dear wife Ninah H. Reilly. I appoint my said wife executrix. Witnessed by Alfred H. Williams and Thomas H. Cassety. Admitted to probate 1 May 1899.

pg 123. 10 Mar 1899. Settlement made with E.W. Smartt and D.H. Wooten, administrators of Mrs. M.J. Davis. The following are the only heirs at law of Mrs. M.J. Davis, dec'd: D.H. Wooten, Sallie Wooten, Nannie E. Smartt, Annie Cowart, George and James Davis by C.W. Sewall their guardian, W.H. Wooten and Sallie Chumbley.

pg 124-125. 6 Mar 1899. Settlement made with Victor Montandon, administrator of F.L. Montandon, dec'd. Reciepts from the heirs given in full for their shares in the personal estate of the deceased as follows: Emma Swindle, Paul Montandon, Maggie Davenport, Rachel Sparkman, Victor Montandon, Henry Montandon, and Fannie Martin. Each received $6.00.

pg 126-128. 21 Dec 1898. **Will of Rhoda Davis.** I,

Rhoda Davis of McMinnville, being in feeble health but
of sound and disposing mind and memory, make and ordain
this my last will and testament. All of my real and
personal property I dispose of in the following manner:
my debts and funeral expenses are to be paid. Second,
I bequeath to my son Lasley McMillin and my two
grandchildren Eddie Clara McMillin and James DeBow
McMillin, children of my deceased son Joseph McMillin,
all my property, to each one third. My executor is to
sell my residence and divide the proceeds between the
above legatees, also my lot in Floral City, Florida and
my household goods. My beds, silverware, and clothing
I give to my said grand-daughter Eddie Clara McMillin.
I appoint James C. Biles my executor and trustee for my
son Lasley McMillin. Witnessed J.W. Irwin and W.B.
Harwell. **Codicil;** I give my daughter in law Mrs.
Lizzie McMillin one bed stead, bed and clothing
belonging to same. Dec 21, 18_88_. Preserted for probate
5 Jun 1899.

pg 129-130. 24 Mar 1892. **Will of G.W. Martin.** I,
G.W. Martin, being of sound mind and memory and
considering the uncertainity of this frail and
transitory life, do therefore make, ordain, publish and
declare this to be my last will and testament. First
after my debts are paid, the residue of my estate I
dispose of as follows: My real estate (400 acres, bound
by A.R. Smith, C.K. Mauzy, Wm. Martin and Jo Cummings)
and my personal property to be equally divided between
my beloved wife Henneyetie Martin, my daughter Mary Ann
Woodard, my daughter Martha Martin, my daughter Maude
Martin, my son Jephey Martin, my son G.W. Martin and my
son T.J. Martin. I appoint John Duncan executor.
Witnessed by Dewey Cummings and J.W. Smith. **Codicil:**
In my will above, made some time ago, I left out two of
my children, to wit: Ben Martin of Fort Worth, Texas and
my daughter Suella _____ of Georgia, I now include both
in my above will. My daughter Mary Ann in Texas for
reasons of my own, I will $5.00. My two sons Bill and
Ransom Martin I only will $5.00 each. My son Thomas in
Texas I have already paid $400.00 which he must account
for with my executor on final settlement. 6 Feb 1894.
Witnessed Don Cummings and Paul Montandon. Presented
for probate 5 Jun 1899.

pg 131-135. 5 Jun 1899. Inventory and sale bill of
John Green, dec'd, reported by G.W. Green,
administrator. Purchases made by Eli Green, Mrs. G.W.
Green, Malinda Green and others.

pg 136-137. 26 May 1899. Inventory of the estate of George W. Mead that came to the hands of Caroline R. Mead, the widow, his executrix.

pg 138-141. 20 Jun 1899. Settlement made with R. Ed. Jones, administrator of Ida E. Jones, dec'd. Equal shares of the estate (1/8th each) were given to: Mrs. Minnie Jones Tucker, Frank Colville as guardian of Emma Jones, Mrs. Ann L. Jones, J.C. Biles as guardian of Annie May and Lucy Jones (2 shares), R. Ed Jones, Will B. Jones, and Mary Lou Brown. C.T. Thurman was also listed as guardian of Emma Jones.

pg 142-143. 10 Jan 1899. **Will of Esther Miller.** I, Esther Miller being of sound mind and disposing memory, do make and publish this my last will and testament. First I desire my debts and funeral expenses paid. Second, I will to Jemima Gribble $1000.00. Third, I will to my brother D.S. Miller all my livestock and farm implements. Fourth, I will to my two nephews D.H. Miller and J.J. Miller all my real estate in Dist 3 of Warren County, to share and share alike. Fifth, D.H. Miller is to have control of my landed estate during his lifetime. Sixth, I appoint D.S. Miller and D.H. Miller my executors. Witnessed by J.T. Hillis and L.L. Rowland. Admitted to probate 3 Jul 1899.

pg 144-146. 27 May 1899. Sale bill of the estate of Nan Collier, dec'd, reported by John H. Collier, administrator. Purchases by C. Collier, Jess Collier, A. Collier, B. Collier, James Collier and others.

pg 147. 2 Aug 1899. List of the personal assets of the estate of John A. Northcutt, dec'd reported by J.R. Northcut, administrator.

pg 148-149. 17 Aug 1899. Sale bill of the estate of John A. Northcutt, dec'd. Purchases made by Abe Northcutt, J.A. Northcutt and others.

pg 150. 7 Aug 1899. Inventory of the estate of B.N. Myers, dec'd, reported by Robert W. Smartt, administrator.

pg 151. 3 Jan 18<u>99</u>. Sale bill of the estate of W.J. Bailey, dec'd held 8 Dec 18<u>99</u> by J.D. Bailey and T.B. Bailey.

pg 152. 27 May 1899. Inventory of the personal estate

of Mrs. Nan Collier, dec'd in the hands of J.H. Collier, administrator.

pg 153. 28 Aug 1899. Sale bill of the estate of G.W.Martin, dec'd made by W.L. Grissom, administrator. Purchases made by Ret Martin, Jesse Martin, J.M. Martin, G.W. Martin and Tom Simmons.

pg 154-156. 12 Sep 1899. Inventory and sale bill of the estate of Rhoda Davis, dec'd that has come to the hands of J.C. Biles, executor.

pg 157-158. 7 Sep 1899. Settlement made with J.F. Thaxton, administrator of William Thaxton, dec'd. The estate owes almost $200.00 above the amount brought in by the sale of the personal assets, and in order to pay same it will be necessary to encroach upon the funds arising from the land sale.

pg 159-161. 5 Sep 1899. **Will of L.B. Brown.** I, L.B. Brown, do make and publish this my last will and testament. First, I direct my funeral expenses and debts be paid. Second, I give to my wife Mariah Brown the house in which we now live with the barn on the north side of the road and the lots around the same. The land and houses to go the Hatton Brown at her death. She is also to have fruit from the orchard and free access to the spring that we use now. She is to have personal property for her lifetime. Third, I give to my daughter Nannie Rodgers a tract of land known as the R.J. Creswell lands. Fourth, I give my son Cyrus Brown $555.00. Fifth, I give my son Hatton Brown lands valued at $650.00. Sixth, I give my daughter Mary Brown all the lands known as my home place and valued at $500.00. She is also to have one horse worth $60.00. Seventh, I will the the steam mill and fixtures be used by the children above named to saw lumber to build them houses and barns and then be sold. I appoint my son Hatton Brown my executor.   Witnesses W.L. Swann and J.E. Jones. Admitted to probate 3 Oct 1899.

pg 162-163. 14 Sep 1899.   **Will of D.W. Ramsey.** I, D.W. Ramsey make, declare and publish this my last will and testament. First I desire the payment of all my debts. Second, I give to my wife Lizzie D. Ramsey my entire estate after payment of debts, realestate consisting of 114 acres in 8th District known as the Ashbury place.. Third, I appoint my wife Lizzie D. Ramsey and my friend E.W. Smartt as executrix and executor. Witnessed by G.W. Ramsey and J.R. Ramsey. Admitted for probate 10 Oct 1899.

pg 164. 2 Jan 18<u>99</u>. Supplemental inventory and sale bill of Elijah Anderson, dec'd reported by J.C. Anderson, administrator.

pg 165. 4 Sep 1899. Sale bill of the estate of Nannie Sherrill, dec'd, sale on 2 Sep 1899 by J.H. Sherrill, administrator. [Names of purchasers not given.]

pg 166-167. 4 Nov 1899. Inventory and sale bill of the estate of L.B. Brown, dec'd made by R.H. Brown, executor.

pg 168-169. 6 Nov 1899. Inventory and sale bill of the estate of O.P. Paris, dec'd reported by Mrs. Sue S. Paris. "I have not asked for my year's support as the widow of O.P. Paris, dec'd, who died intestate leaving myself as the widow and his only child, aged 15 months as his only heirs at law." Signed Mrs. Sue S. Paris.

pg 170. 30 Oct 1899. Inventory of the personal estate of Cindrilla Webb made by James K.P. Webb, administrator.

pg 171. 31 Oct 1899. Final settlement made with J.H. Edwards, administrator of Bettie Mathey, dec'd.

pg 172. 4 Dec 1899. Settlement made with W.H. Bedingfield, administrator of Arminda Fults, dec'd.

pg 173-174. 4 Dec 1899. Sale bill of the estate of L.B. Brown, dec'd made by Hatton Brown, executor. Purchases by C.A. Brown, Hatton Brown, Mary Brown, Cyrus Brown, and others.

pg 175-181. 11 Oct 1899. Sale bill of the estate of Hixie Parkes, dec'd. Purchases by Lou Parks, Mrs Ella Parks, Mrs. Corral Parks, G.W. Parks, D.W. Parks and many others. List of notes due estate. Above reported by G.F. Wagner, administrator.

pg 182. 7 Jan 1899. Settlement made with I.T. Hillis, administrator of the estate of Alfred Elkins, dec'd.

pg 183-184. 11 Feb 1895. **Will of C.R. Morford.** I, C.R. Morford, do hereby make and publish this my last will and testament. I desire that all my debts and my annual

dues to the C.P. Church be paid. I will to my wife all
my household and kitchen furniture and one cow and
$1000.00 to support her and our four minor children
until this will can be executed. I also Will to my wife
Mollie C. Morford for life, my home place on Main
Street, my 1/7th interest in Warren House and my 1/2
undivided interest in Store house on East Main now
occupied by Thurman Bros. & Co. At her death all are to
be sold and the proceeds equally divided between all my
children. I have advanced my daughters Hallie May and
Evie Clair and my son James H. Morford $1000.00 each.
I will to each of my other children $1000.00 to make
them equal with the above. It is my will that my minor
children be made wards of the Chancery Court and that
the money belonging to them be invested and the interest
thereon be paid annually to my wife to cloth, feed and
educate them. If Emma Rowan (col) is in my employ at
the time of my death, I will to her $100.00 for faithful
service. I appoint my wife Mollie C. and my son James
H. Morford executrix and executor of this my will.
Witnessed by J.C. Biles and W.W. Fairbanks. [Mollie and
James H. Morford decline to qualify as executrix and
executor and request that J.C. Biles be appointed in
their stead, 6 Jan 1900.] Will admitted to probate 6
Jan 1900.

pg 185-186. 29 Dec 1899. Settlement with F.M. Womack,
administrator of the estate of William Womack, dec'd.
Heirs listed and amount received from estate: J.M.
Womack $10.00; Ann B. and W.D.P. Womack $10.00 jointly;
James and Susie Dave [or Dove] $10.00 jointly;, A.J.
Womack $10.00; A. Womack $10.00; Arsey Womack $10.00;
F.M. Womack $10.00; J.B. and F.P. Womack, $5.00 each.

pg 187. 15 Jan 1900. Settlement of estate of Martha
Brown, dec'd made by P.H. Winton, executor.

pg 188. 18 Jan 1899. Settlement made with J.C. Biles
and W.L. Newby, administrators of Mary E. Newby, dec'd.
Heirs listed in the settlement to receive $167.62 are:
James M. Newby, Mrs. C.A. Herndon, W.C. Newby, A.J.
Newby, and W.D. Newby. W.C. Pigg (his share $41.92);
J.A.J. Newby and Ann Eliza Roberts (their share
$111.74); E.D. Shed, A.L. Dial and W.F. Coleman (their
share $55.87); Mary Glasebrook (her share $41.90); W.L.
Newby, guardian of the minor children of Louis Pigg,
dec'd (that share $41.90.) The share of Cindrella
Overstreet who administrators are unable to locate
remains in the administrators hands.

Warren County, Tn Will Book 10, cont.

pg 189-190. 17 Jan 1900. Inventory and sale bill of the personal property belonging to the estate of J.H. Sartin, dec'd, except that which was kept by the widow Nora Sartin. Purchases made by Dave Sartin, Mrs. J.H. Sartin and others. W.R. Crouch, administrator.

pg 191-192. 27 Jan 1900. Settlement of the estate of William McKaig, dec'd, by John H. King, administrator.

pg 193. 6 Jan 1900. Inventory of the notes due the estate of Johnathan Bost, dec'd reported by Jerome Collier, administrator.

pg 194-195. 23 Jan 1900. List of the personal property sold at public sale by W.A.Moore and J.B. Roberts, administrators of George W. Cunningham, dec'd 13 Jan 1900.

pg 196-197. 23 Jan 1900. Inventory of the cash on hand and the bank notes and accounts of George W. Cunningham dec'd reported by W.A. Moore and J.B. Roberts, administrators.

pg 198. 27 Jan 1900. Settlement made with J.F. Thaxton, administrator of the estate of William Thaxton, dec'd.

pg 199-200. 27 Jan 1900. Inventory and sale bill of the estate of Jonathan Bost, dec'd. Purchases made by Boy Bost, Jim Bost and others.

pg 201. 6 Feb 1900. D. Bailey, executor of the estate of J.D. Campbell, dec'd, advertised for persons having claims against said estate, none have been filed. Also he can find no effects of said testator.

pg 202-204. 6 Mar 1900. Inventory of the estate of T.F. Mullican, dec'd sold at public sale on 17 Feb 1900. Purchases made by J.D. Mullican, Mary Mullican, J.R. Mullican, S.T. Mullican, F.P. Mullican and others. F.M. Womack was administrator of estate.

pg 205. 10 Mar 1900. Inventory and sale bill of the personal property of the estate of I.T. Green, dec'd, reported by J.T. Green, administrator. Purchases made by J.A. Green, Nancy Green, Jim Green and others.

pg 206. 13 Mar 1900. Supplementary sale bill of the property of Elijah Anderson, dec'd, sold by J.C. Anderson, administrator on 27 Jan 1900. Purchases by J.

Warren County, Tn Will Book 10, cont.

Anderson, Grant Anderson, I.A. Anderson and others.

pg 207-209. 24 Feb 1900. Sale of the estate of Z. Saunders, dec'd, reported by J.K. Saunders, administrator. Purchases by J.K. Saunders, Mollie Sanders, Margaret Saunders, and others.

pg 210-211. 16 Mar 1900. Inventory of the personal property of the estate of C.R. Morford, dec'd that has come to the hands of J.C. Biles, administrator with will annexed. Mrs. M.C. Morford, widow of said dec'd takes a life estate in the 15 shares of Warren House stock.

pg 212. 14 Apr 1900. Settlement made with Robert T. Burt, administrator with will annexed of Tennie Harris (col), dec'd. R.T. Burt qualified as guardian of Martha Scott, the person entitled to the balance of the estate.

pg 213. 14 May 1900. The administrators of the estate of Mary E. Newby report that they have located Cyndrillia Overstreet, one of the heirs of said estate and have paid her the share due her [See pg 188, Will Book 10.]

pg 214-215. 27 Dec 1895. **Will of Elijah Martin.** I, Elijah Martin being of sound mind and disposing memory do make and publish this my last will and testament. First, I desire that my funeral expenses and debts be paid. Second, I will to my beloved wife Harriet Elizabeth Martin, all my real and personal property of every character. Lastly, I appoint my wife Harriet Elizabeth sole executrix of this will. Witnessed by J.J. Northcut and S.H. Wheeler. Admitted to probate 7 May 1900.

pg 216-219. 25 Mar 1891. **Will of Margaretta O. Lewis.** I, Margaretta O. Lewis, widow of George T. Lewis of McMinnville, do make and publish this my last will and testament. First, I will my just debts be paid. Second, I will that my executrix sell the place where I now live, known as River Cliffe and my farm in Warren County and divided the proceeds equally among all my children living and dead. Third, the money I receive from Helen Louise Lewis, dec'd shall be divided between my five living children, the children of my deceased daughter Mary D. Campbell having already received their mother's share of said moneys. Fourth, I give my daughter Blanche L. Lewis all my household and kitchen furniture, my carpets, beds bedding, china, mirrors, silverware, pictures and ornaments about the house. Fifth, my personal effects, wearing apparel, jewelry, books, etc I also give to my daughter Blanche to be disposed of by her as directed by me in a paper I have given her for that purpose. Sixth, the bond for the purchase of the real estate is to be cancelled by Chancery Court. Seventh, I appoint my daughter Blanche L. Lewis executrix. Witnessed by J.C. Biles and Thomas C. Lind. **Codicil:** 19 Dec 1896. Whereas in Item two of my said last will I directed the sale of River Cliffe and the farm, to be equally divided among all my children. My daughter Mrs. Sallie T. Thomas having since died leaving one child Mrs. Blanche Merrill of Thomasville, GA, it is now my will that the proceeds from the said sale be divided as follows: To my sons E.H. Lewis and John S. Lewis 1/6th each; to the children of my deceased daughter Mary Campbell jointly 1/6th; to my daughter Blanche L. Lewis one half. I hereby revoke so much of said Item 2 as gave one share of the money from the sale to my son E.C. Lewis and one share to my daughter Mrs. Sallie Thomas (who is now represented by my grand-daughter Mrs. Blanche Merril). Witnessed as above. Admitted to probate 12 May 1900.

pg 220-221. 28 Apr 1900. Final Settlement of the estate of A.P. Seitz, dec'd reported by administrator of A.P. Seitz, dec'd. Receipts of Jessie Seitz, Alma Seitz, Emma Seitz, Hallie Seitz and Minnie Seitz, in full for the balance due them as heirs at law of said A.P. Seitz, dec'd. The administrator Albert Seitz, the other heir at law, having relinquished to the above named all his interest in said estate.

pg 222. 12 May 1900. Inventory of estate of John C. Watson, dec'd reported by Hattie Johnson and Flora Watson, administratrix of the estate.

pg 223-224. 19 Jun 1894. **Will of Jacob Rogers.** I hereby make my will as follows: I bequeath my son Greek Rogers that portion of my land where I now live, and the tract joining Mrs. Nancy Bouldin. Also half of my mountain tract. I give my son William Rogers the remainder of my land. These two sons are to have the land after the death of my wife Fanny. I give to my son Levy Rogers the son of $5.00. To my daughters Ann Hobbs and Sarah Webb adn their heirs I give $25.00 each. To my daughter Mauda Nunley $50.00. I appoint my sons Greek and William Rogers (or either of them) my executor. Witnesses J.H. Tipton and C.I.L. Barnes.

Warren County, Tn Will Book 10, cont.

Admitted for probate 4 Jun 1900.

pg 225-226. 31 May 1900. Settlement made with C.W. Inglis, administrator of the estate of E. Inglis, dec'd.

pg 227. 18 Jun 1900. Sale of the personal property of the estate of Lucy Etter, dec'd by B.F. Woodlee, administrator.

pg 228-233. 8 Jun 1900. Report of assets of the estate of H.J. Cardwell, reported by W.J. Cardwell, administrator. A balance of $33.45 to be distributed of estate.

pg 234-240. 9 Jun 1900. Sale of the estate of Catherine Gribble, held 2 Jun 1900 reported by J.M. Gribble, administrator. Purchases made by Weathie Gribble, Kit Gribble, J.T. Gribble, Nan Gribble, Holley Gribble, James Gribble, G.P. Gribble, Sam Gribble, T.R. Gribble, and others.

pg 241. 19 Jun 1900. Settlement made with Mrs. S.E. Swann, administratrix of Allie Swann, dec'd. Credits to Cleo Swann, Lizzie Brazier, J.W. Swann, Nannie Snipes, and Lou Morris for $3.05 each and to George L. Hoodenpyl as guardian for two of the heirs for $6.10.

pg 242. July Term 1900. Supplemental report of W.H. Cardwell, administrator of H.J. Cardwell, dec'd.

pg 243-250. 29 Apr 1899. **Will of Mary E. Munford.** I, Mary E. Munford of McMinnville, being of sound mind and disposing memory, and knowing the uncertainnty of life and certainty of death do hereby declare, ordain and establish the following to be my last will and testament. First, I will my just debts be paid and that a marble monument to cost not less than $600.00 nor more than $1000.00 be placed over the grave of my late husband Col. E.W. Munford in the new McMinnville City Cemetery. I wish to be buried by his side, and the stone be constructed that inscription be engraved thereon for both of us. Second, I give to Thomas Munford of Clarksville, TN, a nephew of my late husband my first mortgage on Tennessee Coal, Iron and Railroad Co. Bonds. I give to my cousins Miss Elizabeth B. Holt and Miss Kate Burk Simpson, both of Montgomery AL a similar bond to the one above. I also give another of said bonds to my dear friend Mrs. Mary L. Robertson of Augusta GA. Third, I give another of said bonds to Miss

Mary Ann Gardner of Sand Hills, near Augusta, GA on condition she survives me. In event she dies before me this legacy goes as directed in the next item of this will. Fourth, I will to my namesake Miss Mary Munford Brown of McMinnville, two of my said bonds, plus the above bond should Mary Ann Gardner not survive me. I also give Miss Mary Munford Brown my solid silver cake knife marked M.E.G. and my diamond earrings. Fifth, I give to Samuel Kerr Rosignol of Atlanta, GA, namesake of my much loved uncle Samuel Kerr (by whose will I hold the greater portion of my own estate) three lots Nos. 18, 20 and 23 on Trigg and Kerr Avenues near Memphis, TN. and another of the above named bonds. Sixth, I give to my neice, Mrs. Kate B. Carnes, wife of Samuel T. Carnes of Memphis, Tn all that land on the South side of Kerr Avenue between the railroads in Shelby County, TN, and the silver soup ladle I promised her, my silver tea service, my silverware marked "Kerr" to hold as her own until her brother J.L. Kerr marries, at which time I give said silverware to him. Seventh, "As Miss Jennie M. Harris, since the accident which so seriously crippled and disabled me last winter, has been to me both as a good samaritan and as a devoted daughter, I give to Irwin Craighead of Mobile AL in trust for her, my house and lot on Shelby Street in Memphis, TN. I also give her one bond and my pearl handle knives. Eighth, I give to the Memphis Trust Company in trust for my nephew John L. Kerr, the remaining two tracts of 22 acres each west of the railroad in Shelby County, TN and my plantation in Tunica County, Mississippi known as the OK Landing on the Mississippi River. Ninth, I give to Mollie Gardner, Willie Gardner and Annie Gardner, daughters of Dr. Joseph Gardner of Columbus, GA, jointly, jewelry and my three solid silver plated cake baskets given me by their uncle William R. Gardner. Tenth, I give my dear firend Miss Blanche Louise Lewis my diamond ring and my gold watch and chain. I have recently made a deed to her of other properties. Eleventh, I give my cousin Kate Durr of Montgomery Al, jewelery and the wine cooler of our great grandfather General Samuel Elbert of Revolutionary fame which was brought from England by his father. Twelve, I give $100.00 to Sam T. Carnes in trust for Annie Horton. Thirteen, I give to my cousin Lucy Durr, wife of John W. Durr, Jr. of Montgomery AL, my silver water pitcher. Fourteen, I give to J.H. Johnson of Clarksdale, Mississippi, agent for my plantation, $200.00. Fifteen, I give to Ella Munford, daughter of the late William B. Munford, dec'd at present residing in Nashville, TN all

my stock in the People's National Bank of McMinnville.
Sixteen, The rest of my property, subject to the next
clause of this will, I give to Samuel Kerr Rosignol.
Seventeen, If there is not sufficient funds to cover the
above legacies, my executor is to sell any of my
property not specifically bequeathed above. Eighteen,
I appoint my friend James C. Biles my executor.
Witnessed by George M. Smith and James S. Barton.
Admitted to probate 14 Jul 1900.

pg 251. 4 Aug 1900. Settlement made with William J.
Cardwell, administrator of H.J. Cardwell, dec'd. The
heirs each receive $8.56 (1/7th of the balance of the
estate), to wit: Laura Drake, Paralee Cardwell, F.M.
Cardwell, Florence Lusk, America Cardwell, C.S. Cardwell
and the administrator.

pg 252. 30 Jun 1900. Settlement made with J.C. Biles,
executor of Rhoda Davis, dec'd. Trustees for Laslie
McMillen, E. Clair McMillen and J.DeB. McMillen named
and given funds.

pg 253-254. 16 Aug 1900. Inventory of the personal
property belonging to the estate of Mrs. Mary E.
Munford, dec'd, reported by J.C. Biles, executor.

pg 255-258. 3 Jul 1900. Inventory and sale bill of the
personal estate of Celia Moffitt, dec'd sold at public
sale 18 Dec 1897. Purchasers Laura Moffitt, Venus
Moffitt, A.B. Moffitt and others. E.L. Moffitt, admr.

pg 259-260. 3 Jul 1900. Settlement made with
E.L.Moffitt, one of the executors of G.P. Moffitt,
dec'd.

pg 261. 9 Mar 1900. Settlement made with Elizabeth
Harrison, administratrix of Samuel Harrison, dec'd.
Receipts from heirs for $75.00, to wit: A.G. Harrison,
Sarah C. Welder [Welden] and Albert P. Harrison.

pg 262-263. 30 Jun 1900. Inventory and sale of the
estate of Charlotte Herndon, dec'd made by W.C. Herndon,
administrator.

pg 264-265. 28 Jul 1900. Settlement made with J.C.
Anderson, administrator of Elijah Anderson, dec'd.
Shares of the estate equal to $10.00 given to each of
the following: I.A. Anderson, N.G. Anderson, S.E. Roach,
Mattie Roach, Gendya Burch, J.T. Daniell, guardian and

Warren County, Tn Will Book 10, cont.

J.C. Anderson.

pg 266-267. 1 Sep 1900. Settlement made with J.D. and T.B. Bailey, administrators of the estate of William J. Bailey, dec'd.

pg 268. 19 Jul 1900. Settlement made with W.H. Bedingfield, administrator of the estate of Arminda Fults, dec'd. Receipts for shares of $7.00 each given by the following: A.J. Fults, Lawson Fults, Emma Tipton, Evaline Crouch, W.H. Bedingfield as guardian of the Northcut heirs, W.E. Northcut, Jennie Hobbs, G.M. Fults, and Beersheba Crouch.

pg 269. 13 Sep 1900. Tennie Moffitt and A.R. Hammer, the administrators of F.M. Moffitt, dec'd report rent on the Laurel Creek farm, and rents due on property in Sparta, TN.

pg 270-271. 12 Sep 1900. Inventory and sale bill of the personal property of William M. Meadows, dec'd sold on 1 Sep 1900 by J.J. Meadows, administrator. Purchases by Mrs. Jane Meadows, Marcus Meadows, A.D. Meadows, and othes.

pg 272-274. 3 Apr 1897. **Will of Thomas Mauzy**. I, Thomas Mauzy of Warren County, do make and publish this my last wil and testament. First; I direct that my just debts and funeral expenses be paid. Second, I give to my two beloved daughters Sophia Hash and Julia Biles, all of the estate or property of any kind or description. I have given to my daughter Julia Biles as advancement the sum of $1300.00 and Sophia Hash $1200.00. Third, the share which goes to my daughter Sophia is to be free from the control of her husband G.H. Hash, and my executor is to invest same in real estate for her use and benefit and that of her bodily heirs. Fourth, I appoint J.B. Biles my executor. Witnessed by H.H. Faulkner and E.G. Mead. **Codicil;** 17 Oct 1899. I now declare that it is my will that my beloved grandson Clarence Barbee be paid the sum of $25.00 and the remainder of my property be divided between my daughters as set forth in my said will. Witnessed by Charles Mauzy and Denny Cummings. Admitted for probate 1 Oct 1900.

pg 275. 22 Oct 1892. **Will of Wilmorth [Wilmuth] Stubblefield**. I, Willie Stubblefield, make this my last will and testament. I want my debts be paid. I desire to have a nice tombstone erected at the head of my grave and one at my sister Betsy Sain's and my brother George Stubblefield's. I desire that my nephew Sam Stubblefield to have my bed complete as it stands. My nephew William Rogers to have my chest and my neice Lou Thaxton to have my trunk. The remainder of my bed clothes for my brother William Stubblefield or his grandchildren the heirs of E.L. Stubblefield, dec'd. I appoint James Morrow my executor. Witnessed by G.W. Ramsey and J.R. Ramsey. Admitted to probate 1 Oct 1900.

pg 276-278. 7 Apr 1900. **Will of John Duncan.** I, John Duncan, being of sound mid and disposing memory do make and publish this my last will and testament. First, "that after my death that I be decently buried." Second, my funeral expenses are to be paid. Third, I want my debts paid. Fourth, I desire is to divide my farm between my son Jesse M. Duncan and my son-in-law H.V. Copenhaver and his wife Mollie. Mollie is to have my dwelling house at $1500.00 on a final settlement of the estate. Fifth, Jessie M. Duncan is to have the land above mentioned and he be charged $1500.00 on a final settlement. I have heretofore given Romulus Duncan an advancement of $250.00, advanced Jennie Davis $100.00 and advanced Della Steakley $175.00. I have given all the heirs, to wit: Romulus Duncan, Jennie Davis, Della Steakley and Sallie Cardwell $100.00 when the went to housekeeping. Jessie and Mollie are to be made equal with the above. I want my effects divided equally among all my six children. I appoint my son Jesse M. Duncan and my son-in-law H.V. Copenhaver my executors. Witnessed J.Q. Miller and J.H. Ray. Admitted to probate 5 Nov 1900.

pg 279. 5 Oct 1900. Inventory of the estate of Jeremiah Jaco, dec'd that had come to the hands of Joseph Jaco, administrator.

pg 280-281. 28 Sep 1900. Sale bill of the estate of Bedford Hammer, dec'd, sold at the premises of the late Bedford Hammer on 15 Sep 1900 by F.M. Fennell, administrator.

pg 282-285. 28 Sep 1900. Sale bill of the estate of J.W. Nunley, dec'd, reported by J.S. Nunley, administrator. Purchases made by D.C. Nunley, Ellen Nunley, Ira Nunley, John Nunley, Jonah Nunley, and others.

pg 286. 1 Dec 1900. Inventory of the estate of E. Reeder, dec'd, including account from auditor of Interior Dept. The report made by J.T. Kelton, administrator.

pg 287. 28 Nov 1900. Settlement made with W.R. Crouch administrator of J.H. Sartain, dec'd. Cerditors to receive $0.34 on the dollar.

pg 288-289. 30 Nov 1900. Settlement made with W.T. Pollard, administrator of the estate of George R. Locke, dec'd. Pollard has paid out more than received from assets of estate.

pg 290. 8 Dec 1900. Settlement made with J.T. Kelton, administrator of the estate of Edwin Reeder, dec'd. No balance remains in the administrator's hands.

pg 291-292. 28 Dec 1900. Final settlement made with A.F. Stubblefield, administrator with will annexed of William Stubblefield, dec'd. Receipts for $1107.02 from each of the heirs and legatees, to wit: A.F. Stubblefield, Mrs. E.J. Stubblefield, S.M. Stubblefield, W.R. Stubblefield, E.R. Stubblefield, and Ella Wagner. "In the 3rd item of the testator's will, he directs that the sum of $1000.00 be paid to his daughter Margaret Stubblefield, but just prior to his death, he gave that sum to the said legatee and that it was not his intention that she have another thousand dollars."

pg 293-294. 1 Jan 1901. Settlement made with George T. Miller, administrator of the estate of Robert Miller, dec'd. Mentions long litigation in the Chancery Court with one Hobbs which was necessary to protect his intestate's estate.

pg 295. 31 Dec 1900. List of property sold at the sale of Louisa Cardwell, dec'd made by T.R. Gribble, administrator.

pg 296-298. 31 Jan 1899. **Will of Isaac Grizzle.** I, Isaac Grizzle do make and publish this my last will and testament. First, I will my debts and funeral expenses be paid. Second, I will to the children of Irving Grizzle and wife the farm on which they now live. These children are not to sell said farm until after the death of both Irving and his wife. Third, I will to my son Jno. R. Grizzle's children the farm on which he now lives, not to be sold so long as Jno. R. should live and should he marry again, as long as he or his wife should live. Fourth, I will to the children of my son Ewing Grizzle and wife the farm I own in Pleasant Cove and $1000.00, making my sons Ewing and James Grizzle guardians for the above named children. Said farm not to be sold until after the death of both Ewing Grizzle and his wife. Fifth, I will to my daughter Zona Grizzle and to my son James Grizzle the farm I now live on. Zona is to have the furniture in the kitchen, dining room and room adjoining it. The balance of my residence I bequeath to my son James Grizzle. All my money, stock, farming implements, household goods I bequeath to the above named son and daughter. I appoint my son James Grizzle my executor. Witnessed by Sam Cantrell and H. Leo Boles. **Codicil:;** 31 Oct 1900. I have heretofore given my son F.S. Grizzle all that I intend for him to have. Witnessed by W.W. Fairbanks and H.P. Stubblefield. Admitted for probate 8 Jan 1901.

pg 299. 9 Jan 1901. Settlement made with John B. Biles, executor of the will of Thomas Mauzy, dec'd. Under the terms of the will, the legacy of Sophia Hash will be invested for her benefit. The amount of C.M. Barbee legacy unpaid for the reason that his address was not known.

pg 300. 3 Jan 1901. Settlement made with C.A. Hopkins, administrator of the estate of William J. Hopkins, dec'd. The dec'd yet to receive his distributive share in the estate of Thomas Hopkins, dec'd, settled in Warren County Chancery Court ($46.35).

pg 301-302. 3 Jan 1901. J.R. Northcutt, executor of the estate of John A. Northcutt. The executor is allowed $25.00 for his services.

pg 303-305. 7 Jan 1901. Sale bill of the estate of John Duncan, dec'd, reported by J.M. Duncan, executor. Sale held 14 Nov 1900.

pg 306. 15 Jan 1901. Settlement made with C.I.L. Barnes, administrator of the estate of C.M. Northcutt, dec'd. He has paid out all the assets of the estate, including payments of various amounts to Arminda Fults estate, P.K. Northcutt B.D. Northcutt, H.B. Northcutt, A. Northcutt, W.E. Northcutt and others.

pg 307. 19 Jan 1901. Settlement made with J.H. Collier, administrator of the estate of Nan Collier, dec'd. Receipt for $171.88 given by "Wm. C. Womack, guardian of Frank Collier, only heir of deceased."

pg 308. 9 Jan' 1901. Sale bill of the estate of Mrs. Pheobe Brewer, dec'd as reported by W.A. Hood, administrator. Purchases made by Dock Brewer and others.

pg 309. 5 Dec 1900. List of property sold at the sale of P.H. Hankins, dec'd on 23 Jul 1899. Sale held by D.B. Smith, administrator.

pg 310-314. 25 Jan 1901. Settlement made with J.C. Biles, administrator of the estate of D.W. King, dec'd. The following received their distributive share of the estate: J.K. King, P.W. King, Mrs. T.P. King, Bettie Rhodes, Mrs. Willie Thaxton, Mrs Lyna Paty, Mrs. Mattie Moore and "Nashville Trust Co., guardian of 3 minor heirs" [not named].

pg 315-322. 12 Jan 1901. Sale bill of the estate of James M. Green, dec'd reported by E.N. Green, administrator. Purchases made by E.N. Green, J.J. Green, O.D. Green, J.D. Green, Joe Green, J.M. Green, Lidda Green, Jeff Green, S.A. Green, Homer Green, P.D. Green and others.

pg 323. 4 Feb 1901. Final settlement made with J.R. Northcutt, executor of John A. Northcutt, dec'd.

pg 324. 2 Feb 1901. Settlement made with J.J. Meadows, trustee of the St. Mary School Fund. Vouchers filed: O.S. Hill, teacher and Carlie M. Etter, teacher.

pg 325. 5 Feb 1901. Settlement made with Ed Sparkman, administrator of Elsie Gribble, dec'd.

pg 326-327. 18 Feb 1901. Settlement made with J.N. Hughes, administrator of the estate of Mrs. Racheal Nunley, dec'd. Report made of having paid the share of Margaret Nunley (John C. Hughes, assignee), Lee Nunley, J.I. Teirny (as administrator of Sarah Talleman), and M. Nunley. Mary Ann Freeze's share is held against $22.31 for goods purchased at sale.

pg 328. 4 Mar 1901. Settlement made with N.A.Reeder, administrator of W.M. Reeder, dec'd. Administrator has paid out more that the assets of his intestate.

pg 329.   27 Feb 1901.   List of property sold of the estate of D.C. Dunlop, dec'd on 18 Nov 1899, reported by W.B. Cunningham, administrator. Purchases made by D.S. Dunlop, B.L. Dunlop, D.C. Dunlop and others.

pg 330.   14 Mar 1901.   Inventory of the estate of W.H. Hoover taken 1 Aug 1900 in District 8, reported by D.B. Hoover, administrator.

pg 331.   8 Mar 1901.   Settlement made with J.L. Finger, administrator of the estate of H.W. Finger, dec'd. Balance in the estate to be paid pro rata among the creditors.

pg 332.   20 Aug 1900.   **Will of M.S. Oliver.**   For and in consideration of the love and affection that I have for my wife Melvina Oliver, I hereby give and bequeath all my property both real and personal to her at my death.. I further appoint her executrix.   Witnessed by J.W. Vanhooser and H.H. Holland. Admitted for probate 1 Apr 1901.

pg 333.   18 Mar 1901.   Sale bill of the esate of G.W. Martin, reported by W.S. Grissom, administrator. Purchases made by E.C. Martin, Brite Martin, Jess Martin and others.

pg 334-335.   7 Jan 1901.   Supplemental sale bill of the estate of Catherine Gribble.   Purchases made by J.B. Gribble, Wreathie Gribble, G.P. Gribble, John T. Gribble, William Gribble and others.

pg 336-338.   2 Apr 1901.   List of property sold at the sale of Ellen Miller, dec'd on the 16th of Mar 1901, reported by J.D. Hash, administrator.

pg 339.   16 Apr 1901.   Settlement made with William H. Magness, administrator of the estate of Mrs. J.Ella Magness Simmes.   Under the will of the late W.H. Magness, father of the decedent, the amount in administrators hands belonging to this estate reverts to the W.H. Magness estate. The receipt of W.H. and Edgar Magness, executors of the late W.H. Magness is filed by said administrator.

pg 340.   17 Apr 1901.   Sale bill of the estate of J.K. Saunders, dec'd, reported by R.L. Saunders, administrator.   Purchases by Margaret Saunders, R.L. Sanders, M.F. Sanders and others.

pg 341. 3 May 1901. Inventory of the estate of Levi Woodlee, reported by Ben L. Stanley, administrator.

pg 342-343. 26 Apr 1898. **Will of Bolin Jennings.** I, Bolin Jennings, do hereby make and publish this my last will and testament. First, I wish all my debts paid and a stone placed to mark my grave. Second, I give to my wife Bettie, all my real and personal estate for life, and at her death the estate shall descend to my child Falls Jennings. I nominate Mr. J.F. Morford my executor. Witnessed by W.V. Whitson and W.C. Womack. Admitted to probate 3 Jun 1901.

pg 344-346. 1 Jun 1901. Sale bill of the estate of I.A. Walker, dec'd that had come to the hands of M.E. Walker, administratrix. Purchases by Lee Walker, Losson Walker, Sam Walker, Lizzie Walker, Elijah Walker, Nancy Walker and others.

pg 347. 11 Mar 1901. Sale bill of the personal property of the estate of Levi C. Woodlee, dec'd, reported by Ben L. Stanley, administrator.

pg 348. 1 Jun 1901. Settlement made with J.H. Sherrill, administrator of the estate of Nan Sherrill, dec'd. Balance in estate ($22.68) to be distributed pro rota to creditors of estate.

pg 349-350. 12 Jun 1901. Settlement made with J.T. Gribble, executor of the will of Samantha Cunningham, dec'd. Receipts from the legatees for the amount due them as follows: Sara E. Gribble, $295.13; G.W. Cunningham $296.87; J.M. Cunningham, $296.87; F.R. Cunningham $96.88; F.G. Couch, guardian of Eveleaner Couch $331.85.

pg 351-353. 9 Apr 1901. **Will of Minos Rushing.** I, Minos Rushing, realizing the uncertainty of life and the certainty of death, and being desirous to make a final disposition of my earthly effects in accordance with my will and wishes, though somewhat feeble in body, but of sound mind and disposing memory, do hereby make and publish this my last will and testament. I desire that all my debts and funeral expenses be paid. I give all my household and kitchen furniture to my beloved wife Amanda Rushing. I give to my executor to be by him sold, my horse, wagon and tools and my real estate. Out of the proceeds of the sale of the above he will pay all debts and the balance he will divide equally between my

two brothers Anderson Rushing and Steve Rushing, and my
beloved wife Amanda Rushing. I nominate Robert W.
Smartt sole executor of this will. Witnessed by Robert
W. Smartt and W.A. Johnson. Admitted to probate 10 Jun
1901.

pg 354. 10 Jun 1901. Settlement made with R.C. Barnes,
administrator of Elizabeth Barnes, dec'd. There is no
balance remaining in the hands of said administrator.

pg 355. 22 Jun 1901. Settlement made with F.M.
McDonough, administrator of M.A. McDonough, dec'd. The
administrator is credited with the balance in his hands,
he being the husband of the deceased.

pg 356-357. 21 Apr 1899. **Will of Harriet A. Clark.** I,
Harriet A. Clark of McMinnville, do this day make and
publish this my last will and testament. First, I
appoint Mrs. Betsy M. Long executrix of my personal
property. She is to pay funeral and burial expenses and
all other debts and finish inscription on monument in
City Cemetery with information in large Bible in book
case. To Mrs. Besty M. Long I bequeath $1000.00. To my
brother Rev. Dr. E. Whitaker all the money remaining in
my estate. To Miss Herminia Jeannaire I bequeath my
little chair. To Dr. J.A. Smith, any book or set of
books he may select. To Mrs. Betsy M. Long and her
daughter M. Wave Long, I bequeath all my personal
property of all kinds remaining of my estate. Witnessed
Chas. A. Chaffee and J.A. Smith, M.D. **Codicil:** 20 Jun
1901. I, Harriet A. Clark have this day executed the
$1000.00 clause of the above. Witnessed J.A. Smith and
Jennie Brockman. Admitted to probate 1 Jul 1901.

pg 358-359. 26 Jun 1901. Settlement made with R.W.
Smartt, administrator of Lou J. Roach, dec'd.

pg 360. 29 Jun 1901. Settlement made with J.K.P. Webb,
administrator of Cindrella Webb, dec'd. Due the heirs
as follows: Maude Collier and Belle Womack $24.87;
J.K.P. Webb, $24.87; Heirs of R.A. Webb, $24.87; Heirs
of A.J. Webb, $24.87; and F.P. Webb, $24.87.

pg 361-363. 19 Aug 1891. **Will of Myra L.L. Hartwell.**
I, Myra L.L. Hartwell of McMinnville, being in good
health and sound mind, do hereby make and declare this
my last will and testament. I give to my brother Harvey
E. Scott (if living at my decease) $25.00. If not living
the sum to be paid to his oldest daughter Leila Scott,

both residents of Excelsior, Minn. I give to my neice
Florence E. Haskell, wife of Dr. W.A. Haskell of Alton,
Ill, my silver spoons and one breast pin containing hair
and marked L.E.S. I give to my step-daughter Carrie L.
Hartwell, now living in Shirley Village, Mass., if my
survivor, one-third of all the money I possess. If not
living at my death, it shall be paid with the remaining
two thirds in the following manner. I give to Helen
Nelson, daughter of George Nelson of Hardwick, Vermont
the remaining two-thirds, the interest to be used for
her education. I give to Mrs.M.E. Johnson and Miss
Susie E. Hoyt of McMinnville my wardrobe and table
linen. I appoint Edward P. Crane of Minnapolis, Minn
and R.B.M. Grath of Excelsior, Minn my executors.
Witnessed by Jesse Walling and L.E. West. [Signed Myra
L.S. Hartwell. **Codicil:** 3 June 1895. I give to my step
daughter Carrie L. Hartwell and my two neices Leila
Scott and Bessie Scott (the last two of Excelsior,
Minn.) together one-third of all the money I possess to
be equally divided among the three. Witnessed Jesse
Walling and L.E. West. Admitted for probate 9 July
1901.

pg 364. 27 Jun 1901. Settlement made with A.F. Willis,
administrator of the estate of Charles E. Willis.. "The
deceased was a minor son of the administrator, unmarried
and without issue, therefore the administrator is
entitled to all of his personal estate."

pg 365. 26 Jun 1901. Inventory and sale of the
personal property of the estate of Jordan Fuston, dec'd,
made by Robert W. Smartt, administrator.

pg 366. 26 Jun 1901. Inventory of the estate of James
Newby, dec'd, reported by W.L. Newby, executor.

pg 367-369. 27 Jun 1901. Sale bill of the estate of
B.T. Grove, made by J.R. Groves, administrator.
Purchases made by William Groves, J.R. Groves, Charles
Groves and others.

pg 370. 5 Jul 1901. Settlement of the estate of Sallie
Bowers. "David Miller, administrator of Sallie Bowers,
appointed and qualified at the Jan Term 1898 states to
the Court that he came into possession of some household
and kitchen furniture belonging to the deceased which he
did not sell, but delivered to her sister Liz Edge, her
only heir at law."

pg 371. 17 Jul 1901. Inventory of the estate of Harriet A. Clark, reported by Betsy M. Long, executrix.

pg 372. 15 Jul 1901. Settlement made with E.L. Moffitt, aedministrator of the estate of Celia Moffitt, dec'd. "The Clerk has allowed the administrator $150.00 as compensation for winding up this estate and the estate of G.P. Moffitt, dec'd who was the husband of Celia Moffitt."

pg 373-376. 1 Jul 1901. Sale bill of the estate of Miram[?] Mullican, dec'd, reported by J.J. Mullican, administrator. Purchases by Sol Mullican, J.D. Mullican, Rena Mullican, H.B. Mullican, Sallie Lane, Mary Lane, J.E. Lane and others.

pg 377. 17 Jul 1901. Inventory of the estate of W.D. Edwards, dec'd made by Octa Edwards.

pg 378. 19 Oct 1898. Settlement of the estate of Nancy Wagner, dec'd, made by John Rutledge, executor. Due executor as heir $1029.29, paid Mary A. Lane $1030.29, paid H.B. Bonner $1029.29.

pg 379. 30 Jul 1901. Settlement made with Robert T. Burt, administrator of Ann Scott, dec'd. Administrator has paid out more money than he received.

pg 380. 30 Jul 1901. Final settlement made with R.T. Burt, administrator of Sophia Estil, dec'd. Administrator has paid out more money than he received.

pg 381. 12 Aug 1901. Settlement made with G.S. Shankle, administrator of S.H. Wheeler, dec'd. "The wife of the administrator V.L. Shankle is the only heir at law of the deceased and is credited with the balance of the estate."

pg 382. 24 Aug 1901. Settlement with T.P. Crowe, trustee. "To the chairman of the County Court, whereas I was the Trustee named in a deed of trust made by Mary White, dec'd in her lifetime to me to secure a sum of borrowed money from John Walter on the 11 Dec 1891 and whereas only the interest was paid for a portion of the time, I therefore was directed by the holder of the note, J.L. Garnett, to advertise the property as required by law, beg leave to report to the Court how I have discharged said trust" Mrs. C.C. Murphy became the purchaser of said property. After debts there was left

$41.28 due the heirs of Mary White which was paid to the attorney of the administrator Thomas White.

pg 383. 29 Aug 1901. Settlement made with W.S. Grissom, administrator of George W. Martin, dec'd.

pg 384. 24 Aug 1901. Inventory of the estate of H. Neal, dec'd made by Ewing Grizzle, administrator.

pg 385. 6 Sep 1901. Settlement made with Arch Scott, administrator of Cooper Scott, dec'd.

pg 386. 22 Oct 1901. Settlement made with J.H. Hubbard, administrator of the estate of William Hubbard, dec'd. Receipts for $3.15 each given by: James and John Morgan; W.H. and M.G. Mathis; D.A. Hubbard; L.J. and S.E. Jones; and administrator as his share. Balance due King minors $2.15.

pg 387. 22 Oct 1901. Settlement made with J.H. Hubbard [repeat of page 386]

pg 388. 22 Oct 1901. Settlement made with D.H. and D.S. Miller, executors of the estate of Esther Miller, dec'd. Balance of estate goes to D.S. Miller as the residuary legatee of the testatrix.

pg 389. 18 Nov 1901. Settlement made with T.H. McAfee, administrator of D.S. McAfee, dec'd. There is nothing remaining in estate.

pg 390-399. 24 Sep 1901. List of property sold by the administrator J.L. Miller on 14 Sep 1909, belonging to the estate of Priscilla M. Jaco, dec'd. Purchases made by Jennie Jaco, Sarah Jaco, S.D. Jaco, J.E. Jaco, S.J. Jaco, Mary Jaco and many others.

pg 400. 15 Nov 1909. Settlement made with W.R. Crouch, administrator of the estate of J.H. Sartin, dec'd. Administrator has paid out all the assets of his intestate.

pg 401. 29 Nov 1909. Final settlement made with J.H. Sherrill administrator of the estate of Nan Sherrill, dec'd. There is no balance in the hands of the administrator.

pg 402. 31 Dec 1901. Settlement made with John Blanton, administrator of Joe L. Blanton, dec'd.

[Mentions assets of the estate which are in litigation.]

pg 403-404. 21 Dec 1901. Settlement made with Tennie Moffitt and A.R. Hammer, administrators of F.M. Moffitt, dec'd. Mrs. Tennie Moffitt given $344.25 for years support.

pg 405. 3 Jan 1902. Settlement made with J.R. Grove, administrator of the estate of B.T. Grove, dec'd.

pg 406-407. 28 Dec 1901. Supplemental sale bill of the estate of Priscilla M. Jaco, dec'd, sold by J.L. Miller, administrator on 7 Nov 1901. Purchases by Jennie Jaco, S.D.Jaco, and others.

pg 408. 1 Jan 1902. Settlement made with Charles A. Mitchell, administrator of Leo Groves dec'd. Reciept of George B. Bryan, guardian of Martha Grove_, only heir of deceased.

pg 409. 24 Dec 1901. Settlement made with T.R. Tribble, administrator of the estate of Louisa Cardwell, dec'd. $24.82 to be distributed among the heirs at law [not named.]

pg 410. 3 Jan 1902. Supplemental inventory and sale bill of G.F. Wagner, administrator of the estate of Hixie Parks, dec'd.

pg 411. 29 Mar 1879. **Will of Martha L. Matherly.** I, Martha L. Matherly, being of sound mind and disposing memory, knowing the uncertainity of life and the certainty of death and having no children, and wishing that my husband Hartford Matherly, for whom I cherish the deepest love and affection should own my estate after my death; therefore to accomplish this purpose I do hereby ordain, declare and establish this to be my last will and testament. It is my first wish that all my debts be paid. Second, it is my wish that all of my estate both real and personal be vested in my dearly beloved husband Hartford Matherly. Third, I appoint my husband my executor. Witnessed Elvin Sparkman and Permelia Sparkman. [Probate date not given, but recorded Jan Term 1902.]

pg 412. 16 Jan 1902. Settlement made with Ewing Grizzle, administrator of H. Neal, dec'd. No balance remaining in the hands of the administrator.

pg 413. 8 Jan 1902. Settlement made with N.B. Cummings administrator of D.C. Dunlap, dec'd. Balance for distribution $201.95, there being 7 heirs each receive $28.85.

pg 414. 13 Jan 1902. Final settlement made with J.L. Finger, administrator of the estate of H.M. Finger, dec'd.

pg 415. 12 Feb 1902. Settlement made with Octa Edwards, administratrix of W.D. Edwards, dec'd. Balance of $179.79 retained by administratrix the only heir of deceased.

pg 416-418. 20 Jan 1902. Settlement of the account of J.K. Saunders, dec'd, late administrator of Z. Saunders, made with R.L. Saunders, administrator of said J.K. Saunders.

pg 419. 12 Feb 1902. Settlement made with J.R. Green, administrator of I.T. Green, dec'd. J.R. Green appointed guardian of Charles Green and Nannie Green, minors and only heirs at law of I.T. Green, dec'd.

pg 420. 27 Jan 1902. Sale bill of the estate of E.G. Bess, dec'd, reported by I.P. Bess. Purchases by Rosa Bess, I.P. Bess and others.

pg 421. 3 Feb 1902. Inventory and sale bill of the estate of Lydia Gibbs, dec'd reported by I.G. Gribble, administrator. Purchases by William Gibbs and others.

pg 422. 1 Feb 1902. Inventory and sale bill of the estate of Thomas Brown, dec'd by W.L. Swann, administrator. Purchases by Mat Brown, S.L. Brown and others.

pg 423. 24 Feb 1902. Schedule of personal property of Mrs. Myra L.S. Hartwell, dec'd which came to the hands of Mrs. M.E. Johnson and Miss Susie E. Hoyt, administratrix with will annexed.

pg 424. 30 Jan 1902. **Will of Isaac Tramel.** I, Isaac Tramel being of sound mind and memory, do this day make my last will and testament. First, I bequeath unto my daughter Tennessee Penn $5.00 in cash to be paid out of my personal effects and the same amount to my daughter Emma Clark. The balance of my real and personal effects to my daughter Mary Tramel, consisting of my farm,

household furniture, and stock, except one dark heifer
that I want my grandson Ernest Tramel to have. Also I
bequeath and request that P.G. Potter, if living, be
appointed my daughter Mary's trustee. If P.G. Potter is
unable to serve, then I appoint I.G. Gribble her
trustee. Witnessed by M.J. Phillips and P.G. Potter.
Admitted for probate 3 Mar 1902.

pg 425. 6 Jan 1902. **Will of Thomas William Snipes.**
I, Thos. William Snipes do make and publish this as my
last will. First, for the care and attention Martha and
Amanda have given me, I will them all the stock on the
place now. Second, I want the other personal property
and real estate sold and proceeds equally divided among
the children except $25.00 each for Martha and Amanda
above to be taken out before the equal divide. I want
Baxter's part to satisy the note in favor of Alex
Anderson, the remainder to go to Baxter's heirs.
Witnessed R.L. Owens and W.C. Crisp. Admitted to
probate March Term 1902.

pg 426. 3 Mar 1902. Final settlement made with T.R.
Gribble, administrator of the estate of Louisa Cardwell,
dec'd. Equal shares of $3.40 paid to each of the
following: W.J. Cardwell, America Cardwell, Paralee
Cardwell, F.M. Cardwell, Florence Lusk, C.S. Cardwell
and Laura Drake.

pg 427. 22 Feb 1902. Inventory and sale bill of the
estate of J.W. McGee, dec'd, reported by Van McGee,
administrator. Purchases by Van McGee, J.L. McGee,
Martha McGee and others.

pg 428. 3 Feb 1902. Final settlement of the estate of
G.W. Martin, dec'd made by W.S. Grissom, administrator.

pg 429-431. 13 May 1899. **Will of E.H. Green.** I, E.H.
Green do make and publish this my last will and
testament. Item 1. I will that my debts and funeral
expenses be paid. Second, I give to my grandchildren,
the children of Paralee Locke to wit: Alla Locke, Jessie
Locke, Sam Locke, Lizzie Lawson and William Locke, $5.00
each. Third, I give to my children Harriet Walling,
Mollie Allen, John S. Green, Sam A. Green, Mattie Webb
and J.H. Green and the children of my deceased son
Bailey Peyton Green all the balance of my estate of
every kind and description to be divided equally among
them. I appoint my sons John S. Green, Sam A. Green and
J.H. Green my executors. Witnessed by Thomas C. Lind

and George S. Hoodenpyl. **Codicil:** 13 May 1899. I will that any notes I hold on any of my said children or grandchildren be charged against each before dividing the estate. Witnessed by Thomas C. Lind and George S. Hoodenpyl. Admitted to probate 7 Apr 1902.

pg 432. 13 Jan 1900. **Will of Benjamin Crofot.** I, Benjamin Crofot do make this my last will and testament. I bequeath unto my wife Nancy L. Crofot all my estate both real and personal for her natural life and at her death any profit arising from my estate to be divided among my heirs and the heirs of my wife, except DeWit Clinton Hawn who is to receive $1.00. I nominate Edward Crannell of Troy, New York as executor of this will. Witnessed W.M. Fisher and H.F. Harwell. [Signed as B. Crofoot] Admitted to probate 7 Apr 1902.

pg 433. 17 Mar 1902. Final settlement made with M.E. Johnson and S.E. Hoyt, administratrix with will annexed of Myra L.S. Hartwell, dec'd.

pg 434. 15 Apr 1902. Final settlement made with F.P. Byers, executor of Nathan Byers, dec'd. Voucher filed for Jane Byers $77.80 in full of her distributed share in the estate.

pg 435. 15 Apr 1902. Inventory of the estate of Isaac Tramwell, dec'd made by P.G. Potter, administrator.

pg 436-441. 7 Apr 1902. Inventory and sale bill of the personal property of the estate of P.A. Hoodenpyl, dec'd made 27 Mar 1902 by J.J. Meadows, administrator. Purchases made by Ethel Hoodenpyl, Mrs. P.A. Hoodenpyl, Maggie Hoodenpyl, Laura Hennessee, Mary Gibbs, Marshall Hoodenpyl, Esther Hoodenpyl and many others.

pg 442-443. 4 Mar 1902. **Will of Bethiah L. Colville.** I, Bethiah L. Colville of McMinnville do make and declare this paper writing to be my last will and testament. First, I desire that my debts be paid. Second, I will to Daisey McClarty $100.00. I make this bequest for the kindness to my deceased daughter Lizzie McClarty and to myself by Daisey. Third, I give to A.B. McClarty my gold watch. I hope he will keep it in the family as it was his great grandfather's watch. Fourth, I want Nora McClarty to have my bedstead, also her father's and mother's and my pictures. Fifth, I will to Jessie Fisher my gold thimble, work basket and pin. Sixth, I want my granddaughter Bethiah L. Bell to have my gold chain and cross and jet pin. All my other jewelry to be divided between Willie, Nannie and Lizzie Bell. I want Nannie Bell and daughters to have my furniture and everything in my room not otherwise disposed of. I want my son W.A. Bell to have three volumes of Old and New Testament. Seventh, all the balance of my property of every description I will to my son W.A. Bell and my granddaughter Nora McClarty to be equally divided between them. Eighth, I appoint A.B. McClarty trustee of his sister Nora McClarty's share. Ninth, I appoint my son W.A. Bell and my grandson A.B. McClarty executors of this my will. Witnessed by J.I. Finney and J.C. Biles. Admitted for probate 5 May 1902.

pg 444-445. 18 Apr 1900. **Will of Peter S. Gollady.** I, Peter S. Golladay being of sound mind and desposing memory do this day make my last will and testament. First I direct that my just debts be paid. The residue of my property of every kind shall go to my wife Margaret A. Golladay. She is to act as executor without bond. If I should survive my wife Margaret, I appoint my son Alvadore Golladay my executor to collect debts, sell real estate, etc. He is to divide all that comes into his hands equally between my legal heirs at law. Signed at Vervilla. Witnessed by Jesse Hill and John L. Comer. "My explanation of my last will--My wife Margaret A. and I began our married life in very moderate circumstances and by our united efforts raised our family and started them in life and reserved a part to take care of us if we needed it, bury us, pay our doctor's bills etc and if there is anything left of course we want our lawful heirs to have it and as my wife Margaret A. by her faithful help, industry and economy helped to accumintate whatever of property we have and as we mutually set apart what we now have for the above mentioned purpose, it is my will and wish that she shall have the same rights in and to it after my death as I would or will have if she should die before I do." Admitted for probate 5 May 1902.

pg 446. 19 Apr 1902. Settlement made with W.A. Hood, administrator of the estate of Phebe Brewer, dec'd. There is no balance in the hands of the administrator.

pg 447-448. 26 Apr 1902. Inventory and sale bill of the estate of K.E. Lowry, dec'd reported by William W. Nesmith, administrator.

pg 449. 2 May 1902. Inventory and sale bill of the

estate of O.H. Ford reported by Charles Cunningham, administrator of the estate.

pg 450-456. 3 Mar 1902. Sale bill of the estate of William Snipes, dec'd, reported by J.W. Snipes. Sale held at the house of the deceased in the 1st Civil District. Purchases by Martha Snipes, Mandy Snipes, Albert Snipes, John Snipes, George Snipes, L. Snipes, J.W. Snipes, and many others.

pg 457. 2 May 1902. Settlement made with Charles Cunningham, administrator of the estate of O.H. Ford, dec'd. The administrator has paid out all the assets of the estate.

pg 458-459. 4 Jun 1902. Final settlement made with W.C. Herndon, administrator of the estate of Charlotte Herndon, dec'd. The following gave their receipts for their share of the estate: Lawson Crouch, C.F. Herndon, W.C. Herndon, Jake Herndon, J.J. Garner, A.D. Crouch, and Fannie Herndon.

pg 460-461. 24 May 1902. Settlement made with W.A. Moore, one of the administrators of the estate of George W. Cunningham, dec'd. There being two heirs, Mrs. S.A. Cunningham and Am Roberts, they are each entitled to one half of the balance of the estate.

pg 462. 24 May 1902. Settlement made with J.B. Roberts and W.A. Moore, administrators of the estate of George W. Cunningham, dec'd.

pg 463. 13 May 1902. Settlement made with Jerome Collier, administrator of the estate of Jonathan Bost, dec'd. The administrator has in his hands notes on the heirs of the dec'd as follows: Lizzie Higginbotham, William Higginbotham, J.A. Bost, and J.J. Bost.

pg 464-467. 2 Jul 1902. Settlement made with J.C. Biles, executor of the estate of Mary E. Munford, dec'd.

pg 468. 18 Jun 1902. Settlement made with J.I. Finney, administrator of the estate of Sarah Tallman, dec'd. Ther are no assets remaining in the estate.

pg 469. 2 Jul 1902. Final settlement made with D.B. Hoover, administrator of W.H. Hoover, dec'd.

pg 470. 6 Jun 1902. Inventory of the personal property

of A.T. Webb, dec'd that has come to the hands of Maggie Webb, administratrix.

pg 471-472. 6 Aug 1902. Settlement made with George W. Wagoner, administrator of the estate of Hixie Parks, dec'd. Receipts of heirs for their shares: Frances Hayes, guardian $86.57; Ella Womack $86.57; Luia Cardwell $86.57; J.R. Gratner administrator $86.57; H.S. Parks $173.15; George W. Parks $173.15; Jennie Roach $173.15; and James Cardwell guardian $173.15.

pg 473. 29 Jul 1902. Settlement made with L.P. Gartner, administrator of J.P. Gartner. Credits for the shares paid to: J.E.Jones as guardian of Florence Gartner, L.P. Gartner, H.O. Gartner, Aline Gartner Harrison, and John W. Gartner.

pg 474. 3 Aug 1902. **Will of L.P. Snipes.** Know all men by these presents that I, L.P. Snipes, being in full possession of my mental faculties and beliefing my stay on this earth to be brief, do commend my soul to my God and do publish this my last will and testament. After the payment of my debts and burial expenses I give to Charlietta York, wife of W.C. York all my property both real and personal and at her death what is left is to go to the children of W.C. York. I appoint Charlietta York administratrix without bond. Witnessed by F.M. Fennell, J.H. Rheay, and N.B. Humphrey. Admitted for probate 1 Sep 1902.

pg 475. 19 Jul 1902. Sale bill of the estate of A.T. Webb, dec'd sold by the administratrix Maggie Webb on 19 Jul 1902.

pg 476. 2 Sep 1902. Inventory of the estate of Thomas J. Stroud, dec'd reported by Luther A. Fry, administrator.

pg 477. 3 Sep 1902. Settlement made with Jerome Collier, administrator of the estate of Jonathan Bost, dec'd. Credit vouchers from the following heirs: Lizzie Higginbotham, Nancy Collier, J.A. Bost, William Bost, Amanda Collier and J.J. Bost.

pg 478. 12 Sep 1902. Settlement of the account of G.F. Wagner, administrator of the estate of Hixie Parks. Vouchers for $46.35 each filed by: James Cardwell, Jennie Roach, H.S. Parks, and G.W. Parks. Vouchers for $23.17 each filed by: Luia Cardwell, J.R. Gardner administrator, Ella Womack, and Frances Boyd as guardian.

pg 479-480. 13 Sep 1902. Foss H. Mercer, administrator with will annexed of the estate of Cyrus Richmond, dec'd. The estate cannot be settled until the J.H. Willey estate has been settled.

pg 481-485. 19 Aug 1902. **Will of Blanche L. Lewis.** I, Blanche L. Lewis of McMinnville, do make and publish this my last will and testament. First I will that all my debts and funeral expenses be paid. Second, to my dear neice Eugenia Campbell, youngest daughter of my dear mother's youngest daughter, I give the mahogony workstand used by my mother before her marriage. Third, to my brothers Eugene [Eugence] C. Lewis and John S. Lewis I give in trust $500.00 to be investen and the income paid to my nephew Trigg Campbell until he is engaged is business, at which time he will be paid the full amount. Fourth, to my brother John S. Lewis I give $500.00 and to my sister Stella F. Lewis $100.00. Fifth, should Harriet Lawrence be living with me at the time of my death I give to her $30.00. Sixth, I give $50.00 to the Ladies Aid Society of the Presbyterian Church of McMinnville. Seventh, [donations to charity and church.] Eighth, I give to my brothers Eugene [Eugence] C. Lewis and John S. Lewis and my friend Frank Colville all my remaining property in trust for my nieces Lureta and Eugenia Campbell. Should either of them die without issue, the survivor shall have the full share. If both should died without issue the turst shall cease and the trustees shall pay to my nephew Trigg Campbell one third and the other two thirds divided between all my then remaining neices, daughters of my brothers Eugence C. Lewis, Edward H. Lewis (dec'd) and John S. Lewis and of my sister Sallie Tarwater. Ninth, I appoint my brothers Eugence C. Lewis and John S. Lewis and my friend Frank Colville executors. Witnessed by Thomas C. Lind and Charles Colville. **Codicil:** 1 Sep 1902. [Small personal items to the following]: Blanche Tarwater Merrill, Lureta Campbell, Will Lewis, Kate Burke Simpson of Montgomery, AL, Louise Lewis, Margaretta Lewis, Mrs. T.C. Lind, Trigg Campbell [to have furniture now at "River Cliff"]. Codicil witnessed by Butler and Sallie Smith. Admitted to probate 6 Oct 1902.

pg 486-491. 3 Oct 1902. Sale bill of the estate of F.M. Johnson, dec'd reproted by W.L. Johnson, one of the

Warren County, Tn Will Book 10, cont.

administrators Purchases made by Sam Johnson, S.O.
Johnson, Mrs. Johnson, W.L. Johnson, and many others.

pg 492-496. 23 Sep 1902. Sale bill of the estate of
John W. Cope, dec'd reported by A.T. Cope,
administrator. Purchases made by Ashburn Cope, Ab.
Cope, George Cope, Abner Cope, Lucy Cope, Fred Cope, and
others.

pg 497-498. 10 Oct 1902. **Will of Harmon Walling.** I,
Harmon Walling do make and publish this my last will and
testament. First I direct that my funeral expense and
my debts be paid. Second, I give to my daughter
Elizabeth Martin and her husband A.D. Martin and their
heirs all my property both real and personal, consisting
of 175 acres in Crain Hollow, 4th Civil District. I do
this as a recompense to them for taking care of me and
of my youngest daughter Mary Hitchcock. I appoint A.E.
Crain my executor. Witnessed by W.H. Head and W.M.
Johnson. Admitted to probate 3 Nov 1902.

pg 499-500. 13 Nov 1902. Inventory of the estate of
E.J.Argo, dec'd as reported by Jesse Walling,
administrator. Mrs. E.J. Argo given $10.00 on
allowance.

pg 501. 3 Nov 1902. J.R. Ramsey, administrator of J.W.
Brown, dec'd presents inventory of the estate to be sold
at public sale.

pg 502. Dec 1902. Settlement made with F.M. Fennell
administrator of Bedford Hammer. [Mentions lawsuit
Hammer vs Hammer]

pg 503-504. 1 Nov 1902. Settlement made with J. Morgan
Gribble, administrator of Catherine Gribble, dec'd.
Balance of estate paid to heirs as follows: J.M.
Gribble, C.C. Gribble, S.C. Gribble, M.V. Gribble, Mary
Goddard, Nora Hankins, Sarah Simpson, Margaret Rowland,
A.J. Gribble, the heirs of W.I. Gribble, the heirs of
H.R. Gribble and the heirs of J.T. Gribble.

pg 505-506. 20 Nov 1902. Sale bill of the estate of
James Webb, dec'd reported by A.J. Webb, administrator.
Purchases made by Landis Webb, Mattie Webb, Mrs. James
Webb, I.G. Webb, James Webb, Riley Webb, James K. Webb,
H.B. Webb, and others.

pg 507. 19 Jan 1903. Settlement made wtih J.J.

Warren County, Tn Will Book 10, cont.

Meadows, trustee of St. Mary School Fund.

pg 508. 10 Jan 1903. Supplemental report of the assets of the estate of Levi C. Woodlee, dec'd, reported by Benjamin L. Stanley.

pg 509. 31 Dec 1902. Settlement made with Hattie Johnson, co-administratrix of John C. Watson, dec'd. Clerk allows $10.35 to administratrix, she being a daughter of said Watson, for her trouble in winding up the estate.

pg 510-511. 3 Feb 1903. Inventory of the estate of Miss Blanche Lewis, dec'd reported by Frank Colville, executor.

pg 512. 29 Dec 1902. Settlement made with Charles S. Ivie, executor of the estate of Nancy D. Peay. Credit for the following vouchers: B.T. Paty, guardian of Paty Griffin; Mattie Hicks, nee Paty; and Lucille F. Drake, nee Lou Tilford.

pg 513. 9 Feb 1903. Settlement made with J.J. Mullican, administrator of the estate of Miram Mullican, dec'd. Eight shares of the estate paid as follows: Mattie Mullican, W.I. Mullican, S.E. Lane, Z.C. Dawson, H.B. Mullican and J.J. Mullican each receive $42.00 or 1/8 of the estate. H.P. Davis, S.O. Hendrixon, M.L. Cantrell, J.M. Green, S.T. Green and Mary Green (minor, her share paid to Dent Green) each receive $7.00 or 1/6th of 1/8th of the estate .

pg 514-516. 9 Feb 1903. Settlement made with E.N. Green, administrator of the estate of J.M. Green, dec'd. The following heirs have been paid as shown by their receipts:

O.D. Green, Jr. 1/3rd of 1/12	$ 37.97
Elizabeth Taylor, Tracy City, Tn (1/12)	$113.95
Shadrack Green	$113.95
James M. Green, Jr, Lawrenceburg, Tn	$113.95
W.H. Fisher, gdn of Parker and Sarah D. Green	$ 75.96
Henritta Riggsby	$113.95
Nancy Riggsby	$113.95
J.G. Hendrixson, gdn of C.C. Green	$113.95
Mary L. Webb, 1/4th of 1/12	$ 28.49
Nancy A. Blew, 1/4th of 1/12	$ 28.49
Abraham Potter (minor) 1/4th of 1/12	$ 28.49
Hannah Staffforsheirs, 1/4th of 1/12	$ 28.49
Joseph R. Green, Lawrenceburg, Tn	$113.95

Warren County, Tn Will Book 10, cont.

Mary A. Mallory, Mayfield, KY $113.95
O.D. Green, Sr. $113.95
E.N. Green, administrator's share $113.95

pg 517. 2 Mar 1903. Final settlement made with J.C.
Biles, executor of the estate of Mary E. Munford, dec'd.

pg 518. 20 Mar 1903. Sale bill of the estate of Harmon
Walling made by A.D. Martin, administrator.

pg 519-520. 23 Feb 1903. Sale bill of the estate of
L.J. Holder, dec'd, reported by A.Z. Holder,
administrator. Purchases made by W.F. Holder, F.M.
Holder and others.

pg 521-522. 3 Feb 1903. Inventory and sale bill of the
estate of P.A. Hoodenpyl, dec'd made on 9 Aug 1902.
Among articles included were the distilling aparatus
located near the island ford on the premises of A.C.
Myers.   J.J. Meadows, administrator.

pg 523-524. 31 Dec 1902. Sale bill of the personal
property of J.C. Watson, dec'd, sold by the
administrators Hattie Johnson and Flora Watson on 2 Jun
1900 at the home place of said J.C. Watson.

pg 525. 10 Feb 1903. Supplemental sale bill of the
estate of Kate Lowry, dec'd reported by William M.
NesSmith, administrator.

pg 526. 5 Jan 1903. Sale of the estate of Tempy Ann
Bess, dec'd reported by T.B. Bouldin, administrator.

pg 527. 23 Feb 1903. Inventory of the personal estate
of John B. Berry, dec'd by G.T. Lynn, administrator.

pg 528-529. March 1903. Sale bill of the estate of
J.W. Brown, dec'd by J.R. Ramsey, administrator.
Purchases made by Martha Brown, Estie Brown, Etta Brown,
R.H. Brown, T.B. Brown, Mack Brown, and others.

pg 530. 6 Apr 1903. Inventory of the estate of W.P.
McVey, reported by Sarah E. McVey, administratrix.

pg 531-532. 27 Mar 1903. Inventory and sale bill of
the estate of Marshall Sawyer, dec'd reported by Mrs.
Belle Sawyer, administratrix. The estate is divided
between Mrs. Sawyer and the two minor children.

pg 533.   6 Apr 1903.   Supplemental inventory of the estate of John M. Duncan, dec'd made by J.M. Duncan and H.V. Copenhaven, executors.   They report advances have been made to Romulus Duncan, Jennie Davis and Della Steakley.

pg 534.   15 May 1903.   Settlement made with John B. Biles, executor of the estate of Thomas Mauzy, dec'd. The balance of the estate ($2500.00) was directed by the testator's will to be invested for the benefit of Sophia Hash.

pg 535-538.   9 Mar 1903.   Inventory and sale bill of the estate of Harrison Woodlee, dec'd reported by Frank E. Woodlee, administrator.   Purchases made by E.H. Woodlee, Dee Woodlee, Frank Woodlee, Ed Woodlee and others.

pg 539-545.   7 Jan 1903.   List of personal property sold on 9 Dec 1902 belonging to Sarah D. Jaco, dec'd made by Joe B. Cherry, administrator.   Purchases made by Jennie Jaco, James Jaco, Ann Jaco, Mary Jaco, Leslie Jaco, J.J. Jaco, J.P. Jaco and others.

pg 546-548.   24 Jul 1903.   Inventory and sale bill of the personal property of Welford Luttrell, dec'd, reported by D.C. Oliver, administrator.

pg 549-553.   7 Sep 1903.   Inventory and sale bill of the estate of Martha Lawrence, dec'd, sale held of 15 Aug 1903 by J.D. Hash, administrator.

pg 554-555.   16 May 1903.   Inventory and sale bill of the estate of Martha Martin, dec'd made by J.B. Edge.

pg 556-557.   28 Apr 1903.   Settlement made with H.V. Copenhaver and J.M. Duncan, executors of the estate of John Duncan, dec'd giving each heir their share (less their advancements), to wit: J.M. Duncan, Mollie Copenhaver, Sallie Cardwell, Della Steakley, Jennie Davis, and Romulus Duncan.

pg 1. 20 Aug 1903. Settlement made with Luther A. Fry, administrator of Thomas J. Stroud, dec'd. $229.48 to be divided between the heirs at law of Thomas J. Stroud, dec'd.

pg 2-3. 17 June 1903. Settlement made with J.L. Miller, administrator of Priscilla M. Jaco, dec'd. After payment of outstanding accounts the balance to be divided equally between the bodily heirs of the deceased as follows: Lou York, Alice Clark, Paralee Quick and Bula Potter, each to receive $214.18.

pg 4-5. 23 May 1903. Settlement made with M.E. Walker, administratrix of I.A. Walker, dec'd. Balance of estate paid to heirs: the administratrix, J.T. Walker, Delia and J.H. Warren jointly, I.J. Walker, and L.D. Walker a minor. Each received $35.00. "Above $35.00 carried to Clerk's cash book and paid Sep 12, 1905 to S.J. Walker on Power of Attorney made by said L.D. Walker who became of age June 1905".

pg 6-7. 3 Aug 1903. Settlement made with J.J. Meadows, administrator of the estate of William Meadows, dec'd. Payments of $12.05 made to each of the following: Mrs. Harriet Martin, A.D. Meadows, F.M. Meadows, Thubal Clark, W.D. Meadows, Minnie Lee Douglas, J.J. Meadows, Electra Etter, Ida E.M. Ford.

pg 8-13. 5 Sep 1903. Supplementary inventory of the estate of F.M. Johnson reported by W.L. Johnson, administrator. Mostly doubtful accounts due the estate, totaling $1993.21.

pg 14. Aug 1903. Partial settlement made with P.G. Potter, executor of the will of Isaac Trammel, dec'd.

pg 15. 6 Jul 1903. Supplemental inventory of the estate of Isaac Trammel, dec'd, made by P.G. Potter, executor.

pg 16. 12 Jun 1903. Invoice of the estate of Mrs. C.A. Smallman, dec'd made by William H. Magness, executor. One third of net estate paid to Lillian Smallman, as per will of deceased. Two thirds of net estate paid to Fred, Ernest and John Smallman as per will of deceased. The executor has turned over the house and lot in

Warren County, TN Will Book 11, Cont.

McMinnville to the care and custody of the four heirs above mentioned, they all being of legal and lawful age.

pg 17. 18 Jul 1903. Inventory and sale bill of the personal property of James Keesey, dec'd. Purchases made by Huse Keesey and others.

pg 18-20. 22 Oct 1903. Report of the sale and inventory of the estate of H.A. Hulett made by H.M. Anderson, administrator. Purchases made by W.M. Hulett, John Hullett, Geo. Hullett and others.

pg 21. 22 Sep 1903. M.C. Green, executor of the estate of S. Green, dec'd widow of M.A. Green, dec'd reports notes given for purchases taken from J.G.B. Green, S.M. Green, M.C. Green, J.L. Green, G.B. Green, and others.

pg 22. 4 Dec 1903. Inventory and sale bill of the personal estate of Roland H. Shirley, dec'd, made by John B. Shirley, administrator.

pg 23. 10 Sep 1903. Settlement made with Betsy M. Long, executor of Harriet A. Clark, dec'd. $23.75 legacy to Julien Brassard and the balance to Dr. Whitaker, residuary legatee.

pg 24-25. 12 Dec 1903. Inventory of the personal estate of James Collier, dec'd made by Calhoon Collier, administrator.

pg 26-30. 5 Dec 1903. Inventory of the estate of J.C. Ramsey, Sr. (estate in access of $100,000.00.) Executors James S. Ivie of Shelbyville and W.P. Hickerson Sr. of Coffee County.

pg 31. 21 Dec 1903. Sale bill of the estate of Eli Jones, dec'd, made by J.W. Jones, administrator.

pg 32. 5 Jan 1904. Final settlement made with E.L. Moffitt, administrator of the estate of Mrs. Celia Moffitt, dec'd. Administrator is credited with vouchers for $6.20 each filed as follows: R.S. Moffitt, E.J. Myers as guardian of Maude Myers, Venus Moffitt, A.B. Moffitt, Laura Moffitt, R.G. Martin, William Grove, W.H. Martin and the share of the administrator who was an heir. Vouchers for $1.03 each from: W.M. Johnson, Walter Watson, Emma Groves, G.C. Keesey, Thomas Smith, and G. Grove.

pg 33-34. 21 Jan 1904. Sale bill and inventory of the estate of W.H. Smoot, dec'd, reported by J.C. Smoot, administrator. Purchases made by Jess Smoot, Mrs. W.H. Smoot, Tom Smoot, George Smoot, Doc Smoot, I. Smoot, C.M. Smoot and others. Sale was held 12 Dec 1903.

pg 35-36. 2 Jan 1904. Inventory of the estate of E.H. Green, dec'd reported by Sam A. Green, one of the executors of the estate.

pg 37-38. [Not dated] Inventory and sale bill of the estate of H. Willis, dec'd. Purchases made by Mr. and Mrs. A.F. Willis, Farmer Willis, and others. [Executor or administrator not given.]

pg 39. 30 Jan 1904. Inventory of the estate of Mrs. V.A. Coppinger, dec'd, reported by James L. Coppinger, administrator.

pg 40-41. [Not dated] Inventory and sale bill of the estate of Nancy Fults, dec'd, reported by T.M. Eaton, administrator. Purchases made by H. Fults, Carrol Fults and others.

pg 42-43. 4 Feb 1904. Inventory and sale bill of the estate of Nancy Jaco, dec'd. Purchases made by E.L. Jaco, N.C. Cope, Claud Cope, J.M. Jaco, J.C. Jaco and others.

pg 44-46. 15 Jan 1904. Inventory and sale bill of the estate of Mrs. Myrick Solomon, reported by J.S. Nunley, administrator. Purchases made by Nancy Solomon, Fatha Solomon and others.

pg 47-48. 2 Mar 1904. Settlement made with Sam A. Green, one of the executors of E.H. Green, dec'd. Shares of the estate valued at $561.79 paid to the following: J.S. Green, J.H. Green, H.H. Allen and wife, A.J. Webb and wife, S.A. Green, the heirs of B.P. Green, the heirs of Harriet Walling, not including Clyde Walling's part. Clyde Walling's part $52.10. The four heirs of Polly Locke under the will receive $5.00 each.

pg 49. 27 Feb 1904. Settlement made with G.T. Lynn, administrator of J.D. Berry, dec'd. Octa Parker and G.J. Berry, heirs, paid $140.00 each.

pg 50. 8 Mar 1904. Settlement made with A.R. Hammer, Sr., administrator of the estate of F.M. Moffitt, dec'd.

Mentions F.H. Mercer, attorney, guardian ad litem in court at Spencer.

pg 51-52.   14 Mar 1904.   Settlement made with J.J. Meadows, administrator of P.A. Hoodenpyl, dec'd.   Final settlement shows $475.23 paid to each of the following: P.A.M. Hoodenpyl, J.E. Jones as guardian of Mamie(?) Hoodenpyl, J.E. Jones as guardian of E.V. Hoodenpyl and Maggie Hoodenply.

pg 53.   2 May 1904.   Final settlement of the estate of Isaac Trammel, dec'd, made with P.G. Potter, executor.

pg 54.   1 Apr 1904.   Inventory and sale bill of the personal property of William J. Stroh, dec'd, made by Laura B. Stroh, administrator in DeKalb County, Indiana.

pg 55. 1 Sep 1903. Settlement made with I.G. Gribble, administrator of Lydia Gibbs, dec'd. Mentions the sale of lands in the County Court in cause of Gribble, administrator vs Gibbs.

pg 56.   9 Apr 1904.   Settlement made with Van McGee, administrator of J.W. McGee, dec'd. Receipts for $9.65 for their share of estate given by John Seals, Tobe McGee, Martha McGee, J.R. Farless for his wife Myrtle Farless, John McGee, a minor, and the administrator. "The interest of John McGee a minor has this day been paid into court by the administrator to be held by the court until a guardian is appointed for said minor or he reaches his majority."

pg 57.   28 Apr 1904. Settlement made with J.W. Snipes, executor of the estate of T.W. Snipes, dec'd. Distribution among heirs as follows: Amanda J. Snipes, Martha J. Womack (nee Snipes) "the above receipts include the $25.00 each allowed them by will", S.E. Crawley (nee Snipes), I.A. Anderson "see will of T.W. Snipes", Mary Allison (nee Snipes), executor's share "he being an heir". Each heir received $5.40.

pg 58.   25 Apr 1904.   Supplemental sale bill of the estate of H. Woodlee, dec'd reported by W.T. Barnes co-administrator.

pg 59.   5 Jun 1904.   Inventory of the estate of Abner Woodlee,   dec'd   reported   by   Sallie   Woodlee, administratrix.

pg 60. 6 Jun 1904. Inventory of the goods and chattles of the estate of John H. Savage, dec'd reported by Mrs. O.W. Davis and Frank R. Davis, executrix and executor of the estate.

pg 61. 6 May 1904. Final settlement of the estate of Thomas Brown, dec'd, made with W.L. Swann, administrator.

pg 62-65. 1 Jul 1904. Inventory and sale bill of the estate of Mrs. Mary F. Brasier, dec'd reported by Frank Colville, administrator. Purchases made by George Brasier and others.

pg 66-70. 19 Jul 1904. Inventory and sale bill of the estate of Mrs. Mary A. Gribble, filed by the administrator I.G.H. Gribble. Purchased made by I.G. Gribble, Bob Gribble, and many others.

pg 71-79. 1 Jul 1904. "The first but not final settlement of W.P. Hickerson and Charles S. Ivie, executors of the estate of J.C. Ramsey, Sr., dec'd"...By the fifth term of the testator's will, the executors are directed to divide all bank stock, house hold and kitchen furniture in kind into two equal parts.. "my daughter Laura R. Ivie taking one of said parts and my grandchildren, the children of W.P. Hickerson (naming them) taking the other part" These items have been properly disposed of. To Laura R. Ivie $12600.00 as part of legacy, and to C.R. Hickerson, Georgia Hickerson, W.P. Hickerson, Jr $2400.00 each, to W.P. Hickerson as guardian of Wright, Susie, Laura, Heloise, Lillian and Allen Hickerson $14400.00.

pg 80. 2 Nov 1904. Settlement made with G. Miller, administrator of G.N. Lowry, dec'd.

pg 81. 21 Sep 1904. Settlement made with W.T. Pollard as bondsman for William W. NeSmith, administrator of Kate Lowry, dec'd.

pg 82. 2 Nov 1904. Inventory of the personal property belonging to the estate of G.N. Lowry, dec'd, reported by G. Miller, administrator.

pg 83. 6 Oct 1904. Final settlement made with J.L. Garnett, administrator of the estate of Judah Armstrong, dec'd.

pg 84-85. 30 Oct 1904. Settlement made with A.Z. Holder, administrator of the estate of L.J. Holder, dec'd.

pg 86. 2 Nov 1904. Final settlement made with Gilland Miller, administrator of G.N. Lowry, dec'd.

pg 87-88. 5 Aug 1904. Inventory and sale bill of the personal effects of B.H. Womack, dec'd that has come into the hands of the D.P. Womack, executor of the estate.

pg 89-94. 4 Mar 1904. Settlement made by Frank Colville, executor of Miss Blanche L. Lewis, dec'd, with Conley Tigg Campbell, present guardian of Lureta and Eugenia Campbell, for funds, receipts and disbursements held and made by Miss Lewis, former guardian of such wards. Mentions Chancery Court cause of E.C. Lewis et al vs Lureta Campbell et al.

pg 95-96. 30 Nov 1904. Inventory and sale bill of the property of A.J. Webb, dec'd sold by S.E. Webb, administratrix. Purchases by Bob Webb, I.G. Webb, Jim Webb, J.K. Webb, E.H. Webb and others.

pg 97. 1 Dec 1904. Inventory of the estate of James Webb, dec'd made by I.G. Webb, administrator. Notes on R.L. Webb, A.J. Webb, J.L. Webb, I.G. Webb, James Webb Jr., and H.B. Webb.

pg 98. 3 Oct 1904. Final settlement of the estate of J.W. Brown, dec'd made with J.R. Ramsey, administrator.

pg 99. Oct Term 1904. Final settlement made with R.H. Brown, administrator of Hattie Allison, dec'd (the deceased being a minor). Money from J.L. Thaxton, guardian of deceased used for burial and monument.

pg 100. 12 Aug 1904. Settlement made of the estate of E.G. Bess, dec'd by Byron Bess, the son of I.P. Bess the administrator, who was unable to fulfill the office. Real estate of deceased was sold for payment of debts.

pg 101-102. 28 Jul 1904. Inventory of the estate of J.R. West, dec'd made by Stoke Etter the administrator.

pg 103. 10 Sep 1904. Final settlement made with Maggie Webb, administratrix of A.T. Webb, dec'd.

pg 104. 15 Oct 1904. Settlement made with G.W. Green, administrator of John Green, dec'd. Credits as follow: to Harvey Green 1 full share; to Malinda Green 1/3 share; to Oscar Green 1/3 share; to Eli Green 1 share; to G.W. Green 1 share; to Arnold Green 1/3 share.

pg 105-106. Nov Term 1904. Inventory and sale bill and settlement of the estate of Charles Reynolds made by Mrs. Ann Reynolds, administratrix. Charles Reynolds left as his heirs at law his mother Ann Reynolds, his sister(s) Bettie Miller, Allie Wilcher, Jesse Wilcher, Etna Cantrell, Georgia Stubblefield, Sallie Jennings, Hassie and Regie Etter (heirs of Mattie Etter), Mamie Reynolds and Dillard Reynolds. Each of the above receive $19.94. "Rec'd of William W. Wallace, clerk, my 1/2 of the $19.94 above mentioned due to heirs of Mattie Etter, this March 17, 1906, signed Hassie Etter Lawrence and E.T. Lawrence"

pg 107. 3 Dec 1904. Supplemental sale bill and inventory of the estate of Mary Gribble, dec'd, filed by the administrator I.G. Gribble. Purchases made by I.G. Gribble and others.

pg 108. 19 Nov 1904. Settlement made with T.M. Eaton, administrator of the estate of Patsy Winton, colored, dec'd. Property sold to pay debts.

pg 109-110. 8 Dec 1904. Settlement made with J.D. Hash, administrator of Martha Lawrence, dec'd.

pg 111. 3 Jan 1905. Settlement made with J.J. Meadows, trustee of St. Mary's School Funds.

pg 112. Jan Term 1905. Inventory of the personal estate of W.P. Faulkner, dec'd made by John L. Willis, administrator with will annexed.

pg 113. 10 Jan 1905. Inventory of the assets that have come into the hands of George T. Riggs, administrator of the estate of Miss Mary J. Brown, dec'd.

pg 114-115. 23 Jan 1905. Final settlement of the estate of James Collier, dec'd made by Calhoun Collier, administrator. The following heirs, each to receive $145.56: Jerome Collier, A.M. Cummings, Authur Collier, Margaret Higginbotham, Sallie Myers, and Calhoun Collier. The following heirs receive $48.52: Tobe McGee, Levander McGee and Myrtle Farless. The following heirs receive $29.11: Jennie Collier, Claude Collier, Horace Collier, Sam Collier and Doc Collier.

pg 116. Feb Term 1905. Settlement made with William Thurman, administrator of Osie Brown, dec'd.

pg 117. 24 Jan 1905. Inventory of the personal estate of Mrs. Elza J. Griswold, dec'd reported by Mrs. F.M. Smartt, executrix of the estate.

pg 118-121. 2 Jan 1905. Sale of the personal assets of Archibald Scott, dec'd by E.L. Moffitt, administrator of the estate. Purchases made by Cooper Scott, Victoria Scott, Lilly Scott, J.H. Scott, Levi Scott and others. "There is due the estate of Archibald Scott a sum of money arising from the lands of Cooper Scott, dec'd sold in Chancery Court of Warren County in the cause of Arch Scott, executor of Cooper Scott, dec'd vs L.V. Scott et al. This interest is one seventh of the net proceeds of said land sale less such amount as may be due from the estate of Arch Scott on lands purchased at said sale by him and for which he executed his notes. Such notes have not been paid in full."

pg 122. 9 Feb 1905. Settlement of the estate of Mrs. E.J. Griswold, dec'd made with Mrs. F.M. Smartt, executrix. Balance due the heirs of the estate [not named here] $102.65.

pg 123. 5 Feb 1905. Settlement made with T.B. Bouldin, administrator of Tempy Ann Bess, dec'd. Henry Bouldin received $70.10 as guardian of N. Bess.

pg 124. 11 Feb 1905. Settlement made with J.W. Jones, administrator of Eli Jones, dec'd.

pg 125. 1 Apr 1905. Final settlement of the estate of Nancy Fults, dec'd, made by T.M. Eaton, administrator.

pg 126. 18 Mar 1905. Settlement made with A.R. Hammer, one of the administrators of F.M. Moffitt, dec'd. Willie J. Moffitt reciept for $46.83.

pg 127. 4 Apr 1905. Settlement made with D.C. Oliver, administrator of the estate of Wilford Luttrell, dec'd. "The balance of $57.96 in the hands of the administrator and the clerk allow him this sum for his services based on the fact that Luttrell and wife were murdered and the administrator has been faithful and dillegent in his efforts to locate the perpetrators of the crime and his incured expenses in this effort is not properly chargable to the estate."

pg 128. 3 Apr 1905. Inventory of the estate of Mrs. Sarah A. Cunningham reported by W.A. Moore, executor.

pg 129-130. 24 Mar 1905. Settlement made with A.T. Cope, administrator of the estate of John W. Cope, dec'd. Receipts from J.M. Hobbs, administrator of Georgia Cope, Lucy D. Hobbs, Lucy Cope, Hallie Walling and Sallie Brown ($135.00 each)

pg 131. 15 Dec 1904. Inventory and sale bill of the personal property of Alice Smartt, dec'd made by R.W. Smartt, administrator.

pg 132-133. 14 Apr 1905. Settlement made with _____ Johnson, administrator of the estate of F.M. Johnson, dec'd.

pg 134. 17 Apr 1905. Final settlement made with Mrs. S.E. McVey, administratrix of W.P. McVey, dec'd.

pg 135. 19 Apr 1905. Sale bill of the personal property of the estate of Miss Mary J. Brown, dec'd, returned by the administrator George T. Riggs.

pg 136-137. 3 Jul 1905. Inventory of the personal estate of W.F. Stubblefield, dec'd presented by his wife Mrs. Belle Stubblefield.

pg 138. 20 Apr 1905. A.C. Myers, administrator of the estate of M.T. Gillentine, dec'd, reports insolvency.

pg 139. [Not dated] Sale of the personal property of Miss Margaret Stubblefield, dec'd on 17 Jun 1905. Purchases made by A.F. Stubblefield, W.R. Stubblefield, and others.

pg 140. 18 Sep 1905. Sale bill of the estate of Parlee York, dec'd reported by S.F. York, administrator. Purchases made by B.H. York, Mrs. Sam York, Mrs S.F. York, and others.

pg 141. 4 Sep 1905. Inventory of the estate of Emeline Hoodenpyl, reported by P.E. Hennessee, administrator.

pg 142-145. 25 Sep 1905. Sale bill of the estate of

L.V.A. Hash, made by T.F. Hash, administrator.

pg 146. 2 Oct 1905. List of the personal property of the estate of I.D. Cummings, dec'd.

pg 147-148. 2 Oct 1905. Supplemental inventory and sale bill of the estate of Emeline Hoodenpyl, dec'd sold at public auction at the late residence of the deceased in the 5th Civil District of Warren County by P.E. Hennessee, administrator.

pg 149-151. 14 Oct 1905. Sale bill of the estate of Mrs. I.D. Cummings, dec'd reported by G.P. Cummings, administrator. Purchases made by Mat Cummings, G.P. Cummings, Mr. and Mrs. G.P. Cummings, Mattie Cummings, and others.

pg 152. 21 Oct 1905. Inventory of the estate of W.N. Russell, reported by J.C. Safley, administrator.

pg 153. 16 Oct 1905. Final settlement of the estate of R.H. Shirley, dec'd made with John B. Shirley, administrator. J.W. Shirley had been paid $369.50 during his lifetime. A.J. Brewer, administrator of J.W. Shirley, dec'd received $186.63 as final settlement of the R.H. Shirley estate.

pg 154-155. 6 Nov 1905. Inventory and final settlement of the estate of John Mathews, dec'd reported by his administratrix Mary Louise Mathews. Estate wholly insolvent.

pg 156. 28 Nov 1905. I.W. Webb, trustee vs heirs of Stephen Mayfield, dec'd. Webb reports that on 28 Oct 1902, Stephen Mayfield and wife Delphia Mayfield conveyed to him in trust a tract of land in the 15th District of Warren County to secure L.M. Mayfield a note of $50.00. On 25 Nov 1905 at the request of the beneficiary and according to the terms of said trust deed Webb sold said land to T.M. Templeton.

pg 157. 7 Nov 1905. Inventory and sale bill of the estate of Mary T. Stubblefield, colored, reported by N.W. Ware, administrator. Sale held at the residence of deceased on 13 Apr 1905.

pg 158-159. 25 Nov 1905. Settlement made with I.B. Edge, administrator of the estate of Martha Martin, dec'd. Balance of the estate divided between the following: I.B. Edge as administrator, William Martin, Robert Martin, F.M. Helton, A.Z. Holder as guardian, J.B. Martin, A.Z. Holder and Mattie Holder, Zeb Martin, and H.H. Martin. Each received $3.50.

pg 160. 23 Nov 1905. Inventory of the estate of H.L. Stanley, dec'd, made by John L. Willis, administrator. Mentions judgment in favor of H.L. Stanley against P.H. and L.J. Huddleston in Bedford County, TN.

pg 161-162. 4 Dec 1905. List of the sale of the entire household and kitchen furniture of Martha A. Cantrell, dec'd held 4 Sep 1905, made by J.L. Coppinger. Purchases made by W.K. Cantrell and others. Final Settlement.

pg 163. 23 Dec 1905. Inventory and sale bill of the estate of I.D. Cummings, dec'd, G.P. Cummings, administrator.

pg 164. 12 Dec 1905. Final settlement of the estate of Mary T. Stubblefield, dec'd, made with N.W. Ware, administrator.

pg 165-166. 9 Dec 1906. Inventory of the personal estate of John D. Hennessee, dec'd, filed by Florence Hennessee administratrix. Final Settlement.

pg 167. 3 Jan 1906. Settlement made with Mrs. F.M. Smartt, executrix of Mrs. E.J. Griswold, dec'd. Vouchers filed for the following shares in the balance of the estate; Mrs. Lillia Johnson, Mollie Christian, W.A. Griswold and Mrs. F.M. Smartt (executrix's share), each receive $16.72. S.M. Griswold and Norman Griswold each receive $16.50.

pg 168-171. 1 Jan 1906. Inventory and sale bill of the estate of V.A. Dunlap, dec'd reported by D.A. Safley, administrator. Purchases made by D. Dunlap, D.S. Dunlap, B. Dunlap, Sherman Dunlap, B.L. Dunlap, and others.

pg 172-173. 16 Jan 1906. Inventory of the personal estate of Myrick Smartt, dec'd returned by the administrator F.M. Smartt. F.M. Smartt being the husband of Myrick Smartt, dec'd is entitled to the balance of the estate after expenses.

pg 174. 17 Jan 1906. Settlement made with G.T. Lynn

and W.T. Parker, bondsmen fo A.L. Willis, administrator of H. Willis, dec'd.

pg 175-176. 16 Jan 1906. Inventory and sale bill of the estate of James P. Edwards, dec'd reported by George W. Darnell, executor.

pg 177. Feb Term 1906. Settlement made with George W. Darnell, executor of J.P. Edwards.

pg 178. 23 Jan 1906. Supplemental inventory of the estate of L.V.A. Hash, dec'd made by T.F. Hash, administrator.

pg 179. 30 Jan 1906. Inventory of the estate of Georgia Cope, dec'd made by J.M. Hobbs, administrator. Funds from 1/4 of land in cause of Cope vs Cope.

pg 180. 30 Jan 1906. Final settlement made with John M. Hobbs, administrator of the estate of Georgia Cope. Lucy Hobbs receipt for $314.58 to wind up estate.

pg 181-185. 10 Feb 1906. Inventory and sale bill of the estate of Mrs. R.A. McGee made by W.T. McGee and G.E. McGee. Purchases by Mrs. Tom McGee, Sallie McGee, Tom McGee, Ada McGee and others.

pg 186. [Not Dated] Inventory and sale bill of the estate of Mollie Adamson, dec'd reported by Lina Earls Newby, administratrix.

pg 187-188. 20 Mar 1906. Final settlement of the estate of Mary F. Brasier, dec'd made with Frank Colville, administrator. The following heirs listed: Martha Bell, Ida Gilliam, Allice C. Lewis, Annie Luck, Ruth Gribble, George Brasier, and W.E. Brasier.

pg 189. 24 Mar 1906. Sale bill of the estate of Jackson Booman, dec'd reported by I.T. Hillis, administrator. Purchases made by Harley Booman and others.

pg 190. 9 Feb 1906. Final settlement of the estate of Joseph Miller, dec'd made with D.S. and E.W. Miller, administrators. Shares of the estate given to John J. Miller, D.H. Miller, and J.M. Gribble.

pg 191-192. 7 Feb 1906. H.F. Peers and R.H. Peers, executors of the will of Susan Peers submit the settlement of her estate. They report that their testatrix, Mrs. Susan Peers was the wife of William Peers who died several years ago testate, leaving Susan life estate in $1000.00, the remainder to his daughter Mrs. E.J. Foster; also life estate in $1000.00, the remainder to go to his son H.L. Peers; also a farm which was to go to R.H. Peers. G.W. Foster was former husband and sole representative of said Mrs. E.J. Foster.

pg 193. 6 Apr 1906. Settlement made with D.C. Oliver, trustee of J.A. Cates.

pg 194. 5 Jun 1906. Final settlement made with James L. Coppinger, administrator of the personal estate of Mrs. V.A. Coppinger, dec'd. Heirs, each receiving $6.90 are: Bettie Coppinger, Lynchie Coppinger, Ethel Coppinger and Hubert, Eliza and Virginia Coppinger (the last three by their guardian).

pg 195-196. 5 Jun 1906. Inventory and settlement of the personal estate of J.W. Gribble, dec'd filed by the administratrix Mary Lou Gribble. Credit recieved to S.A. Gribble, widow.

pg 197-199. 2 Apr 1906. Inventory and final settlement of Frank Colville, sole acting executor of the will of Miss Blanche L. Lewis, dec'd. Includes cash received from Eugene C. and John S. Lewis out of the trust estate in their hands formerly belonging to Miss Blanche Lewis. (See Warren County, Tn Chancery Court Minute Book 14, pages 171-180.)

pg 200-201. 6 Jul 1906. Inventory and sale bill of the estate of E. Montgomery reported by John Seal, administrator. Purchases made by Florence Montgomery, Mrs. E. Montgomery, and others.

pg 202-203. 15 Mar 1906. Settlement made with J.B. Cherry, administrator of Sarah D. Jaco, dec'd. Heirs of the deceased receiving 1/7th of the estate are: Jennie Ann Jaco, Buela Potter, Mary Cherry, Paralee Quick, Lou York, and Alice Clark. Heirs receiving 1/35th of the estate are: A.F. Cunningham, William Cunningham, Dora Howard, Minnie Cunningham, and Mabel Cunningham.

pg 204-205. 7 May 1906. Final settlement made with J.J. Meadows, administrator of James Keesey, dec'd.

pg 206. 2 May 1906. Settlement made with George T.

Riggs, administrator of the estate of Miss Mary J. Brown, dec'd. One-fifth of the estate given to: W.H. Brown, Mrs Sallie Riggs, W.C. Brown, and Nannie Gray and one-seventh of one-fifth of the estate to J.W. Brown, Clay Brown, Frank Brown, Ella Moffitt, Mrs. Trousdale Lusk, and Hallie Brown (a minor). [The seventh devisee of the last 1/5 of the estate not named.]

pg 207-208. 15 Mar 1906. Settlement made with D.P. Womack, executor under the will of B.H. Womack, dec'd.

pg 209. 26 Jun 1906. Settlement made with John C. Smoot, administrator of the estate of W.H. Smoot, dec'd. Mrs. E.F. Smoot, widow given year's support.

pg 210. 10 Apr 1906. Settlement made with J.M. Anderson, administrator of H.A. Hulett, dec'd. Insolvent estate.

pg 211. 10 Jul 1906. Settlement made with P.E. Hennessee, administrator of the estate of Emeline Hoodenpyl, dec'd. Insolvency proceedings.

pg 212. 12 Jul 1906. Settlement made with Ed Sparkman, administrator of the estate of Elsie Gribble. "Elsie Gribble left the county about 17 years ago and since his departure this fund belonging to him has come into the hands of said Ed Sparkman who qualified as his administrator but it is not known whether Elsie Gribble is dead or not or what became of him."

pg 213-214. 7 Aug 1906. Inventory and sale bill of the estate of W.M. Akers, dec'd, reported by J.R. Akers, administrator. Purchases made by J.R. Akers, Lucy Akers, and others

pg 215. 23 Aug 1906. Settlement with J.J. Meadows, trustee of St. Mary School Fund. Beatrice Hill, teacher, paid.

pg 216. 30 Aug 1906. Settlement made with A.W. Rowland, administrator of James Rowland, dec'd. Heirs listed with amounts received as follows: Isaac W. Dulaney ($5.10), J.B. Rowland ($5.10), Addela Coffee ($5.10), G.M.D. Rowland ($15.30), J.N. Rowland ($15.30), P.M. Jaco ($15.30), S.A. Wilson ($5.10), G.W. Rowland ($5.10), Mattie Watson ($5.10), L.J. Dulaney ($15.30), R.P. Rowland ($15.30), John L. Rowland ($15.30), J.H. Rowland ($15.30), and A.W. Rowland ($15.30).

pg 217. 31 Aug 1906. Inventory of the personal estate of Mary J. Gardner, dec'd returned by J.R. Gardner, administrator.

pg 218-219. 31 Aug 1906. Inventory and sale bill of the estate of Mrs. Nancy Hash, sold on 16 Dec 1905 and reported by W.V.D. Miller. Purchases made by G.W. Hash, Henry Hash, W.H. Hash, J.D. Hash and others.

pg 220. 31 Aug 1906. Final settlement of the personal estate of Mary J. Gardner, dec'd, made with J.R. Gardner, her husband and administrator. He is entitled under the law to said personal estate.

pg 221-228. 6 Aug 1906. Inventory and sale bill of the estate of Mrs. Hixie Fuston, sold 16 Aug 1906 reported by M.L. Sellars, administrator. Purchases made by Emma Fuston, A.T. Fuston and many others.

pg 229. 5 Mar 1906. Inventory and sale bill of the estate of Steven Mayfield, reported by I.G. Webb, administrator. Property sold to Delphia Mayfield, S.S. Mullican and Pink Davis.

pg 230. 29 Aug 1906. Final settlement made with Lina Earls, now Newby, administratrix of Mollie Adamson, dec'd. She reports that there in nothing left in the hands of the administratrix.

pg 231. 31 Aug 1906. Settlement made with W.V.D. Miller, administratror of the estate of Mrs. Nancy Hash, dec'd. There is $60.90 remaining in the hands of the administrator which will be distributed among the heirs less the administrator's allowance of $5.00.

pg 232. 31 Aug 1906. Final settlement made with J.K. P. Webb, administrator of Cinderella Webb, dec'd. John Collier's heirs receive 12.43; Bell Womack's heirs receive $12.43; A.J. Webb's heirs receive $24.86; F.P.Webb and J.K.P. Webb each receive $24.86. "$19.91 in hands of the administrator belonging to the heirs of R.A. Webb who live in Texas. As the administrator has an old and unpaid account against their father they have refused to draw this account and it is now given to the administrator..."

pg 233. 21 Aug 1906. Inventory and settlement of the estate of Mrs. C.B. Swann, made by W.L. Swann, administrator. "As this is all personal property it reverts by law to the administrator who was the husband of the deceased."

pg 234. 31 Aug 1906. Settlement made with J.C. Safley, administrator of W.M. Russell. $25.00 was derived from a pension from the state. The administrator filed a bill in this cause to sell the land to pay debts.

pg 235-241. 16 Oct 1906. List of the personal property of the estate of Mrs. _____ Wagner, dec'd, reported by T.J. Wagner, administrator. Purchases made by T.J. Wagner, Myrtle Wagner, Lem Wagner, W.W. Wagner, Sallie Wagner and others. "Mrs. Wagner died 1 Oct 1894."

pg 242. 23 Nov 1906. Inventory and sale bill of the estate of V.A. Dunlop, dec'd reported by D.A. Safley.

pg 243. 4 Dec 1906. Inventory of the personal estate of B.J. McCollum, dec'd filed by B.S. McCollum, administrator.

pg 244. 24 Dec 1906. Sale bill of the personal property of the estate of B.J. McCollum, dec'd. Purchases made by B.S. McCollum, I.W. McCollum, J.W. McCollum and others.

pg 245-249. Dec Term 1906. Inventory and sale bill of the personal property of the estate of Mrs. Eliza Davis, dec'd filed by G.J. Davis, administrator. Purchases made by Charles Davis, D. Cantrell Davis, H. Davis, G. Davis and others.

pg 250. Jan Term 1907. Final settlement made this day with Ed Sparkman, administrator of Elsie Gribble, "supposed to have been dead but is living... Elsie Gribble having left this state some 18 years ago and not being heard from in this time was supposed to have been dead, but leaving estate. Ed Sparkman acted thereupon and some time since Gribble has returned..."

pg 251. 12 Jan 1907. "I, Elsie Gribble now a resident of Closa, CA, formerly a resident of Bishop or Rowland, Tennessee do be these presents acknowledge the payment of $73.30 in full due me from Ed Sparkman who has held a fund belonging to me and due me from the estate of Lodd Rowland, dec'd. Said sum was turned over to said Sparkman by order of te Court to be held in trust... 12 Jan 1907" Signed Elsie B. Gribble.

pg 252. 14 Jan 1907. Supplemental inventory of the estate of B.J. McCollum, dec'd reported by B.S. McCollum, administrator.

pg 253. 25 Jan 1907. Inventory of the personal estate of Daniel Green, dec'd by T.C. Green, administrator.

pg 254. 28 Jan 1907. Inventory of the personal estate of J.B. Grissom dec'd, returned by Mrs. L.D. Grissom, administratrix.

pg 255. 5 Mar 1907. Supplemental inventory of the personal estate of Mrs. R.A. McGee, returned by W.T. and G.E. McGee, administrators.

pg 256-257. 5 Mar 1907. Final settlement of the estate of Archibel Scott, dec'd, made by E.L. Moffitt, administrator. Payments of $88.10 made to G.R. and C. Barnes jointly, L.F. and Mary P. Painter, Alex and Lillie P. Painter, Hughy and Vic S. Slaughter, and J.C. Scott. L.V. Scott and others received $125.00.

pg 258. 11 Mar 1907. Inventory of the personal estate of C. Hayes, dec'd returned by A.C. and A.G. Hayes, administrators.

pg 259-260. 16 Mar 1907. List of property sold of J.B. Grissom, dec'd returned by his administrator. Purchases by Mrs. L.D. Grissom, John Grissom, Creed Grissom and others.

pg 261-262. 1 Apr 1907. Sale bill of the estate of W.P. Faulkner, dec'd made by John L. Willis, administrator with will annexed.

pg 263-268. 2 Apr 1907. "The Clerk respectfully reports to the court that he has this day taken the first but not the final account of John L. Willis, administrator with will annexed of W.P. Faulkner, dec'd". Advancement made to Annie Lee Faulkner, now Mrs. Orton (daughter). Advancement to Allie Grisswold and to the dec'd son Herman Faulkner. Mrs. Mary Faulkner paid for a year's support. Paid Mrs. Lilla Martin on her claim against the estate of her father. Amounts paid the distributees and legatees as follows: $1800.00 each paid to Mrs. Mary Faulkner the widow, Ben Faulkner, Mrs. [Madison] Orton, W.P. Faulkner, Jr., Mrs. Lilla Martin, Mrs. Allie Grizzie, and Herman Faulkner.

pg 269-270. 4 Mar 1907. Settlement made with J.T. Wagner, administrator of the estate of Mrs. M.E. Wagner, dec'd. Receipt for $62.50 from Myrtle and Lillie Wagner, children of G.G. Wagner, heir. Receipt of Ella Locke, heir for $62.50; receipt of the administrator (who is a full heir) for $62.50. Administrator holds $62.50 the share of Willie Mansfield who is a granddaughter of Mrs. M.E. Wagner and whose whereabouts in unknown.

pg 271-273. 6 Mar 1907. Inventory of the personal estate of W.M. Bonner, dec'd which has come into the hands of James B. Bonner, administrator.

pg 274-276. 8 May 1907. Inventory of all the goods and chattels of the estate of C.C. Paris, dec'd reported by Mrs. Nannie Paris, administratrix.

pg 277. 16 May 1907. Settlement made with W.T. Darnell, administrator of Rebecca Ramsey, dec'd. He reports nothing in the hands of the administrator.

pg 278-280. 16 Mar 1907. List of property at sale of J.B. Grissom, dec'd 16 Feb 1907 reported by L.D. Grissom, administratrix. Purchases by: Mrs. L.D. Grissom, John Grissom, Creed Grissom, and others.

pg 281. 27 May 1907. Inventory and sale bill of the personal property of the estate of James M. Basham, held at his residence 22 May 1907. Mary Ann Basham administrator. Purchases made by Ed Basham.

pg 282. 30 May 1907. Final settlement of the estate of W.M. Akers, dec'd made with J.R. Akers, administrator.

pg 283. 22 May 1907. Final settlement made with A.Y Phillips, administrator of the estate of Mrs. Octa A. Phillips.

pg 284-286. 31 May 1907. Sale bill of the estate of Mrs. Octa A. Phillips, dec'd reported by A.Y. Phillips.

pg 287-291. 3 Jun 1907. List of property sold on 17 May 1907 belonging to the estate of Eliza C. Hunter, dec'd reported by William B. Teeters.

pg 292-298. 5 Jun 1907. J.J. Meadows, administrator of the personal estate of W.C. Bonner, dec'd reports sale of stock of general merchandise on 13 Apr 1907 at

Steppsville owned by W.C. Bonner at time of his death. Purchases made by Oscar Bonner, J.W. Bonner, J.B. Bonner, Oma Bonner, Mary Bonner, Willie Bonner, Joe Bonner and others.

pg 299. 15 Jul 1907. Inventory of the estate of J.H. Milstead reported by G.W. Perry, administrator.

pg 300. 10 Jun 1907. J.B. Bonner, administrator of W.M. Bonner, Sr., dec'd reports public sale of the property of the deceased at the residence of Enoch Bonner on 1 Jun 1907.

pg 301-303. 11 Jun 1907. Settlement of the estate of H.L. Stanley, dec'd made by John L. Willis, administrator. The distributive share of Mrs. J.E. Thompson (Nannie Stanley Thompson), and Mrs. Mary McAlister noted.

pg 304-307. 22 Jul 1907. Final Settlement of the estate of John R. West, dec'd made with Stoke Etter, administrator. Receipts of widow and children as follows. Mrs. Anna West (widow), Oscar West, Della West, guardians receipt for shares of Harry West, Elevis West, Audrey West, Pauline West and Johnnie West, minor heirs of John R. West, dec'd. "One of the children had died since his death and after she was 21 years of age, hence had a vested estate after the death of her father, and the widow not being her legal mother, her interest would vest in her brothers and sisters who were her half brothers and sisters."

pg 308-309. 19 Jul 1907. Supplemental inventory and sale bill of the personal estate of E. Montgomery, dec'd, returned by John P. Seals.

pg 310-311. 2 Aug 1907. Partial settlement made with John P. Seal, administrator of the estate of E. Montgomery, dec'd. Mrs. Mary Montgomery given $250.00 for part of a year's support.

pg 312-317. 14 Aug 1907. Sale bill and inventory of the estate of Mrs. M.E. Roberson, dec'd reported by James H. Todd, administrator. First report made Mar 1905. Balance in estate divided as follows: $22.64 to Mrs. R.M. Graham's heirs, some of which are minors without a guardian, and $7.12 is due Mrs. L.A. Smith.

pg 318-319. 17 Jul 1907. Inventory of the estate of

Mrs. Susan Ann Reynolds, dec'd reported by Dillard C. Reynolds, administrator.

pg 320-321.   27 Aug 1907.   Final settlement of the personal estate of Margaret Stubblefield, made with J.R. Ramsey, administrator.   Receipts from Mary Stubblefield, administratrix of W.H. Stubblefield, heir, $420.00; A.F. Stubblefield, W.A. Stubblefield, E.P. Stubblefield, and S.M. Stubblefield, sons of J. Stubblefield, $84.00 each; Mrs. Ella Locke, daughter of J. Stubblefield, $84.00.

pg 322-326. 2 Sep 1907. Report of the sale of personal property of the estate of Mrs. Ann Reynolds, dec'd, made by Dillard C. Reynolds, administrator.   Purchases made by Mamie Reynolds and many others.

pg 327-329. 11 oct 1907. Inventory and sale bill of the estate of Mrs. Mary Ann Basham. The administrator T.E. Basham reports that he sold all of said property at her late residence in the 9th District of Warren County on 23 Sep 1907.   Purchasers were Noah Basham, Isiah Basham, Adam Basham and others.

pg 330.   24 Oct 1907.   Inventory of the estate of Mrs. S.C. Fuston, reported by A.T. Fuston, administrator.

pg 331-332.   11 Nov 1907.   Final settlement of the estate of Mrs. R.A. McGee, dec'd made with G.E. McGee, one of the administrators of the estate, the other administrator being W.T. McGee.   The following heirs received $129.37 each: S.L. Cardwell, W.B. Cardwell, Wash and Lena Long, Floy Bost.   The following heirs received $258.75 each: W.L. McGee and G.E. McGee.

pg 333-334.   6 Nov 1907.   Final settlement of the personal estate of Mrs. Ann L. Jones, made with J.C. Biles, executor.   Legacy of $91.02 each paid to R.E. Jones, Lucy Jones and Annie May Jones.

pg 335-340.   _ Dec 1907.   Report of the sale of the personal property of the estate of C.C. Paris, dec'd by Mrs. Nannie Paris, administratrix of said estate. Purchases made by J. R. Paris, Jessie Paris, Mrs. Paris and many others.

pg 341-344. [Not dated]. Inventory and sale bill of the estate of Robert Keaton made by A.D. Keaton and Robert Gribble, administrators of said estate.   Sale held 18 Aug 1906.   Purchases made by Jennie Keaton,

Charley Keaton and others.

pg 345-346. 30 Sep 1907. Inventory and report of sale of the personal property of the estate of Robert Keaton, dec'd made by Robert Gribble and Allen Keaton, administrators of said estate. Sale was held 11 Nov 1905. Pruchases made by Mrs. A.D. Keaton and others.

pg 347. 14 Sep 1907. Inventory and sale bill of the personal estate of "my late husband G.R. Bonner, dec'd" made by Catherine Bonner. Sale held 31 Aug 1907, with pruchases made by James Bonner, Jr., J.W. Bonner and M.L. Bonner.

pg 348-354. 23 Dec 1907. Final settlement of the estate of W.P. Faulkner, dec'd by John L. Willis administrator. To each of the following there is due $365.66: Mrs. Mary Faulkner, Ben Faulkner, Mrs. Lyda Martin, William P. Faulkner, Jr., and Mrs. Allie Griswold. Receipt of Mrs. Orton: "Received of John L. Willis, administrator with will annexed of W.P. Faulkner, dec'd, the sum of $515.66, the same being the balance in full of my share of the estate of my father, having heretofore received of said administrator the sum of $1650.00. This Dec _, 1907." Signed Mrs. Annie Lee Orton and M. Orton. Mrs. Allie F. Griswold is the wife of S.M. Griswold and resident of Parker County, TX. Lyda Martin is the wife of C.P. Martin. Herman Faulkner received $105.71 making final distribution of the proceeds of said estate on 6 Jan 1908.

[Letter clipped to page 355, dated 10 Sep 1908]. To Mr. Clay Faulkner, McMinnville stating that his nephew Herman Faulkner of Salt Lake City has hired an attorney to represent him concerning the estate of said Herman's father W.P. Faulkner, dec'd.

pg 355. 6 Jan 1908. John L. Willis, administrator with will annexed of the estate of W.P. Faulkner, dec'd reports that he has distributed the assets of the estate and is therefore discharged of his trust.

pg 356-362. 7 Feb 1908. Inventory and sale bill of the estate of A.M. Womack, dec'd reported by L.P. Womack and A.D. Womack, executors. Purchases made by Joe Womack, J.T. Womack, Mrs. Cleo Womack, L.P. Womack, Sam Womack, W.C. Womack, Mrs. D. Womack, J.C. Womack, W.L. Womack, Frank Womack, Mrs. Willard Womack, Alton Womack, F.B. Womack, Mrs. and Mrs. A.M. Womack, C.M. Womack, Mrs.

D.D. Womack, Dick Womack, S.P. Womack, Claude Womack, R.A. Womack. Receipt filed for Tempy Womack for $450.00 for her claim to the estate of her late husband A.M. Womack. Receipt for $450.00 for his share or interest in the estate of A.M. Womack signed by J.J. Womack.

pg 363. 2 Jan 1908. Sale bill of the estate of Mrs. Eliza C. Hunter, dec'd reported by William B. Teeters.

pg 364. 2 Jan 1908. List of notes come to the hands of Wm. B. Teeters, administrator of Mrs. E.C. Hunter.

pg 365. 7 Dec 1907. The account of A.T. Fuston, administrator of Mrs. S.C. Fuston, dec'd. $26.00 paid to each of the following: M.E. Mears, S.M. Fuston, T.H Fuston, W.N. Fuston, A.T. Fuston and B.D. and G.B. Mears (the last two jointly to receive $26.00).

pg 366. 10 Jan 1908. Inventory of the estate of W.C. Lock, dec'd, by J.B. Lock, administrator.

pg 367-368. [Not dated] Settlement of Robert Gribble and A.D. Keaton, administrators of the estate of Robert Keaton, dec'd.

pg 369. 20 Jan 1908. Inventory of the estate of John Bouldin, dec'd filed by George Bouldin.

pg 370. 15 Mar 1908. Final settlement of the personal estate of W.H. Stubblefield made with Mrs. Mary F. Stubblefield, administratrix.

pg 371-372. 13 Mar 1908. Sale bill of the estate of Daniel Green, dec'd, reported by T.C. Green, administrator. Purchases made by T.C. Green, John Green, Hervy Green, Ferris Green and others. Payments made out of the estate to J.T. Green ($100.00), Malisse Massie ($78.91), J.J. Green ($80.00), J.M and Bettie Smith ($80.00), Andy Green ($78.91), and to administrator T.C. Green (his interest in the estate, $78.91.)

pg 373-375. 12 Mar 1908. Inventory and sale bill of the personal property of G.M. Smartt at his late residence 22 Jun 1904 by the administrators A.W. and J.P. Smartt. Purchases made by G.D. Smartt, Mrs. G.M. Smartt, Furman Smartt, and others.

pg 376-377. March Term 1908. Settlement of the estate

of G.M. Smartt by Robert W. and J.P. Smartt, administrators. C.A. Smartt years support (24 Jul 1907) $237.50.

pg 378-379. 2 Mar 1908. Inventory of the estate of R.G. Belcher, dec'd reported by J.R. Belcher, executor.

pg 380-384. 25 Mar 1908. The second, but not final settlement of W.P. Hickerson and Charles S. Ivie, executors of the estate of J.C. Ramsey, Sr., dec'd. Upon the death of Laura R. Ivie, one of the legatees, on 6 Oct 1905, it was agreed by and between them that in as much as she had devised her 1/2 interest in the old home place to her nephew Wright Hickerson and the balance of her interst to her husband Charles S. Ivie that the rents collected on the place should be distributed among the persons entitled thereto. The executors state that the amounts expended by them in payment of the debts owing by J.C. Ramsey, Jr and W.T. Ramsey, sons of J.C. Ramsey, Sr., out othe funds of this estate shall cover their compensation for services rendered as executors of this estate.

pg 385-388. April Term 1908. Sale of the personal property of Mrs. A. Bradford by J.R. Ramsey, administrator.

pg 389-391. _ Apr 1908. Final settlement of the estate of H.L. Stanley, made by John L. Willis, administrator. There are three distributees, Mrs. Nancy Jane Thompson, Mrs. Mary A. McAlister and Newton Stanley, the only children of H.L. Stanley.

pg 392-400. 13 May 1908. Settlement with Frank R. Davis and Mrs A.W. Davis, executor and executrix of the estate of John H. Savage, dec'd.

pg 401. 18 May 1908. Settlement of the personal estate of Mrs. L.V.A. Hash made by the administrator T.F. Hash. The following "full heirs" received $43.99 each: H.L. and N.J. Sherrill; Thomas A. and Daisy B. Scott; W.A. and T.H. Kinnard; G.W. Hash; and T.F. Hash. An additional $43.99 still in the hands of the administrator belonging to Thomas E. Hash who is a full heir and who the administrator has been unable to locate.

pg 402. 1 Jun 1908. Inventory of the estate of A. Crain, reported by A.M. Crain, administrator.

pg 403. 18 Jul 1908. Final settlement of the estate of J.P. Edwards, dec'd, made with G.W. Darnell, executor.

pg 404. 10 Jul 1908. Inventory of the personal property from the estate of Henry C. Martin, dec'd made by Neety Martin, administratrix.

pg 405. 13 Aug 1908. Inventory of the personal estate of J.W. Dodd filed by H.N. Dodd, administrator.

pg 406. 13 Aug 1908. Final settlement of the estate of J.W. Dodd, made with H.N. Dodd, administrator. The balance of the estate goes to the administrator who is the father of J.W. Dodd.

pg 407. 19 Sep 1908. Inventory of the estate of E.G. Mead, dec'd, reported by his wife Mrs. Mary A. Mead as administratrix.

pg 408-410. 22 Sep 1908. Inventory and sale of the estate of Creed Taylor, dec'd reported by J.A. Taylor, administrator. Purchases made by Ninnie Taylor, Jim Taylor, and others.

pg 411. 23 Sep 1908. Inventory of the personal property of the estate of John W. Shirley, dec'd, including amount received from John B. Shirley as administrator of Rowland Shirley, dec'd. John B. Shirley is also administrator of the John W. Shirley estate.

pg 412-413. 2 Nov 1908. Inventory of the funds received by W.L. Hillis as administrator of Maude Hillis, dec'd.

pg 414. 2 Nov 1908. Inventory of the personal estate of W.L. Adamson, returned by J.H. Adamson, admr.

pg 415-417. 17 Oct 1908. Report "but not final report" of the assets of the estate of William C. Bonner, Jr., dec'd, made by J.J. Meadows. Years support given Mrs. Mary Bonner, widow of deceased.

pg 418. 14 Nov 1908. Sale bill of the estate of W.T. Adamson, reported by J.H. Adamson. Purchases made by Robert Adamson, Alte Adamson, Joe Hale and Fred Hale.

pg 419-420. 20 Nov 1908. Final settlement of the estate of A.J. Webb, dec'd made with the administratrix

Mrs. S.E. Webb. Includes the amounts received from I.G. Webb, administrator of James Webb, dec'd.

pg 421-422. 21 Nov 1908. Complete inventory of the estate of A.J. Webb, made by Mrs. S.E. Webb, administratrix. Purchases made by Bob Webb, I.G. Webb, Jim Webb, J.K. Webb, E.H. Webb, and others.

pg 423. 15 Dec 1908. Final settlement of the personal estate of E. Montgomery, made by J.P. Seal adminstrator. Several receipts given by Mrs. Mary Montgomery.

pg 424-425. 1 Dec 1908. Final settlement made with M.L. Sellers, administrator of the estate of Hixie Fuston, dec'd. Settlement shows payment of $74.00 each to the following: R.M. Smartt as assignee of Ed Warren; R.W. Smartt as assignee of Martha DeLong; H.P. Stubblefield, clerk and master in the case of T.J. Potter vs Willie Warren in Chancery Court; E. Parsley; Thomas Parsley; Amanda Moore; Miss Tennie Smith; Bethel Parsley; Amon Parsley; and Hattie Potter. The following received $18.50 each: Mary Cantrell, Owen Parsley, Bettie Irving, and Thomas Parsley.

pg 426-427. 19 Jan 1909. J.H. Jarrell, administrator of the estate of A.J. Williams, dec'd files inventory of that estate.

pg 428. 27 Jan 1909. Settlement made with J.J. Meadows, trustee of St. Mary School Fund.

pg 429. 27 Jan 1909. Final settlement of the estate of Mrs. Eliza Davis, made by G.J. Davis, administrator. Receipts filed by Flossie Cotten and Mable A. Bryant, the heirs of this estate.

pg 430-431. 3 Feb 1909. Final settlement of William F. Elkins, administrator of the estate of G.T. Davies, dec'd. Mrs. Flora Davies's balance in full $83.09. Amount due the minors paid to Oliver Towles, guardian, $932.40.

pg 432. 3 Feb 1909. Final settlement of the personal estate of Mrs. M.E. Wagner, dec'd made by F.J. Wagner, administrator. The administrator "on 4 May 1907 made a full settlement except as to the interest of Mrs. Willie Mansfield whose residence was unknown at that time. He now comes and files receipt of the said Mrs. Mansfield for her share..."

pg 433-434. 19 Feb 1909. The undersigned Jesse Lock, administrator of the estate of W.C. Locke, dec'd submits the following report. Receipt of Sarah A. Locke, widow of said dec'd for a year's support. There are four shares in said estate, to wit: Sarah A.Locke (widow), Jesse Locke, Buck Locke and Mrs. Maddux and Mrs. Stubblefield [the last two jointly].

pg 435. 19 Feb 1909. Final settlement of the estate of J.B. Grissom, made by Louisa Grissom, administratrix.

pg 436-439. 1 Mar 1909. Settlement of the estate of C.C. Paris, dec'd reported by Mrs. Nannie Paris, administratrix. Miss Jessie Paris paid $60.00 for support of minor Berlin Paris. The clerk reports that there are six distributive shares of the estate of C.C. Paris, he having had five children and leaving his widow who takes a child's part. Payment in full made to the following: C.C. Paris, Jr., Mrs. Ruby Hawkins, Jesse Paris, and Ed Paris. A share also paid to C.C. Paris, Jr. as guardian of the minor Berlin Paris.

pg 440. 1 Mar 1909. Sale bill and inventory of the personal assets of Joe Durley, dec'd made by James H. Todd, administrator.

pg 441. 4 Mar 1907. Final settlement made with Frank Colville, administrator of W. Lester Stroud. Payment of $363.00 made to Allie Hart, J.M. Stroud and J.A. Stroud.

pg 442-443. 20 Mar 1909. Final settlement of the estate of Mrs. Nancy Hash, made with W.V.D. Miller, administrator.

pg 444. 30 Mar 1909. Final settlement made with C.J. Hill, administrator of J.N. Hill, dec'd. Payments made to Manda J. Hill, the widow.

pg 445-448. 9 Apr 1909. Inventory and sale of the personal property of the estate of B.C. Wilkinson, dec'd, made by H.B. Evans and T.A. Wilkinson, administrators of said estate. Purchases made by Mrs. T.A. Wilkinson, W.E. Bluhm, and others. Notes on C.L. Wilkinson and G.L. Wilkinson made to deceased.

pg 449-450. 9 Feb 1909. Inventory and sale of the personal property of the estae of John Green, dec'd made by H.B. Evans, administrator. Purchases made by Mrs. John Green, Sam Green, John Green and others.

pg 451-452. 19 Apr 1909. Statement of the funds received by G.B. Ramsey as administrator of the estate of Isaac Ramsey, dec'd. The following heirs each received $7.39: Alice Rouse, T.J. Ramsey, Hannah Smartt, I.C. Ramsey, Joe Ramsey, Laura B. Parker, Cassie Morris, G.W. Ramsey and Lidia Spurlock, as well as the administrator who is an equal heir.

pg 453. 24 Apr 1909. Inventory and sale bill of the estate of Henry Martin, dec'd made by the administratrix [not named here].

pg 454-460. 26 Apr 1909. Inventory of the personal estate of Mrs. M.A. Golladay who died intestate on 2 Feb 1909 which came or should have come into the hands of A. Golladay, administrator of said deceased.

pg 461-462. 27 Apr 1909. The final accounting of B.S. McCollum, administrator of the estate of B.J. McCollum, dec'd. $15.83 in the hands of the administrator for distribution among the distributees of the deceased [not named.]

pg 463-465. [Not dated] The first and final account of William B. Teeters, administrator of the estate of Mrs. Eliza C. Hunter. The sum of $399.25 is distributed among the "brothers and sisters of Mrs. Hunter, namely W.A. Miller, A.O.Miller, Margarett Owens and Mary Jane Gribble, all of whom are dead execpt W.A. Miller, leaving children."

pg 466. 14 May 1909. Inventory of the property of S.C. Gribble, reported by T.A. Wommack, administrator.

pg 467-468. 17 May 1909. "The following are the names of those who bid off stuff of the late deceased Gribble:" Bob Smith, Will Grissom, R.E. Womack, John Hankins, Nora Hankins, George Roberts and others.

pg 469. June Term. Settlement of the estate of G.R. Bonner, made by his wife Mrs. Catherine Bonner, administratrix. Balance in hand, $20.00, is due the widow as heir of her deceased husband.

pg 470. 21 Jun 1909. Inventory of the estate of Cooper Scott, dec'd which has come into the hands of L.V. Scott, administrator with will annexed, as successor to Arch Scott, executor (deceased).

pg 471. 25 June 1909. Settlement of the estate of
W.L.Adamson, made with J.H. Adamson, administrator.

pg 472-473. 13 July 1909. Inventory and sale bill of
the estate of Henry Stroud, dec'd made by John A. Boyd,
administrator.

pg 474. 13 Jul 1909. Inventory of the estate of Edward
T.   Annable,   dec'd   reported   by   A.H.   Faulkner,
administrator with will annexed.

pg 475-476. 28 Jul 1909. Sale bill of the property of
J.H. Milstead, dec'd by G.W. Perry, administrator. Sale
held 20 Jul 1907.   Final settlement of the personal
estate   shows receipt of Ada Milstead, widow of J.H.
Milstead for balance in full.

pg 477. 3 Aug 1909. Final settlement of the personal
estate of Grant Anderson, dec'd.   S.E. Roach, Mattie
Roach, Genelga Burch, I.A. Anderson, each received
$178.97.   J.A. Brixey, W.H. Brixey and Arie Darnell
received $178.97 jointly. J.C. Anderson, administrator,
received $178.97, he being a full heir.

pg 478-480. 31 Jul 1909. Inventory and sale bill of
the property of Ross Swoap, sold a public sale at the
homestead of the late Ross Swoap by Adam West,
administrator.   Distribution of the estate as follows:
one third to Mrs. Annie Swoap, the widow, and one third
to each of the two minor children Lizzie and Cora Swoap.

pg 481. 7 Sep 1909. Final settlement with Mrs. Ann
Reynolds, guardian of Mamie Reynolds, made by D.G.
Reynolds, administrator of Mrs. Ann Reynolds. Receipt
of $503.12 for the "full settlement of of my estate in
the hands of my guardian Mrs. Ann Reynolds, me being 21
years of age" Signed Mamie Reynolds.

pg 482. 29 Sep 1909. Inventory of the estate of J.
Swancutt, dec'd reported by Jacob Schmitz,
administrator.

pg 483-484. 9 Oct 1909. Settlement with Jim B. Bonner,
administrator of the estate of William Bonner, dec'd.
The total of $2356.25 is distributed among the heirs, to
wit: E.F. Bonner, T.M. Bonner, and the heirs of Jacob
Bonner, leaving a balance of $1500.15 yet to be
distributed.

pg 485-490. 11 Oct 1909. Inventory and final settlement of the estate of James H. DeBard, made by his wife Mrs. Laura Debard as administratrix. The balance remaining in the hands of the administratrix belongs to herself as widow and to Davis M. Debard and Eunice Debard as children and sole heirs at law of James H. DeBard, dec'd.

pg 491. 31 Oct 1909. Settlement made with J.J. Meadows, Trustee of St. Mary School Fund.

pg 492-494. 16 Nov 1909. Inventory and sale bill of the estate of J.G. Reynolds, sold at public sale, reported by James Grizzell, administrator. Balance of $312.50 paid to Court for distribution among the creditors of the deceased.

pg 495. 16 Nov 1909. Inventory of the estate of H.C. Williamson, reported by J.R. Akers, administrator.

pg 496. 6 Nov 1909. Inventory of the estate of Mrs. Emma Seitz, reported by Albert Seity, administrator.

pg 497-502. 8 Sep 1909. The first and final settlement of the estate of Mrs. Ann Reynolds, dec'd, made by Dillard G. Reynolds, administrator. "There are 9 distributive shares as follows: 1) Mamie Reynolds; 2) Mrs. Allie Wilcher; 3) Jessie Wilcher; 4) Mrs. Georgia Stubblefield; 5) Mrs. Bettie Miller; 6) Mrs. Edna Cantrell; 7) Mrs. Sallie Jennings; 8) Dillard G. Reynolds and 9) Mrs. Etter who is dead and leaves only 2 children, namely Reggie Etter and Mrs. Hassie Lawrence who are each entitled to the distributive share of $77.76 except Reggie and Hassie who are entitled to $38.82 each, all of whom have been paid by the administrator..." Allie Wilcher is wife of R.H. Wilcher, Sallie Jennings is wife of R.W. Jennings, A.P. Wilcher is husband of Jessie Wilcher, W.K. Stubblefield is husband of Georgia Stubblefield, E.T. Lawrence is husband of Hassie Lawrence, and R.R. Etter is guardian of Reggie Etter.

pg 503-507. 3 Jan 1910. List of articles sold at the sale of the personal property of R.L. Stubblefield, dec'd reported by J.R. Stubblefield, administrator. Purchases made by G.H. Stubblefield, J.R. Stubblefield, and many others.

pg 508-511. 8 Dec 1909. Inventory and sale bill of the

estate of Nancy Gross, dec'd filed by R.W. Smartt, administrator. Sale held 13 Nov 1909.

pg 512-517. 1 Jan 1910. Report of inventory and sale bill of the personal effects of Mrs. O.W. Davis, dec'd. [Names of purchasers not given]. "Under a compromise and family settlement sometime during the past year with Mrs. Worley and Mr. Fairbanks, representing my mother for the sake of peace I surrendered the greater part of the above property with was mine individually. I am still content to stand by this family settlement and account for this property as belonging to my mother provided her daughters will abide by the same, but they are now seeking to avoid said settlement and in the event of their doing this, then this property belongs to me." Signed Frank R. Davis.

pg 518. 24 Jan 1910. Inventory and sale bill of the personal property of the estate of R.K. Rains, sale being held at late residence of said R.K. Rains, dec'd in Oct 1907 reported by I.R. Rains, administrator. "This inventory does not include one horse which had been given to Crit Rains by R.K. Rains in his life time, and which was turned over to him with the consent of all the heirs of th estate, afterward being purchased from Oscar Rains for $100.00."

pg 519-521. 4 Feb 1910. Settlement with A.D. Womack and Levander Womack, executors of the estate of A.M. Womack, dec'd. This settlement leaves for distribution among ten heirs $5209.48. With interest collected, each or the following heirs received $555.00: C.L. Keaton and wife S.P.; John B. Womack; Minnie Jones; A.D. Womack; L.P. Womack; S.L. Brown and wife; S.G. Womack; Joe L. Womack; J.T. Womack; and J.E. Martin.

pg 522-524. 10 Feb 1910. Inventory and settlement of the estate of J. Fred Murphy, dec'd made by H.B. Evans, administrator. The balance of the estate in given to Mrs. A.D. Murphy, mother of the dec'd.

pg 525. 24 Feb 1910. Inventory of the estate of R.L. Stubblefield, dec'd filed by J.R. Stubblefield, administrator.

pg 526-528. 28 Feb 1910. Final settlement of H.B. Evans, administrator of the estate of John Green, dec'd. There being originally six children of the deceased and his widow, as follows: John Green, Jr; J.M. Green; Sam

A. Green; Mandy McCollum; Minnie Minton [or Winton]; Ida Killian, dec'd; and the widow, making seven distributive shares of $148.48 each.

pg 529-530. 17 Mar 1910. Inventory and sale bill and final settlement of the estate of H.L. Moffitt, dec'd made by W.T. Moffitt, administrator. The administrator makes oath that there are no debts against said estate and that he was the only heir at law of the said deceased.

pg 531. 9 Apr 1910. Settlement of the estate of W.S. Rogers, made with his administrator W.M. Rogers of Warren County.

pg 532. 26 May 1910. Final settlement of the personal estate of E.C. Hunter, dec'd made with William B. Teeters, administrator. There were four origianl shares, viz: A.O. Miller, dec'd, Margaret Owens, dec'd, Mary Jane Gribble, dec'd and W.A. Miller. The heirs of A.O. Miller are Sarah J. Miller, Margaret Miller, Martha J. Miller, Laura Miller and Floy Miller. The heirs of Mary Jane Gribble are James H. Gribble, J.C. Gribble, Frank Gribble, W.R. Gribble, George T. Gribble, Josie Gribble and Mrs. J.M. Lively. The heirs of Margaret Owens are George A. Owens, Mrs. Florence Lister and Laura B. Huffaker.

pg 533. 18 Jun 1910. Settlement and statement of the estate of William Biles. "Under the last will and testament of my husband William Biles, I was made residuary legatee and beneficiary of the personal estate of decedent, after the payment of special bequests named in the will and the indebtedness of the estate, and whereas Mr. J.C. Biles as executor of said will has paid the indebtedness of the estate and has delivered a large portion of the estate coming to me under such will...I desire that J.C. Biles be required to make an inventory of said estate..." Signed Mrs. Bettie Biles.

pg 534-537. 7 Mar 1910. Inventory and sale bill of the estate of Dr. W.H. Moore, dec'd [administrator or executor not named here]. Purchases made by J.B. Moore, Mrs. Moore, Kate Moore and many others.

pg 538-539. 13 Jul 1910. Settlement made with John A. Boyd, administrator of the estate of Henry Stroud, dec'd.

pg 540. 4 Jul 1910. "As administratrix of the personal estate of my deceased husband James A. Cleghorn, there is no property that comes into my hand...by use of property diligence. I was well acquainted with his affairs and his business and know that he had no personal property..." Signed Mrs. N.A. Cleghorn.

pg 541-543. [Not dated] Final settlement made with J.R. Belcher, executor of the will of R.G. Belcher, dec'd. There was a balance of $4240.99 in the hands of the executor to be distributed to the heirs of said R.G. Belcher which has been paid, to wit: 1) J.R. Belcher a son; 2) Robert Belcher a son; 3) Mrs. Lou Ella Brewer, a daughter who died leaving the following 6 children, Ethel Brewer, William B. Brewer, James Brewer, Tennie Brewer, Clarence Brewer and Thomas Oliver Brewer; 4) William Belcher a son who died before the testator leaving three children, J.A. Belcher, Mrs. Fanning P. Massey and Mrs. Willie Carson who died since the testator leaving the following six children, Nellie Pearl Carson, Loron Louise Carson, Fannie Belle Carson, Claud Raymon Carson, Mattie Lou Carson and James Walter Carson; 5) Mrs Henriette B. Riddle who died before the testator leaving five children, Mrs. Lillie P. Green, W.B. Riddle, Richard Riddle, Charlie Riddle and John Riddle; and 6) Mrs. Fannin Riddle.

pg 544-545. 11 Jul 1910. Inventory and final settlement of the estate of O.D. Hinkley, dec'd reported by G.W. Hinkley, administrator.

pg 546-547. 9 Jul 1910. Statement and final settlement made with J.R. Akers, administrator of H.C. Williamson, dec'd. The balance in his hands due the widow and children is $157.04, this being equally divided between the widow and the nine children, to wit: the widow, being the natural guardian of the minor children received $78.50, and receipts filed from Ida Williamson, H.J. Williamson, B.A. Williamson, Oscar Williamson, and Nannie Jordan for $15.71 each.

pg 548. [Not dated]. Final settlement made with the unnamed administrator of the estate of Jackson Bowman, dec'd. Harley Bowman is the only heir of Jackson Bowman.

pg 549. [Not dated]. Sale bill of the estate of S.D. Walker, dec'd. Purchases made by J.D. Walker, S.E. Walker, L.D. Walker, Della Walker, and others. [No

Warren County, TN Will Book 11, Cont.

administrator named here].

pg 550-553. 2 Sep 1910. Inventory and sale bill of the estate of C.J. Heath, dec'd, reported by W.A. Johnson, including a draft from Minneapolis, Minn. Insurance company for C.J. Heath's portion of his mother's estate.

pg 554-559. 30 Oct 1910. Final settlement made with J.J. Meadows, administrator of W.C. Bonner, dec'd. Mentions case of J.J. Meadows, admr, et al vs Bonner, et al, Warren County. Oscar Bonner paid one half the estate as a distributee and the other half as guardian.

pg 560. Nov term 1911. Sale bill of th estate of Isaac Anderson, dec'd. Purchases made by Nancy Anderson, John Anderson, James Anderson, Jim Anderson, and others.

pg 561. 28 Oct 1910. Inventory of the estate of W.A. Connell, dec'd made by William B. Connell, administrator.

pg 562. 29 Nov 1910. Additional inventory of the estate of A.J. Williams, dec'd reported by J.H. Jarrell, administrator.

pg 563-565. 1 Dec 1910. Final settlement made with J.H. Jarrell, administrator of A.J. Williams, dec'd.

pg 566. [Not dates]. Sale bill of the estate of Adeline Van Hooser, dec'd. [No administrator given.]

pg 567. 3 Dec 1910. Inventory of the estate of Mary F. Humphery, dec'd, reported by J.N. Walling, executor.

pg 568. _ Dec 1910. Final settlement of the estate of Mary F. Humphrey, dec'd, made with J.N. Walling, executor. Distributive shares of the estate given to N.B. Humphrey, D.E. Humphrey, Ninah H. Ross, and Nell H. McAfee. "Ivory Box" delivered to beneficiaries N.B. and D.E. Humphrey, Ninah H. Ross and Nell H. McAfee.

pg 569-572. 3 Dec 1910. Inventory and settlement of F.P. Byars, administrator of Miss Jane Byars, dec'd. Purchases made by Mary Byars, J.G. Byars, H.H. Byars, S.H. Byars, Joe Byars, S.J. Byars, and others.

pg 573-575. 6 Dec 1910. Report and settlement of F.P. Byars, administrator with will annexed of Nathan Byars, dec'd. "That decedent died seized and possessed of the real estate hereafter discribed, which under the last will and testament of decedent, was devised for life to his daughter Miss Jane Byars, and after her death the land was to be sold by the executor named in the will and proceeds divided among his children equally." Land in question contained 333 acres in lying in the 14th Civil District of Warren County.

pg 576-578. 27 Aug 1910. Settlement of the estate of E.G. Mead, dec'd reported by Mrs. Mary A. Mead, administratrix with will annexed.

pg 579-582. 2 Jan 1911. Inventory and sale bill of the estate of Joseph Young, dec'd, reported by James Young, executor.

pg 583-585. 28 Dec 1910. The first and final account of the estate of Edward T. Annable, dec'd by A.H. Faulkner, administrator. The administrator had paid the indebtedness of the estate with money in his hands arising from the sale of the house and lot of the deceased, the deed to which was executed by the heirs of Mrs. Annable, Mr. Annable having willed it to her and she having died only a few days after him.

End of Will and Settlement Book 11.

WARREN COUNTY, TN WILLS
Volume 1

Aug 1888-May 1926

[This Will Book contains wills not recorded in the Will and Inventory Books, although covering the same years. These were entered in no special order and the date of probate not always given.]

pg 1. 1 Apr 1899. **Will of Thomas C. Lind.** It is my will that all my debts be paid. I give to my beloved wife Ida C. Lind all my property of every kind. I request that she purchase and give to each of our two sons Samuel Colville Lind and Warner E. Lind a gold watch. I appoint my wife Ida executrix of this will. [Witnesses not given]

pg 2-3. 27 Aug 1888. **Will of Cordelia Alta Smallman.** I give to my daughter Lillian a featherbed, silver-ware and gold watch. I also give her 1/3rd of all the balance of my estate. Should she die without issue, her share is to go to her brothers. I give to each of my sons [not named] a bedstead and the remainder of my estate to share and share alike. I appoint W.H. Magness Sr. and W.H. Magness Jr. my executors. Witnessed by Robert Cantrell and Julia E. Harrison.

pg 4-7. 9 May 1903. **Will of J.C. Ramsey.** First I desire all my debts and funeral expenses be paid. Second, I desire my executors to erect a monument on my lot in the new cemetery at McMinnville in memory of my deceased wife and two sons and myself, as my daughter Mrs. Laura Ivie and my son-in-law W.P. Hickerson may suggest.   Third, in appreciation of the long and faithful service of Flora Rowan, colored, I leave in trust for her $800.00. Fourth, I direct my executors to sell all the real estate I may die the owner of. Mrs. Laura Ivie is to take my homeplace in McMinnville at such price as may be agreed upon between her and W.P. Hickerson. Fifth, I desire the balance of my estate to be divided into two parts--one part to my daughter Mrs. Laura Ivie, wife of C.S. Ivie of Shelbyville, Tn and the other part to my grandchildren, to wit: W.P. Hickerson, Jr, Chisum Hickerson, Georgia Hickerson, Wright Hickerson, Insa__ [Naison] Hickerson, Laura Hickerson, Helloise Hickerson, Lillie Hickerson and Allan Hickerson to share and share alike. My bank stock and household furniture is to be divided likewise. Sixth, I nominate

W.P.Hickerson Sr., and C.S. Ivie my sons-in-law the executors of this my last will and testament. The piano belongs to my daughter Laura Ivie and the center table belongs to my granddaughter Georgia Hickerson. If the debts for medicine and medical services contracted for my son James Ramsey during his last sickness have not been paid before I die, I direct these paid out of my estate. Witnessed by F.H. Mercer, Jesse Walling and Frank Colville.

pg 8. 10 May 1900. **Will of Elizabeth Edge.** First, I want my debts and burial expenses paid. Second, I will to my friend J.C. Biles my house and lot in McMinnville that was deeded to me by Mr. J.C. Biles. Third, I appoint Frank Colville executor of this will. Witnessed by J.S. Burroughs and H.P. Stubblefield.

pg 9-10. 1 May 1894. **Will of J.M. Webb.** I want my lot divided into three lots and my wife Elizabeth Webb to have the middle lot for her home for her lifetime and if S.C. Webb, my youngest daughter lives with her mother and takes care of her, she is to have lot 2 for her own. I want my upper lot to be rented out if possible or sold, along with the lower lot 3 to pay the mortgage. I want the balance to be divided equally among my heirs [not named.] I want R.A. Thatch and J.B. Webb to attend to this matter. Witnessed by J.W. Smith and A.R. Hammer.

pg 11. 17 Aug 1870. **Will of Middleton Rowan.** I will to my beloved wife Lucy the house and lot on which I now live, all the household furniture, provisions, money, notes and accounts. It is my will that my daughter Jane live with my wife Lucy as long as she conducts herself right and proper. I nominate my wife Lucy executrix of this will. Witnessed by J.W. Mitchell, A. Knox, and T.H. Mabury.

pg 12. 13 Dec 1903. **Will of Mrs. E.J. Griswold.** First, I give and bequeath to my daughter Lucy Smartt all my household furniture except my carpet in my bedroom which I give to my granddaughter Sadie Smartt. Second, any money which I may possess at my death I desire to my equally divided among my children. Third, I appoint Lucy Smartt to be executrix of this my will. Witnessed by M.D. Smallman and Annie Johnson.

pg 13-14. 26 Mar 1898. **Will of B.H. Womack.** I, B.H. Womack of Dibrell, TN, do make this my last will and testament. First, all my debts and funeral expenses shall be paid. Second, I give the rest of my estate to my sons, to wit: J.T. Womack, James A. Womack, W.W. Womack, G.M. Womack, H.B. Womack and D.P. Woamck and the bodily heirs of A.R. Griffin, M.P. Newby and M.P. Marler when of age. The minors are to have such an amount as would have been their mothers, in other words, each set to have 1/9th. I direct that my wife E.E. Womack be provided for as the law directs with homestead, etc. "Respectable tombs with proper inscriptions are to be set up over each myself and wife." I appoint my sons G.M. and D.P. Womack executors of this my will. Witnessed by John C. Gilbert and W.H. Phelps.

pg 15-20. 30 Mar 1903. **Will of John H. Savage.** I, John H. Savage made a will about 1890 and have made several wills and codicils since that time. I am in better health now apparently than I have been since 1890 and I now by this will revoke and annul all wills and codicils made by me before this time. I now will to my sister Mrs. O.W. Davis for her life, all that part of my home farm which is now enclosed by fence (800 acres) together with so much of the land as lies north of the river and which is not now enclosed. This life estate is given upon the experss conditions that she shall reside upon the land and use it as she is now doing. I also will to Mrs. O.W. Davis all my stock, household goods, etc. I prefer that the two south rooms of my law offices in McMinnville shall not be sold but kept as a convenient stopping place for the family. Miss Florence Davis has lived unmarried and has divided her time and toil to aid and care for her mother, sister and brothers--I give to her $1000.00. Witnessed 20 Jun 1903 by J.F. Morford and J.C. Biles. **Codicil:** 26 Dec 1903. I appoint Frank R. Davis executor to my will to act jointly with Mrs. O.W. Davis. He is to take management of my lands in DeKalb County, Tn and dispose of same. Witnessed by J.F. Morford and J.C. Biles. **Codicil:** 15 Jan 1904. It is my will that the home place whereon Mrs. O.W. Davis now lives shall remain as part of my estate for 10 years after my death. Witnessed J.F. Morford and J.C. Biles. **Codicil:** 27 Jan 1904. I have $8000.00 in bonds at People's National Bank of McMinnville. These bonds are not to be subject to division among my heirs for the term of 10 years. Witnessed by J.F. Morford and J.C. Biles.

pg 21-22. 29 Jun 1903. **Will of J.H. Phelps.** First, I direct my debts and funeral expenses be paid.

Secondly, I give to my beloved wife Jennie A. Phelps the farm upon which I have resided for some 20 years in the 1st Civil District of Warren County, containing 146 acres. Thirdly, I give to my said beloved wife all my personal property of whatsoever kind.. Lastly, I nominate my wife Jennie A. Phelps my executrix. Witnessed by Jesse Walling and John L. Willis.

pg 23. 7 Apr 1904. **Will of M.V. Hunter.** First, I direct my funeral expenses and debts be paid. Secondly I bequeath all my personal property, money, stock, etc to my wife Eliza C. Hunter. I do hereby appoint my wife executrix. Witnessed by W.B. Cummings and J.W. Sherrill.

pg 24-27. 18 Nov 1898. **Will of W.P. Faulkner.** First, I commit my soul to the God that gave it, then I wish my body decently buried in my lot in the new Cemetery by the side of my wife Mattie M. No costly expenditure either in burial or monument to be made. Secondly, I hereby nominate and appoint my sons Ben F. Faulkner and Hermon Faulkner my executors to sell my property and after all debts are paid to divide the remainder equally between my seven heirs, that is to say my six children and my wife Mary A., each to share and share alike. The portion going to my minor children Lida and William P., Jr. to be held in trust until their majority. The share going to my wife Mary A. to be held in trust for her and she is to get the interest semiannually during her life. After her death the principal to be equally divided between my children. Witnessed by J.C. Kirby and J.L. Mitchell. The following are the items in the little book [of accounts against the heirs.] Heirs listed there are: Herman Faulkner; Lida Faulkner; Annie Lee Faulkner, now Orton; Mrs. Mary Allien Griswold and husband S.M. Griswold.

pg 28. 7 Aug 1903. **Will of W.H. Redmon.** I will that my land that lies on the east side of Hickory Creek and known and the Old Mill Tract be sold and the proceeds be used to pay my debts. I further will all my personal property to my wife Henrietta Redmon, my house and lot in Vervilla, my timber lot in Vervilla known and the Callahan property to my wife. Witnessed by G.W. Stroud and W.M. Riddle.

pg 29. [Undated Will]. **Will of Susan Peers.** First, all just debts to be paid. Second, I bequeath to my son Harvey Fletcher Peers $2200.00, which sum includes one thousand dollars willed him by my husband William Peers and held by me during my life. Third, I bequeath to the trustees of the Ebenezer Cemetery, Excelsor, Wisconsin $100.00 to be used to keep my lot and the cemetery in good repair. Fourth, all the property which comes to my estate from the estate of my sister Hester Jorgas to be equally divided between my grandchildren George Peers and Susie Peers, children of Reuben Peers. Fifth, all the rest of my estate to be equally divided between my sons Reuben Peers and Fletcher Peers and my grand-children George and Susie Peers. Sixth, I appoint my sons Reuben and Fletcher Peers administrators of this my last will. Witnessed by N.G. Witmon and Freda Lauge.

pg 30-31. 9 June 1904. **Will of Sarah A. Cunningham.** First I direct my debts and funeral expenses be paid. Secondly, I give to my daughter Amanda M. Roberts furniture and $10.00 in cash. I give to my grandson James B. Roberts furniture and $5.00 cash. I give my granddaughter Lou Bryant and my grandsons G. Thomas Roberts, Charles S. Roberts and Firm Roberts, each $5.00 cash. I give to my grandson W.A. Moore and heirs, all the balance of my personal effects. Lastly I nominate W.A. Moore my executor. Witnessed by Francis M. Womack and W. Earnest Moore.

pg 32. 5 Feb 1905. **Will of William A. Cotton.** First, I direct that my funeral expenses and debts be paid. Second, for the love and affection I have for my two daughters Martha Wright, wife of Alford Wright and Mary Wright, wife of Marion Wright, I will the balance of my estate to be equally divided between them. Lastly I nominate H.C. Cotton my executor. Witnessed by W.I. Huston and Wamon Hutson.

pg 33-35. 28 Aug 1902. **Will of James P. Edwards.** First, my will is that all my debts be paid. Second, I will to my beloved wife Mollie Edwards 100 acres of land out of the west portion of the lands on which I now live to include the dwelling house, barn and other houses thereto attached. Third, it is my will that my wife have a horse and buggy and all the household furniture. Fourth, it is my will that the balance of my land be equally divided among my heirs and my wife. Sixth, I nominate my friend G.W. Darnell my executor. Witnessed by A.R. Hammer and R.W. Smartt.

pg 36. 27 Aug 1904. **Will of Shadrach L. Green.** First, I direct that my funeral expenses and debts be paid.

170

Secondly, I give to Amanda Mullican and Opha Green the remainder of my estate. Lastly I nominate W.D. Green my executor. Witnessed by J.R. Davis and M.G. Green.

pg 37. 22 Nov 1902. **Will of Herbert A. Clark.** First, I resign my soul to the hands of Almighty God, hoping and believing in a remission of sins by the merits and mediation of Jesus Christ. My body I commit to the earth, to be buried at discretion of my executor. And my worldly estate I give and devise as follows: First, I give to my wife Dora E. Clark my "Home Farm" containing 41 acres. Second I give to my wife, after the payment of my debts, all the stock, furniture and other personal property belonging to me. Third, I appoint my wife Dora E. Clark sole executrix. Witnessed by John D. Tewksbury, Charles E. Tewksbury and Edward F. Annable.

pg 38-40. 19 Sep 1904. **Will of M.H. Wilson.** First, I desire that my debts and funeral expenses be paid. Second, I desire to be decently interred without unnecessary expenses or ceremony. Third, I will to my beloved children all my property both real and personal, except 100 acres of land in the east protion of the home tract. At my death my executors are to sell the said 100 acres. I appoint my friends W.M. Kennedy, J.A. Cunningham and my oldest girl living M.B. Wilson my executors. It is my will that if Mannie A. Wilson stays and looks after the interest of the children until he is 21 years old he shall have one horse or the value of same. The proceeds of the sale of the 100 acres of land are to be kept by the executors for the expenses of the family. Witnessed 1 Mar 1905 by E.D. Crowley and E.M. York.

pg 41. 18 Sep 1905. **Will of Benjamin F. Palmer.** I direct that my funeral expenses and debts be paid. I give all my property both real and personal to my sister Mrs. W.C. Pierce, also known as Maggie Pierce. I appoint George L. Beech my executor. Witnessed by E.W. Crowder and W.W. Fairbanks.

pg 42. 24 Jan 1905. **Will of Fult Marbury.** First I give to Minnie Louise Spencer an heir's part, equally sharing with my daughter Martha Julia Marbury and son Ewin Boyd Marbury of my real and personal property. Second, I nominate my wife Lizzie Bell Marbury executor of this my last will and testament. Witnessed by J.P. Bostick and Lizzie M. Durley.

pg 43. 3 Aug 1905. **Will of M.A. Cummings.** First, I give to my daughter Mattie Cummings furniture and a calf. Second, I give to my daughter Mattie Cummings a notes that I hold on Arthur Collier, Jerome Collier, James Higginbotham and Aaron Higginbotham. I give to G.P. Cummings one bed and bed clothing. I appoint Arthur Collier my executor. Witnessed by J.T. Hillis and Helen Patterson.

pg 44. 20 Jul 1901. **Will of G. Permelia Lusk.** First, after my debts are paid, the residue of my personal estate I bequeath as follows: To my beloved daughter Josephine S. Lusk who has taken care of me, I give all my personal property including notes, money and accounts, stock, furniture, etc. Witnessed by J.T. Hillis and B.F. Smith.

pg 45-47. 25 Nov 1890. **Will of Caswell C. Roberts.** I, C.C. Roberts of 3rd District of Warren County, bequeath to my daughter Talitha Ann Crawford the north half of my land including the homestead, to her and the heirs of her body. I bequeath to Robert Lee St.John and Ustacin St.John the south half of my land, jointly to be equally divided between them when they arrive at their majority. I give to J.K. Roberts power of attorney and he is to be my executor. My son James L. Roberts having already received from me much more in value that I am now able to give the remainder of my children. I bequeath to my son W.W. Roberts $50.00. Witnessed by James D. McGiboney and J.K. Roberts.

pg 48. 16 Jan 1899. **Will of Adrain Northcutt.** First, I order and direct my wife E.W. Northcutt to pay all debts. Second, I give to my wife E.W. Northcutt all my property both real and personal for as long as she lives. Third, my wife has made a will and she is to see that it is to the interest of our daughter Susan Ann Ramsey and our grandson H.B. Northcutt. Fourth, my wife E.W. Northcutt is to have full controll and possession of all I own at the time of my death to do as she thinks best. Witnessed by J.L. Thaxton and Jesse Thaxton.

pg 49-50. 4 Sep 1880. **Will of E.G. Hardcastle.** First, I will my soul to God who gave it and my body to be buried in a Christian manner after the directions of my friends. Secondly, I direct that my funeral expenses and debts be paid. Thirdly, I direct that my wife Nancy Hardcastle (should she out live me) shall have support and maintanance out of my farm and property during the

term of her natural life. I have heretofore given my
sons J.P. Hardcastle and B.T. Hardcastle all my property
that I expect them to have and whereas my five
daughters, Mary Ann Hardastle, Jane Hardcastle, Frances
Emeline Hardcastle, Martha Cordelia Hardcastle and Ruth
Carander Hardcastle are now in possession and hold in
their own right all of the personal property now on my
farm. Fourthly, I direct that all my land of which I
die possessed of shall be equally divided between the
aforementioned five daughters and my son G.L.
Hardcastle, share and share alike. I appoint my son
J.P. Hardcastle my executor. WItnessed by J.C. Blair
and W.H. Newby.

pg 51-55. 5 Jan 1892. **Will of William Bouldin.** First,
I direct my funeral expenses and debts be paid.
Secondly, I bequeath to my son Henry Bouldin, Lot No. 1
on the Spencer Road between Isaac Barnes and William
Bouldin. "If Henry Bouldin intermarried with first or
second cousins this shall be null and void". Thirdly,
I bequeath to my son Charley Bouldin a tract of land
(Lot No. 2) on the Spencer road near Sink Gulf.
Fourthly, I bequeath to my son Jackson Bouldin a tract
on land in the gulf known as the big Hurricane Gulf.
Jackson is to pay $25.00 each to Henry, Tempy Ann and
Amanda. Fifthly, I bequeath to my son Thomas Bouldin my
interest in a tract of land on the top of Cumberland
Mountain in Van Buren County during his natural life
after which to go to his son Dalton. Also another tract
of land south of Nancy Bouldin's lands during his life
then to his daughter Cora. If she dies without heirs
said land is to descend to her brother Dalton. Sixthly,
I bequeath to my daughter Maude and Tempy Ann the
remainder of my land, the place on which I live and the
other lying in Big Sink, all of which lies on the south
side of the Spencer road. Should my wife outlive me she
is to be supported. The heirs may sell the above land
to one another, but I forbid the sale of any share to
anyone outside of the family. Witnessed by Frank Hill
and John Panter. **Codicil.** 7 Mar 1898. First I give to
Tempy Bess part of the old Lewis Bouldin tract. Second,
I give to my son Henry Bouldin 50 acres on the top of
Cumberland Mountain on which I now live. Third, I give
to my daughter Amanda Clark, nee Amanda Bouldin, part of
the old Lewis Bouldin tract in the Big Sink. Witnessed
by Frank Hill and John Panter.

pg 56-57. 28 Feb 1906. **Will of Mrs. Ann L. Jones.** I,
Ann L. Jones, widow of E.W.B. Jones, dec'd make this my

Warren County, TN Will Book, Vol 1, cont.

last will and testament: First, I desire that my
funeral expenses and debts be paid. Second, I give to
my two daughters Anna May Jones and Lucy E. Jones all my
furniture goods, share and share alike. Third, I give
to my three children Anna May Jones, Lucy E. Jones and
Ed R. Jones the balance of my estate. Fourth, I
nominate James C. Biles executor of this will.
Witnessed by Mrs. Elsie Crosser and Foss H. Mercer.

pg 58-59. 30 Jul 1906. **Will of Mary Jennett Telford.**
First, let all just debts and funeral expenses be paid.
Second, I will to the Womans Christian Temperance Union
of Colorado plots 12 and 13 in the city of Denver.
Third, I will to Mrs. Alla M. Shaw of Evanston, Ill one
acre formerly owned by George Gribble. Fourth, all the
rest of my estate I bequeath with instruction already
given. Witnessed by Maud Julia Vollmer, Martha Better
and Eugene Crosby all of Hinsdale Sanitariam, Hinsdale,
Ill.

pg 60-63. 14 Dec 1904. **Will of H.A. Cunningham.** I
give to my wife Sara J. Cunningham all my property for
her lifetime and at her death to go as follows: All
property I may be the owner of at the time of my death,
as myself and wife have helped out older children namely
Charles Cunningham, Fletcher Cunningham, Albert
Cunningham, and G.B. Cunningham and having given my
daughter Nora Parker $25.00, I give the remainder of my
estate of my youngest son Rona [Rono,Rana] Cunningham,
subject to the life estate of his mother and in
consideration that he pay to Frank Parker our grandson
and daughter Nora and child $75.00. He is also to pay
off the indebtness of the estate and have $75.00 for his
share. This share be his full share of the estate of
myself and also of the estate of my mother. The balance
of this personal property which remains shall be divided
equally among my children Charley, Fletcher, G.B. and
Rona Cunningham. I appoint Rona Cunningham my executor.
Witnessed by G.W. Byford and H.M. Anderson.

pg 64. 8 Jun 1899. **Will of Sallie T. Spurlock.** First
it is my will that all my just debts be paid. Second,
I give to my brother Cicero Spurlock $300.00. Third,
all the remainder of my property of every kind I give to
my sister Josie M. Spurlock. I nominate my friend E.M.
Neal of Nashville the executor of this my will.
Witnessed by Ida C. Lind and Thomas C. Lind.

pg 65-66. 3 May 1907. **Will of Pamelia Jones.** First,

174

I will my soul to God who gave it and my body to be decently interred in the ground from whence it came. Second, I will to my dear brother Rufus H. Stanley my house and lot where I now live on Spring Street. Third I bequeath to the same Rufus H. Stanley all my furniture enjoining him to pay my funeral expenses and debts. He is last to pay my grandson Horace Owen $10.00. I appoint my friend Jesse Walling my executor. Witnessed by E.D. Hammer and A.R. Hammer.

pg 67-68. 12 Oct 1896. **Will of Robert K. Hesseltine.** I give to my beloved wife Lucy L. all my goods and estate during her natural life for her suppport or the support of her children. I give to my three children, (namely Herbert E., Emma A. and Florence M.) all that remains after the decease of my wife, provided that my son Herbert E. shall pay a note of $909.52 made to R.K. Hesseltine and signed over on back of same to Emma A. Hesseltine. I appoint my wife Lucy L. my sole executrix. Witnessed R.G. Hutchins, Sr. and S.E. Hutchins.

pg 69. 6 Jul 1900. **Will of Mrs. Susan J. Woodlee.** First, I desire my debts be paid. Second, I will to Mrs. Bethiah L. Hendrix who is now living with me $150.00. Third, all the balance of my property both real and personal I will to my brother James P. Hendrix, and appoint him executor. Witnessed by J.C. Biles and William Biles.

pg 70-72. 5 Dec 18<u>54</u>. **Will of Robert Sargeant.** First, I give to my beloved wife Mary 150 acres in the 12th District of Bledsoe County, it being one half of the tract I purchased from Jacob Foust of Rhea County, TN, also 50 acres deeded to me by Bennet Roberts of Van Buren County, TN along with all the stock, furniture, farming utensils, books and papers. At her death all the real estate bequeathed to my wife be equally divided between her two sons (John William Powell and Henry Powell). I will to my son Clement Augustas Sarg<u>ent</u> $5.00 in addition to what I have already given him. I will to my son Robert Webb Sargeant $10.00 in view of former gifts I have render he and his brother. To John William Powell, son of my present wife Mary, 100 acres in Bledsoe County (it being part of a 5000 acre tract entered by Isaac Hinkle), deeded to me by Thomas Silver and his wife Anna N.L. Silver. To Henry Powell, also son of my present wife I will 150 acres in Bledsoe County being half of the 300 acre tract I purchased of

Jacob Foust. It is also my will that should my stepsons died before my wife Mary or without heirs, the whole of the bequest made to them shall go to her, and at her death to the pastor of the Cumberland Presbyterian Church at Liberty Campground so that public services can be held every Sabbath day. I appoint my wife administratrix of my real and personal estate. Witnessed Thomas A. Pope, Nap Pope, Jno. Pope.

pg 73. 31 Jan 1907. **Will of A.M. Womack.** First, I desire my natural body be given a decent burial. Second, I desire that my executors do express my entire estate to public sale, and that they sell same in lots. Third, I desire that my wife Tempie Womack share equally with my children [not named] in my estate. Fourth, I nominate my sons L.P. Womack and A.D. Womack my executors. Witnessed by A.C. Womack and F.P. Womack.

pg 74. 19 Apr 1907. **Will of Griffith T. Davies.** First, all my just debts and funeral expenses to be paid. Second, I give all the rest of my estate to my beloved wife Flora Davis and to her heirs namesy: David Lusk Davies, Walter Griffith Davis, Bessie Lou Davis, and John Morris Davis. Third, I appoint Wm. F. Elkins with my wife Flora Davies as executor and executrix. Witnessed by George B. Henegar and Elvin Elkins.

pg 75-77. 7 Feb 1907. **Will of R.G. Belcher of Viola.** First, I direct my debts be paid. Second, I order my home be sold. Third, I will that the proceeds of the sale be equally divided between five of my bodily heirs and the heirs of deceased members of my children, namely: John R. Belcher, the heirs of W.B. Belcher, dec'd, Robert Belcher, M.F. Riddle and the heirs of H.E. Riddle, dec'd (W.M. Riddle representing the heirs of H.E. Riddle, dec'd). Fourth, I have made no provision for my daughter Louella Brewer, dec'd since I had deeded her a tract of land on Barren Fork. Fifth, I will that my personal property and stock be sold, except my household furniture which I will shall be divided between my six bodily heirs. Sixth, I will that the heirs of my deceased daughter Louella Brewer be equal with the other five in the division of the personal effects. Thomas Brewer is guardian of these heirs. Seventh, I appoint John R. Belcher as my executor. Witnessed by P.H. Winton and Robert Belcher.

pg 78-79. 26 Oct 1901. **Will of John Bouldin.** First I will my soul to God who gave it. Second, my will is

that all my debts and funeral expenses be paid. Third,
I will to my beloved son George Bouldin and his children
my home place in the 14th district of Warren County.
Fourth, I also will to my beloved son George all my
furniture.   Fifth, I will my horse named Joe to my
grandson Johnnie Bouldin.   Sixth, I will my grandson
Will Bouldin my shot gun and my musket to my grandson
George Bouldin.   Seventh, I will to my granddaughter
Hattie Ann Bouldin my clock.   I appoint my son George
Bouldin my executor. Witnessed by A.R. Hammer, R.W.
Smartt and George Bouldin.

pg 80-83. 6 Dec 1900. **Will of A.R. Smith.** First, I
direct my debts be paid. Second, I give to my beloved
wife Emma Hite Smith all my household furniture, farming
implements, one horse and buggy, livestock, groceries,
farm products. I have provided her a home in a deed
executed to Butler and Byron Smith and J.J. Walker.
Third, I direct that all the balance of my estate be
equally divided between my five living children, to wit:
Butler Smith, Bryon Smith, William Smith, Lela Walker,
wife of J.J. Walker and Jennie P. Massie, wife of
Merritt Massie, and my four grandchildren, to wit:
Clarence, Rayborn, Bryon and Mary Gribble, minor
children of my deceased daughter Emma Gribble. Fourth,
advancements made to my children should be charged
against their share of the estate. Fifth, the share
given to my daughter Jennie P. Massie be vested in my
son Butler Smith in trust for her. Sixth, I direct that
the share of my estate given to my four grandcildren be
vested in my son Byron Smith as trustee. Seventh, I
appoint my son Bryon Smith my executor. Witnessed by
Frank Maddux, J.B. Biles, and J.D. Elkins. **Codicil:** 6
Apr 1904. First I direct my executor to have a marker
erected over the graves of myself and wife. Second, I
direct him to pay to Butler Smith $200.00 for the
education of my granddaughter Mary Gribble, an orphan of
tender age. Third, since making my will I have advanced
my son William $200.00 more, making to date $510.75 for
which he is to account. Fourth, after paying for the
monument and the $200.00 to Butler Smith for Mary
Gribble, I direct that the balance of my estate be
disposed of as directed in my aforesaid will. Witnessed
by William Biles, Frank Maddux and J.D. Elkins.

pg 84-85. 23 Jan 1908. **Will of J.F. Morford.** First, I
will that all my debts and funeral expenses be paid.
Second, I give to my son J.J. Morford one-half interest
in the two store houses owned jointly with Hallie Leiper

and my brick residence where I now live on Chancery Street. Third, I give to my daughter Florence M. Carson $6000.00 in stock in the 4th National Bank of Nashville. Fourth, I will that the above bequests are to be equalized between my two children, then I direct my son Charles M. Morford be made equal with them. Fifth, I will that the advancements made my children in my lifetime be equalized between them. Sixth, I will the remainder of my estate to be equally divided between my three children, J.J. Morford, Charles M. Morford, and Florence M. Carson. Seventh, I appoint my son J.J. Morford, C.M. Morford and D.B. Carson executors of this my will. Witnessed by J.C. Biles, J.P. Bostick and James Gribble.

pg 86-87. 8 Apr 1905. **Will of E.G. Meade.** First, I direct my debts and funeral expenses be paid. Second, I will to my wife Mary A. Meade all my property real, personal and mixed during her natural life. Third, at the death of my wife it is my will that all my estate be sold and paid out as follows: First retain sufficent funds to give my wife a decent interment The remainder to be distributed as follows: one half to Mrs. Minnie Smith, widow of Dr. Joseph Smith, dec'd of Ridgedale, a suburb of Chattanooga. Out of the remaining half I direct it to be equally divided into two parts, one part to E.G. Ransom of Warren County, Pennsylvania and the other part to the Presbyterian Church at McMinnville, Tn, to be used by them in payment of pastor's salary. Fourth, I appoint my friends H.H. Faulkner and Charles Colville executors. Witnessed by M.B. Harwell and W.L. Swann. Filed for probate 8 Sep 1908.

pg 88. 29 Nov <u>1886</u>. **Will of Mary Hill.** I, Mary Hill, widow of James W. Hill of Warren County, make this my last will and testament. First I desire all my burial expenses be paid and all my debts. Secondly, I desire that my son Albert Sidney Hill have all my personal property of every kind. Thirdly, I desire what money of cash notes that may be on hand be equally divided between my son William I. Hill and my son S.A. Hill. Fourthly, I appoint Andrew B. Myers my executor. Witnessed by Thomas S. Myers, Octa Myers, and Mattie Myers. Filed for probate 7 Sep <u>1908</u>.

pg 89-90. 8 Oct 1907. **Will of James P. Elkins.** First, it is my desire that all my debts be paid. Second, I desire that my wife shall have the use of my house and lot in McMinnville recently purchased of Ed Mitchell and his children on Spring Street during her widowhood. Should our daughter Mary J. Elkins remain single and live with me and my wife until our death then she shall have the house and lot free from the debts of any husband she may subsequently marry. Third, I desire my wife shall have the rents of my Cannon County farm which I got from my father in the 7th distract of that county. At my wife's death the property is to be sold and equally divided between all my heirs. I appoint my son James D. Elkins my executor. Witnessed J.C. Rankin and L.H. Barnes. Filed for probate 5 Sep 1908.

pg 91-94. 3 Jun 1898. **Will of Mrs. Virginia A. Hill.** First, I desire my debts and burial expenses be paid. Second, I direct my executors to keep $1000.00, invest it, and pay the interest quarterly to my sister Harriet Coopwood, provided that she continue to reside in Tennessee. At the death of my said sister the $1000.00 less her burial expenses be distributed among my heirs as if I had died intestate. Third, I direct that all the balance of my property be distributed among my legal heirs as though I had died intestate. Fourth, I appoint Frank Colville my executor. Witnessed by John Panter and E.L. Moffitt. **Codicil:** 16 Dec 1904. I direct that after my death, that portion of my estate as would be vested in my son Frank Hill by paid over to John C. Myers and William S. Cain to be held by them as trustees for said Frank Hill. Payment out of this trust will be directed by my daughters Sue E. Myers and Athelia Cain. Witnessed by H.S. Coopwood and W.M. Cardwell.

pg 95. 20 Apr 1907. **Will of A.S. Coffee.** First, I direct that my debts and funeral expenses be paid. Second, I give to my beloved niece Bettie Smithson all money in my possession, togther with all other of my personal property of any kind. Lastly I nominate Bettie Smithson my executrix. Witnessed F.L. Leeper and Hallie C. Leeper. Probated at April Term 1909.

pg 96-98. 25 Jan 1906. **Will of J.B. Ritchey.** First I will my debts and funeral expenses be paid. Second, I give to my beloved wife Myra Ritchey all my dividends and personal property, also one half of my interest from the use of my stock of drugs, medicines and other goods not in possession of Ritchey and Smartt. The other half of the proceeds to go to the use of my two children Alfred and Mary. To my two children A.S. Ritchey and Mary Hill Hume I will the balance of my property, all my real estate including my Texas land in Young County except my home place. Said home place I give to the children of A.S. Ritchey to be held in trust for them by their father. Lastly, I appoint my son A.S. Ritchey and my son in law Alfred Hume executors and my beloved wife Myra Ritchey executrix of this my last will and testament. Witnessed by J.F. Morford, J.J. Morford and Charles M. Morford. Probated April Temr 1909.

pg 98-101. 4 Feb 1899. **Will of Mary V. Hill.** First I will that all my debts and funeral expenses be paid. Second, I give to my sister Myra Ritchey my home place (7 acres in McMinnville) and at her death said home place is to go to my niece Mary Hill Hume and her heirs. Third, I give to Mary Hill Ritchey, infant daughter of A.S. Ritchey, my brick office and lot on the public square in McMinnville and the frame house on Spring Street, also my jewelry and piano. This is to be held for her by her father A.S. Ritchey until she is 21 years old. Fourth I will to my nephew Charles I. Smartt and Benjamin Hervey Prince 400 acres of land in Texas, a part of the 640 acre survey I own in Young County, Texas. Fifth, in view of the fact that J.B. Ritchey and wife Myra Ritchey have had the principal care and support of sister Martha Smartt, I will to my sister Myra Ritchey my furniture, books, and all household goods. Sixth, I will to Alfred Brown Ritchey, son of A.S. Ritchey, all other property, real and personal. Seventh, I appoint J.B. Ritchey executor of this my last will and testament. Witnessed by T.C. Smartt, Thomas K. Bostick and R.G. Hutchins, Jr. Probated at April Term 1909.

pg 102-104. 2 Apr 1909. **Copy of will and bond, etc. of J. Carroll Stark.** Ida Grove Iowa, Sept 29, 1907. I, J. Carroll Stark of Hamilton, Hancock County, Ill, do make this my last will and testament. First, is case of my demise, I will that all my property borh real and personal be sold and the proceeds used to pay all my indebtedness. After payment of such claims, I want my lawful wife Phebe E. Stark to take one half the balance and the rest to be divided among my five children. The balance divided so as to give my son Fred E. Stark one fifth since I have never helped him as much as the other boys. To my son Ernest E. Stark I give one fifth less $100.00. To Ben B. Stark, one fifth less $500.00. To Bertha a full one fifth if her husband makes no charge for doctor bills but let such go on certain moneys I paid Mr. Wirt for him in about 1893 or 94. To the heirs of my oldest daughter Mrs. Ella M. Wirt, one fifth of my

estate with my dying thanks to their dear mother for her
kindness to the whole family. To the heirs of my oldest
son Wilson L. Stark the sum of $10.00 to be divided
among the three children. At the death of my wife her
dower shall be equally divided between my boys: Ernest
C., Ben B. and Fred E. Stark and the heirs of Mrs. Ella
M. Wirt and to Bertha E. Pease, my two daughters. I
appoint my wife Phebe E. Stark executrix. Witnessed by
A.M. Record, H.T. Lynch and A.D. Creighton. Probated
March Term 1909, Hancock County, Illinois. On 4 Nov
1908 the will was admitted to probate. The widow
stated that J.Carroll Stark was at the time of his death
a resident of Hancock County and departed this life near
McMinnville, Tennessee on or about 28 Oct 1908 and left
surviving him Phebe E. Stark of Hamilton, Ill, his widow
and the following heirs at law: Ben B. Stark,
McMinnville, Tn.; Mrs. Bertha Pease, Keokuk, Iowa;
Ernest C. Stark, Carlyle, Montana; Fred E. Stark,
McMinnville, Tn; Edna Wirt, Kansas City, Missouri; Fred
Wirt, Kirksville, Missouri; Edith Wirt, Kansas City,
Missouri; Edward Wirt, Kansas City, Missouri; Leroy
Wirt, Kansas City, Missouri; Ernest Carroll Stark, Rolla
Stark, and Myrtle Stark, addresses unknown. Endorsed 25
Mar 1909. Phebe E. Stark gives bond in both Tennessee
and Illinois.

pg 115. 18 Apr 1906. **Will of William Biles.** After
all my debts and funeral expenses be paid I give the
remainder of my estate both real and personal to my wife
Bettie A. Biles. My one half interest in the old homestead with what notes due J.C. and William Biles I give
to my brothers and sisters. To my sister Bettie Brown
and brother T.B. Biles I give the old Biles farm and
$1000.00 as they are not as well able to take care of
themselves as the others. I appoint J.C. Biles
administrator. [No witnesses]. Probated May Term 1909.

pg 116-118. 13 May 1909. **Will of William T. Earls.** I
have heretofore given to my daughter Mollie Scott all
that I desire her to have. To my son Alex Earls, I have
given property which he has invested in land which we
divided, my part being on the south side of Frank's
Ferry Road. To my son John Beach Earls I give him
$400.00 and a bay horse. I give my daughter Annie Earls
a horse valued at $100.00 when she marries or reaches
the age of 18. All the remainder of my property I give
to my wife Sophia Earls and at her death equally to her
four children Willie, Anne, Charley and Tom. I appoint
my wife Sophia Earls my executrix. Witnessed by R.W.

Smartt and W.A. Coldwell. [No probate date.]

pg 119. 10 Oct 1904. **Will of Edward T. Annable.** I give all my real and personal estate to my wife Carrie Annable. Witnessed by Herbert A. Clark and E.H. Gens. Probated 13 Jul 1909.

pg 120-121. 2 Oct 1907. **Will of William Vaughn.** For the love and esteem I have for my granddaughter Sarah Davis and her husband Thomas J. Davis, Jr. I give my home place. This is the land I made a contract with to Venus Cope but he became dissatisfied with the contract and we set it aside. In view of my age and bodily infirmities, my grand-daughter and grandson agree to care for all my wants. I appoint them my executors. Witnessed by Wm. V. Whitson and J. Fred Murphy. Probated 9 Aug 1909.

pg 122-126. [Will not dated.] **Will of Annie Eggleston.** I want Lula Appleman to have my house and lot in Morrison. I want "the boys" to have the corn and my bed clothes and dishes and carpet. I want State Young, Sister Frank and Brother Deacon each to have one featherbed. Give my neighbors whatever they want of my furniture. If you sell the farm give "the boys" $500.00 and the rest to go to Lula Appleman. Witnessed G.W. Stroud and W.W. Kell. Probate Court of St. Joseph, Michigan, 29 Jun 1909 appointed Lula Appleman administratrix. (The deceased died on 22 January 1909 and at the time was living in Three Rivers, Michigan.)

pg 127-129. 12 Jul 1909. **Will of Florence E. Biglow.** First, I want to be decently buried. Second, I want my just debts be paid. Third, I will to my husband George D. Biglow my farm during his natural life or until he marries again. Fourth, after my death and after the termination of my husband's estate in the farm, I will that my executor sell the farm and pay to my three children Osman N. Biglow, Henry Etter [Henrietta] L. Cummings, and Willard L. Biglow $1800.00 to be equally divided between them. Fifth, I will that my executor pay to my husband the balance of the money my farm brings. Sixth, I hereby authorize that my executor sell said land and make deed to same. Seventh. I appoint my friend A.H. Faulkner executor of this will. Witnessed by A. J. Trail, MD and Eugene E. Northcutt, MD. **Codicil.** 19 Aug 1909. First, I desire that my daughter Henretta L. Cummings shall have no part of my estate and that my sons will get $900.00 each. Second, I want my executor to sell enough of my property for all my debts to be paid. Witnessed by Eugene E. Northcutt, MD and Bettie C. Kirby.

pg 130-131. [Will not dated.] **Will of R.L. Stubblefield** of Viola. First, I want all my debts and funeral expenses be paid. Second, I give to my wife Mary Stubblefield all my household and kitchen furniture. The balance of my personal estate shall be sold and divided equally between my children (Earnest and Pearl Bonner receiving their mother's share and Mary Wilson her mother's share.) Third, I give to my wife Mary Stubblefield my home place during her lifetime and appoint my son J.R. Stubblefield as her agent. Fourth, at my wife's death I give to my son J.R. Stubblefield my farm after paying the following: his mothers funeral expenses; Laura Lipscomb $100.00; Mattie Reagor $420.00; Haskel Stubblefield $420.00; George Stubblefield $300.00; Ernest and Pearl Bonner $150.00 each; and to Mary Wilson's guardian $200.00. Fifth, I appoint my son J.R. Stubblefield guardian of my grand-daughter Mary Wilson. Sixth, I appoint my son J.R. Stubblefield executor of this my last will. Witnessed by W.H. Moore, W.E. Garner and A.J. Brewer. Probated at the Dec. Term 1909.

pg 132-133. 1 Jan 1907. **Will of A.J. Denton.** Mt. Ida, Arkansas. I, A.J. Denton, born and Quebeck, Tennessee where my parents are buried, make the following statement of what I wish done with my property when I am dead: viz: At this date I owe no debts, but if at death I owe anything I wish it to be paid, also funeral expenses and a plain square white marble tombstone erected at my grave inscriber "A.J. Denton, born 1856, died 190_" costing about $25.00. I wish what I bequeath to my sister Nannie J. Wright be invested in realestate and a clear deed given to her and her natural heirs. I wish $100.00 paid to the Fanning Orphan School and to the Bible College at Nashville. I give my Burriett College Stock to Charles J. Denton; my gold watch to Otto Denton, my silver watch to Elijah Denton (T.F. Denton's son); my gold ring to Charles J. Denton; and my other personal effects to T.F. Denton. My other cash I bequeath as follows: E.C.L. Denton, J.H. Denton, Mary C. Johnson, S.J. Denton, Chellie Wright, Ethel Wright, Daisy Denton Womack, Horace Andrew Denton each to receive $100.00. To Nannie J. Wright and T.F. Denton $600.00 each. To F.R. Denton and Clyde Underwood $300.00 each. To C.C. Denton (T.A.C. Denton's son),

J.A. Denton (E.C.L. Denton's son), W.K. Dyer, A.J. Underwood and Clarence Wright each to receive one gold watch. The remainder of my estate is to be divided among my living brothers and sisters. I appoint Jesse Walling Sr. my executor. [No witnessed given.] Probated Jan. Term 1910.

pg 134-135. 14 Mar 1905. **Will of Philip F. King.** I desire all my debts be paid. I give to my beloved wife Lou King all my personal property and all my landed estate. At her death I desire my lands be sold and the proceeds divided equally among my brothers and sisters and their heirs. I appoint my wife Lou King and my friend R.W. Smartt as executors of this will. Witnessed J.B. Biles and Joe R. Biles. Probated May Term 1910.

pg 136. 29 Jul 1908. **Will of Mary Francis Humphery.** I, Mary Francis Humphery, widow of the late David Humphery, dec'd make this my last will. To my surviving children namely: N.B. Humphery, Nina H. Ross, Nell B. McAfee and David E. Humphrey I give all my property both real and personal, all to have equal shares taking into account sums I have loaned some of them in the past. An ivory box given me by my mother Mrs. Peninah Camfield, shall become part of my estate. I request J.N. Walling to act as my executor. Witnesses J.J. Morford and T.C. Smartt. Probated at May term 1910.

pg 137. 18 Feb 1910. **Will of William B. Ellsworth.** I, William B. Ellsworth, husband of Jane C. Ellsworth, being of sound mind publish this as my last will. First I desire all my debts be paid. Second, I give to my beloved wife Jane C., all my property, real, personal and mixed to be hers absolutely. Third, I nominate my wife Jane C. Ellsworth the executor of this will. Witnessed by Francis Martin, George T. White and J.W. Waggoner. Probated at May term 1910.

pg 138-140. 18 Jul 1906. **Will of Columbus Arnold.** I, C. Arnold, make this my last will and testament. I devise to my wife Clera May Arnold and my granddaughter Lena May Cooper jointly all my realestate, my wife to have full control during her life. My money on hand and insurance policy to be equally divided between said beneficiaries. My granddaughter's part not subject to the debts or control of her husband. Should my granddaughter die having issue, at her death her interest is said estate should descend to them. Should both my wife and granddaughter die without issue, the estate to be equally divided among the legal heirs of myself and my wife. I appoint A.H. Faulkner and J.O. Snodgrass my executors. Witnesses A.H. Faulkner and F.A. Rutledge. Probated 6 Jun 1910.

pg 141. 23 Apr 1910. **Will of R.L. Saunders.** I, R.L. Saunders, do this day will and bequeath to my wife Mrs. Helen Saunders all my real estate belonging to me, and also all my personal property after my debts are paid. Witnesses S.B. Jones, J.B. Davis, Major Jones, J.K.P. Webb. Probated at July Term, 1910, Warren County Court.

pg 142-143. 18 Jan 1908. **Will of Martha J. White.** I, Mrs. Martha J. White of McMinnville, do make this will. I give to my daughers Flora Harvey, widow of the late John Harvey of Lawrenceburg, TN and Martha J. McGuire, wife of John McGuire of McMinnville the house on Smithville Street in McMinnville where I now reside. Upon the death of either of these daughters, her half share shall go to her lawful heirs. It is not my desire to bequeath anything to my sons William White and Thomas White as I have heretofore given them more than a equal share. Witnessed by R.G. Hutchins, Jr. and William Thurman. Probated at Aug term 1910, Warren County Court.

pg 144-145. 9 Jul 1910. **Will of Mollie Ware.** I, Mollie Ware of District 11 of Warren County make this my last will. After my lawful debts are paid, I give my personal estate as follows: to my relatives Robert Ware, Constance Luttrell, Edd Neblett, John Neblett, Robert Snipes, Lula Snipes, Mabel Whitlock, Edd Luttrell, Roy Luttrell and Ida Lance $50.00 each, the remainder of my estate to my sister Constance Lutrell. I appoint my sister Constance Luttrell my executor. I authorize my sister Constance to pay G.W. Snipes, husband of Lula Snipes $50.00 for her three minor children. Witnessed by J.D. Herndon, Lucy Akers and J.R. Akers. Probated in Warren County Court at its Aug Term 1910.

pg 146-149. 13 May 1902. **Will of Charlie Finger.** I, Charley Finger, do make this my last will and testament. 1) I desire all my just debts and funeral expenses be paid. 2) I desire to be decently and modestly buried. 3) I will to my beloved wife Mary Finger, all my property both real and personal, except what may be necessary to pay my debts. My real estate consists of the place whereon I now live. At the death of my wife,

I will that the balance of my estate be sold and equally divided between my children or their heirs. 4) I nominate my friend J.L. Finger my executor. Witnessed by G.W. Darnell and W.S. Martin. **Codicil.** 10 Oct 1902. My property to be sold after the death of my wife and the proceeds equally divided between my two children Sam Finger and Pus Hammonds. I am not unmindful of the fact that I have other children, but I do not desire them to have a part of my estate. Witnesses G.W. Darnell and W.S. Martin. Probated at October term of court 1910.

pg 149. 19 Sep 1910. **Will of A.L. Kessinger.** I, A.L. Kessinger of McMinnville, do make this my last will and testament. My age is 73 years and am sound of mind though feeble in body. I bequest all my property to my nephew John Peak in consideration that he may have with me during my sickness through life, and for erecting tombstones over both my own and my deceased wife's grave. Witnessed by W.H. Askew, F.S. Griffith and J.P. Mullican. Probated in Oct term of court 1910.

pg 150. 5 Jul 1909. **Will of A.J. Mattison.** I, A.J. Mattison, is full possession of my mental faculties do make this my last will and testament. I will my real estate, consisting of my home place in the 1st Civil District, 44 acres, to my wife Martha V. Mattison for her life and at her death to my daughter Ora Mattison Crawley, wife of Clarence Crawley. In making this disposition I am not unmindful of the fact that I have other children. I appoint my wife Martha V. Mattison executrix of this, my last will. Witnesses R.W. Smartt and L.R. Turner. Probated at Oct term of court 1910.

pg 151-152. 18 Jun 1910. **Will of Joseph Young.** Know all men by these presence, greeting. Knowing that life is uncertain and death is certain, I make the following my last will. First, I will that all doctor bills be paid. Second, I owe my son in law S.C. Barnes and wife S.E. (Betty) Barnes $200.00 that I want paid. I also owe as security for my son Hop $50.00 due 6 Jun 1910. In 1865 I let Laura Ready (my daughter) and her husband T.B. Ready have a tract of land on Sycamore Creek in Cannon County which they have not paid for, which is as much as I can give them until the other children get $450.00. I want my two sons Will Young and Hop Young to pay the amount each owes out of their distributive share of my estate. After the above, I will that equal division be made of my estate between my children: Sarah Elizabeth Barnes and husband S.C. Barnes, Laura Ready and husband T.B. Ready, Mary Truitt and husband D. Truitt, Will Young and heirs, Hop Young and his heirs, Holly Wheeler and husband N.B. Wheeler. I have made provision for my son James Young. I name J.C. Smoot, Esq and James Young as my executors. Witnesses J.B. Shirley and J.N. Shirley. Probated in Court at Dec term 1910.

pg 153. 3 Dec 1910. **Will of Miss Margaret Smith.** I, Margaret Smith, hereby make this my will and testament. I devise to my cousin George W. Smith all my property, both real and personal. I desire him to pay my debts. I appoint him my executor and excuse him from giving bond or taking oath or making inventory. Witnesses Mrs. Lucy B. Searle, J.L. Norris, G.W. Crim, E.H. Crim. Probated at court, Jan term 1911.

pg 154. 14 Sep 1910. **Will of John B. Blair.** I, John B. Blair have made my last will and request James P. Blair is to have my house and lot where I now live and he is to see after me when I am not able to see after myself. If he does not do so the lot is to be sold and the money divided between Joise Crouch, Maude Bonner, and Bular Turner. Maude Bonner and Bular Turner, Vance and Dorsey Blair, Ruby and Pearl Blair, Elsie and Nelly Blair, Albert Blair, Latia Bonner, Carroll Blair, and John Edgar Blair are to have personal items. Maud and Bular are to have the other things in the house. James P. Blair to have the tools if he sees to burying me. [No witnesses given]. Probated Feb term 1911.

pg 155. 28 Nov 1908. **Will of Hans Nelson.** I, Hans Nelson of Warren County make this as my last will. First, I direct that my funeral expences and just debts be paid. Secondly, I give to my wife Jane Nelson all my property both real and personal during her natural life, and at her death to go to my children or their descendants, except that my daughter and her husband, Ella and Roy Gross, shall not have any part. I appoint my wife Jane Nelson my executrix. Witnessed by T.F. Stratton and John L. Willis. Probated at April term 1911.

pg 156. 18 Jul 1903. **Will of J.P. Mullican.** I, J.P. Mullican, being of sound mind and memory and considering the uncertainty of this frail and transitory life, do make and declare this to be my last will and testament. I give to my wife Jane Mullican and her bodily heirs by me my land in Dist. 12 of Warren County. My wife is to have control of said farm during her natural life and her death it is to be divided among her bodily heirs by me. Witnessed by J.G. Goff and R.L. Southerland. Probated April Term 1911.

pg 157-158. 24 Jun 1910. **Will of R.H. Mason.** I, R.H. Mason, being of sound mind and memory, but knowing the uncertainty of life do make this my last will and testament. First, I desire that all my debts be paid. Second, I desire that all my property be sold and converted into money and what is left after debts and administration of estate be equally divided "between Maud Austin Joe Mason Pollard Floren Mason the afflicted daughter of E.J. Mason and I.B. Mason children who are to represent one unit or one share Edith Thach and Willie Blake if Floren Mason should die I desire that her share shall go the improvement of the family home" [sic] I want I.B. Mason's children's share to be used to improve their family home or loaned out and the interest only used for the family except in case of necessity or sickness. I appoint W.L. Swann trustee to this fund. Third, I have heretofore advanced my daughter Dora Wilson several years ago $950.00 to pay off the home where she now lives in Texas. I have advanced my son Thomas B. Mason various amounts at various times which would more than cover his interest in my estate. Fourth, I authorize my executors to sell my real estate or personal property. I nominate H.C. Thatch and Frank Colville my executors. Witnessed by William J. Hagan and T.E. Gilbert. Probated June term 1911.

**The above are wills found in
Warren County Will Book
Volume 1
written before 1910 and probated before 1911**

Volume 1 contains wills
recorded thru 1926.

[This will was omitted from Volume 1 of this series of books of the wills of Warren County. The author apologizes for and inconvenience this may have caused]

pg 22. Last Will and Testament of Levi Rodgers.
I, Levi Rodgers do make and publish this, my last will and testament. Hereby revoking and making void all other wills by me at any time made. First, I direct that my funeral expenses and all my just debts be paid as soon after my death as possible out of any money that I may be possessed of, or may first come to the hands of my Executor. 2nd, I give and bequeath to my daughter Cyrena Stubblefield, all my old tract of land whereon I now live, except about 18 acres adjoining the land of my son Jacob Rodgers. Also I give to her 100 acres of a tract of land I purchased of Josiah Rodgers to be taken off the end of said tract. Also, I give to her my negro woman Dice for the purpose of taking care of my sister Polly Rodgers. 3rd, I give and bequeath to my son Jacob Rodgers the above named 18 acres of land, or that portion under fence adjoining his land, as above stated. 4th, I give and bequeath to my daughter Jane Rodgers, $100.00. 5th, I give and bequeath to my son Elijah Rodgers $400.00 out of the price of five negroes which I have sold him, and $150.00 which he has received heretofore, in all $550.00. Also I give to him the balance of the tract of [land] I bought of Josiah Rodgers not willed to my daughter Cyrena Stubblefield. 6th, my will and desire is that the balance of my property that I may die possessed of be sold and out of the proceeds I give to my children Polly Woodlee, Enoch Rodgers, John Rodgers, Reece Rodgers, Levi Rodgers and Cela Dodson, each $550.00 including what I have already given them, or may yet give them (an account of which will be kept) so as to make them shears equal to what I have given my son Elijah, and if there should be anything left then the balance to be equally divided amongst these my last named children including Elijah. 7th, I do hereby nominate and appoint Elijah Rodgers my executor. In witness whereof I do to this my will set my hand and seal this 18th day of December 1849.
Witnessed by George Etter and James Cope. Proven in open court _____ Term, 1850.

===

BEECH,(cont)		. J.B.	109,177,184	. James	83
. Mariah	59	. J.C.	3,10,17,26,36,42	. Joe L.	83,119
. V.H.	66	.	44,50,58-60,70-71,91	. John	83,119
. V.H. Mrs.	83	.	92,99-100,102,104-105	BLEW,Nancy A.	129
. Virginia	65	.	108,113,124-125,130	BLUHM,W.E.	157
. Virginia D.	65	.	151,162,167-168,175	BLYLOCK,J.	66
. Virginia H.	64	.	178,181	BOLES,H.Leo	112
BELCHER,Elizabeth	15	. James C.	98,108,174	BONNER,A.J.	19
. J.A.	163	. Joe R.	184	. Audy	91
. J.R.	29,154,163	. John B.	112,131	. Catherine	152,158
. John R.	15,176	. Julia	109	. E.F.	159
. R.B.	176	. Sarilda	58	. Elizabeth	88
. R.G.	154,163	. T.B.	181	. Enoch	150
. Robert	163,176	. Thomas	58	. Ernest	183
. Thomas	15	. Thomas M.	33	. G.R.	152,158
. W.B.	176	. W.H.	33	. H.B.	50,80,91,118
. William	163	. William	29,162,175,181	. J.B.	150
BELL,Bethiah L.	123	BISHOP,C.H.	72,88	. J.W.	150,152
. J.L.	19	Sam	97	. Jack	7
. Lizzie	124	BLACK,C.G.	32	. Jacob	159
. Martha	143	. C.G. Jr.	58	. James	152
. Nannie	124	. Charly	32	. James B.	149
. W.A.	124	. Jane	27	. Jennie	7
. Willie	124	. Jodie	32	. Jim B.	159
BENNETT,L.L.	55	. Mary	32,71	. Joe	150
N.E.	55	. Mary M.	58	. Latia	187
BERRY,G.J.	134	. Sallie	32	. M.L.	152
. J.D.	134	. Sam	18	. Mary	150,155
. John B.	130	. Susie M.	69	. Maude	187
BESS,Byron	137	. Thomas	2,11,96	. Miles	7,10,15,18-19,22
. E.G.	121,137	. William T.	27	. Miles Sr.	10
. Elenza G.	92	BLACKMAN,Daisey E.	50	. Milton	19
. Frankie	39,46	BLACKMORE,Daisy E.	80	. Oma	150
. I.P.	121,137	BLAIR,Albert	187	. Oscar	150,164
. John Sr.	92	. Carroll	187	. Pearl	183
. N.	139	. Dorsey	187	. Polk	19
. Rosa	121	. Elsie	187	. Pope	7
. Tempy	173	. J.C.	173	. Reding	91
. Tempy Ann	130,139	. James P.	187	. T.M.	159
BETHEL,Artomisa	21	. John B.	187	. T.P.	40
BETTER,Martha	174	. John Edgar	187	. W.C.	149-150,164
BIGLOW,Florence E.	182	. Nelly	187	. W.M.	149
. George D.	182	. Pearl	187	. W.M. Sr.	150
. Osman N.	182	. Ruby	187	. William	7,19,159
BILES,Bettie	162	. Vance	187	. William C. Jr.	155
. Bettie A.	181	BLAKE,Willie	188	. Willie	150
. J.A.	1,19	BLANTON,Hanah	83	BOOMAN,Harley	143

==

==

===

Name	Pages	Name	Pages	Name	Pages
CHRISTIAN,A.L.	22	. Beene	99	. Samuel L.	32
. F.C.	70,79	. Berner	99	. Warner E.	74
. H.J.	8	. Bud	14	COMER,F.A.	59
. Josie	79	. C.	99	. George	27
. L.M.	22	. C.M.	14,22,33,42	. George P.	59
. May	19	. Calhoon	133	. J.L.	10
. Mollie	142	. Calhoun	138	. John L.	124
CHUMBLEY,Sallie	95,97	. Charley	14	. Mai	27,50
CLARK,A.C.	64,90	. Claude	139	. S.E.	10
. A.M.	66	. Dal	14	. Thomas	29,50,59
. Absalom	59,70	. Doc	139	CONNELL,W.A.	164
. Absolum C.	81	. Frank	42,113	William B.	164
. Alice	73,132,144	. Horace	139	COOK,Jesse	12
. Amanda	173	. J.H.	22,39,42,100,112	S.A.	12
. C.T.	35,82	. J.T.	14,22,42	COOPER,Lena May	184
. Dora E.	171	. James	14,39,99,133,138	COOPWOOD,H.S.	179
. Emma	121	. Jennie	139	Harriet	179
. Harriet	133	. Jerome	14,103,125-126	COPE,A.T.	10-11,26,128
. Harriet A.	116,118	.	138,172	.	140
. Harriett A.	23	. Jess	22,99	. Ab.	128
. Herbert A.	171,182	. Jesse	14	. Abner	128
. J.B.	35,37,42,59,82	. John	14,146	. Adrian	11
. J.E.	73	. John H.	14,99	. Ashburn	128
. Johnson P.	23	. June	42	. B.C.	87
. Levisa	73	. Maude	116	. B.F.	56
. Martha E.	79	. Nan	99-100,112	. Buck	82,87
. Thubal	132	. Nancy	14,39,126	. Buck C.	80
CLEGHORN,James A.	163	. Nannie	14	. C.D.	34
N.A.	163	. Sam	139	. C.L.	34
CLENDENON,A.J.	22	. W.P.	14,22,42	. Claude	134
J.M.	22	. Widow	14	. E.A.	11,26
CLENNY,Heloise	55	. William	14,39,42	. Edmon	82
S.M.	55	COLSON,Mary	50	. Elizabeth	11
COE,J.F.	30	COLSTON,Mary	80	. F.	34
COFFEE,A.S.	63,179	COLVILLE,Bethiah L.	74	. Fannie	7
. Addela	145	.	123	. Fred	128
. C.	11,34,41,69	. Charles	74,127,178	. G.A.	34,47,56
. Halley	11	. Frank	27,29,38,47-48	. G.P.	34,47,56
. Hallie M.	63	.	50-51,54,74-75,77,80	. George	128
. Jessee	11	.	84,89,99,127,129,136	. Georgia	140,143
. Mary E.	11	.	137,143-144,157,167	. H.B.	10
. Patrick H.	63-64	.	179,188	. J.B.	34,47,56
COLDWELL,W.A.	182	. Frank R.	34	. J.N.	34,56
COLEMAN,W.F.	102	. J.F.	63	. J.W.	7,10-11,18
COLLIER,A.	99	. James Fulton	63	. J.W.M.	10-11,26
. Arthur	172	. S.L.	41	. James	10,189
. Authur	138	. Sam L.	36,74	. Jim	47

==

===

DUNLOP,(cont)	. Z. 20,42,44	. Electra 132
. V.A. 147	. Zebeda 23	. Elizabeth 45
DURHAM,W.D. 90	EDWARDS,B.R. 32	. Emer 45
DURLEY,Furman 12	. Bettie 32	. George 44,47,64,73,75
. Furmon 4	. J.C. 32,43	. 189
. H.D. 4	. J.H. 85,101	. George H. 45,70,73
. Houston 4,12	. J.P. 23,143,155	. H.R. 5,70,75
. Jinnie 12	. James C. 23	. Harriet Rowan 45
. Joe 157	. James H. 32	. Hassie 138
. Lizzie M. 171	. James P. 143,170	. Henry 45
DURR,John W. 107	. John H. 32	. Henry R. 45
. Kate 107	. Lucy 32	. J.C. 70,73
. Lucy 107	. Martha C. 23,43	. J.E. 45
DYE,John 27	. Mollie 170	. J.P. 6
. Margaret Ann 27	. Octa 118,121	. Jane 45
. Marguritte 66	. W.D. 118,121	. Jesse C. 45
DYER,W.K. 184	. William 32	. Lucy 45,47,70,73,106
EAKINS,W.F. 62	. William D. 32	. Maggie 47,70
EARLES,A.W. 71	EGGLESTON,Annie 182	. Margaret 45
. M.V. 71	ELKINS,Alfred 75,101	. Martha B. 15
. Nancy 5	. Elvin 176	. Mary 45
. T. 71	. J.D. 6,9,22,177	. Mattie 138
. Tabitha 71	. James 6,9	. Mollie 35
. Tom 71	. James D. 22,179	. Nancy 45
. Willie 71	. James P. 178	. R.R. 4,45,64,70,73,75
EARLS,Alex 181	. Jane 22,68-69,90	. 95,160
. Anne 181	. John 6	. Reggie 160
. Annie 181	. Mary J. 179	. Regie 138
. Charley 181	. Susan 22	. Stoke 137,150
. John Beach 181	. William F. 156,176	. Stokley 45
. Lina 146	ELLSWORTH,Jane C. 184	. Sue 35
. Sophia 181	William B. 184	. T.H. 35,70,92
. Tom 181	ESHMAN,J.B. 70	. Thomas H. 45,75
. William T. 181	ESTES,Jane 43	. W.G. 6,33,45,82
. Willie 181	W.B. 43	. William G. 63
EARP,Martha L. 80	ESTIL,Sophia 118	EVANS,Druselah H. 53
EATON,T.M. 134,138-139	ESTUS,Jane 51	H.B. 157,161
EDGE,Elizabeth 87,167	W.B. 51	FAIRBANKS,David 44
. G.W. 44	ETTER,Bettie E. 82	. Mr. 161
. I.B. 141-142	. Boysdon R. 45	. W.W. 102,112,171
. J.B. 23,44,131	. C.H. 6	FAIRCHILD,M. 14
. J.R. 23,44	. C.M. 70,73	W. 14
. Liz 117	. Carlie M. 60,113	FANCHER,Ann 12,14,19
. M.A. 44	. Charles M. 45	. Charles S. 14
. M.E. 44	. Charlotte 33	. J.M. 14
. Mary A. 42	. E.B. 6	. J.W. 19
. Mary Ann 23,44	. E.Bruce 81-82	. John 12,14,19

===

===

GIBBS,(cont)	GREEN,A.W.	74 . Lillie P.	163
. S.J.	43,61 . Andy	153 . M.A.	133
. William	121 . Arnold	138 . M.C.	93,133
GIBSON,L.C.	79 . B.P.	134 . M.G.	171
O.T.	79 . Bailey Peyton	122 . M.K.	78
GILBERT,John C.	168 . C.C.	129 . Malinda	98,138
T.E.	188 . Charles	121 . Margarett	2,14
GILLENTINE,M.T.	140 . Coleman	43 . Mary	129
GILLEY,A.Y.	9 . Colman	27 . Nancy	1,103
J.A.	9 . Daniel	148,153 . Nannie	121
GILLIAN,Ida	143 . Dent	129 . O.D.	113
GLASEBROOK,Mary	102 . E.H.	14,122,134 . O.D. Jr.	129
GLASEBROOKS,E.J.	84 . E.N.	113,129-130 . O.D. Sr.	130
GLENN,Harrison	37 . Eli	98,138 . Opha	171
. J.R.	56 . Ferris	153 . Oscar	138
. Levi	37 . G.B.	133 . P.D.	113
. Martha	36 . G.W.	98,138 . Parker	129
. Pheba	36 . G.W. Mrs.	98 . Rachel	14,18,22,26
. Phebe	37 . George	96 . S.	133
GODDARD,Mary	128 . Harvey	138 . S.A.	113,134
GOFF,J.G.	188 . Hervy	153 . S.M.	133
GOLLADAY,A.	158 . Homer	113 . S.T.	129
M.A. Mrs.	158 . I.T.	103,121 . Sam	14,157
GOLLADY,Alvadore	124 . J.A.	103 . Sam A.	122,134,161
. Margaret A.	124 . J.C.B.	28 . Sarah D.	129
. Peter S.	124 . J.D.	113 . Shadrach L.	170
GOODSON,A.J. 37,42,48,50 . J.G.B.		133 . Shadrack	28,129
.	74 . J.H.	93,122,134 . T.C.	148,153
. A.J. Sr.	59 . J.J.	113,153 . W.D.	171
. A.T.	59 . J.L.	133 . Willie	26
. E.	42 . J.M.	113,129,161 GRIBBLE,A.J. 54,58,66,73
. Eliza	59 . J.R.	121 .	75-76,128
. I.J.	74 . J.S.	134 . A.J. Jr.	54
. J.R.P.	21,74 . J.T.	1-2,103,153 . Alex	58
. Jack	42 . James	59 . Bob	136
. John	21,74 . James M.	113 . Bryon	177
. Milas	59 . James M. Jr.	129 . Buck	59
. N.A.	48,50,59 . Jeff	113 . C.	59
. R.V.	21,74 . Jim	103 . C.C.	128
. T.A.	59 . Joe	113 . Carroll	90
. Tempie	21 . John 98,138,153,157 . Catherine	106,114,128
. Tennessee	74 .	161 . Charles	59
GORE,Nancy C.	84 . John Jr.	161 . Clarence	177
GRAHAM,R.M. Mrs.	150 . John S.	122 . D.C.	59,90
GRATH,R.B.M.	117 . Joseph R.	129 . D.L.	54
GRAY,J.W.	50 . Lidda	113 . Elsie	82,94,113,145
Nannie	145 . Liddie	74 .	147

===

==

==

LEPPER,F.L.	11	LOCK,Emma	70,75	. Edd	185
LEWIS,Alice C.	143	. George R.	85-86	. Roy	185
. Blanch	24	. J.B.	153	. Welford	131
. Blanch L.	17,20	. J.L.	86	. Wilford	139
. Blanche	38,129	. J.T.	86	LYNCH,H.T.	181
. Blanche L.	104-105,127	. Jesse	157	LYNN,G.T.	130,134,142
.	137,144	. Sam	86	LYON,Matthew	70
. Blanche Louise	107	. Sarah	19	MABRY,T.E.	21,29
. Delila	8	. W.C.	19,153	MABURY,T.E.	43
. E.C.	17,105,137	. Will	86	T.H.	167
. E.H.	105	LOCKE,Alla	122	MADDUS,Julia A.	69
. Edward H.	127	. Buck	157	MADDUX,Frank	177
. Eugence C.	127	. Ella	149,151	Mrs.	157
. Eugene C.	127,144	. Emma	73	MAGNESS,E.J.	29,35
. George T.	104	. George R.	111	. Eddy	30
. Helen Louise	38,104	. Jesse	157	. Eddy E.	30
. J.D.	5	. Jessie	122	. Edgar	35,114
. J.K.P.	8,20	. Paralee	122	. J.E.	30
. John S.	105,127,144	. Polly	134	. J.Ella	35,114
. Leila	63	. Sam	122	. W.H.	29,35,114
. Lela	11	. Sarah A.	157	. W.H. Jr.	166
. Louise	127	. W.C.	157	. W.H. Sr.	166
. Margaretta	127	. William	122	. William H.	114,132
. Margaretta O.	104	LOGUE,Mary	88	. William Harrison	30
. Martha E.	20	LONG,Betsy M.	116,118	. Willie	30
. Russell	20	.	133	MALLOY,Mary A.	130
. S.H.	20	. Lena	151	MANSFIELD,F.	50
. Sam H.	8	. M.W.	96	Willie	149,156
. Stella F.	127	. M.Wave	116	MARBURY,Ewin Boyd	171
. Trigg	127	. Wash	151	. Fult	171
. Will	127	LORANCE,J.H.	83	. John	3
LILLARD,Martha	61	LOWRY,G.N.	136-137	. Lizzie Bell	171
LILLIARD,Martha	94	. J.S.	14	. Martha Julia	171
LIND,Ida	74	. K.E.	124	MARLER,G.B.	37
. Ida C.	166,174	. Kate	130,136	. M.P.	168
. Samuel Colville	166	. W.R.	14	. Pearl	37
. T.C.	8,50	LUCK,Annie	143	MARTIN,A.D.	128,130
. T.C. Mrs.	127	LUDWICK,Amanda B.	84	. Albert	24
. Thomas C.	27,105	LUSK,Florence	108,122	. Ben	98
.	122-123,127,166,174	. G.Permelia	172	. Bill	98
. Warner E.	166	. J.B.	29	. Brite	114
LIPSCOMB,Laura	183	. J.D.	31	. C.P.	152
LISTER,Florence	162	. John D.	60	. E.	6
LIVELY,J.M.	4,66	. Josephine S.	172	. E.C.	114
. J.M. Mrs.	162	. Louise	60	. Elijah	45,104
. Jodie M.	70	. Trousdale Mrs.	145	. Elizabeth	128
. W.S.	3,66,70	LUTTRELL,Constance	185	. Fannie	97

===

MARTIN,(cont)
. Francis 184
. G.W. 98,100,114,122
. George W. 119
. H. 6
. H.C. 10
. H.E. 6
. H.H. 142
. Hariet 132
. Harriet Elizabeth 104
. Henneyetie 98
. Henry 158
. Henry C. 155
. J.B. 142
. J.E. 161
. J.I. 75,78
. J.M. 100
. Jephey 98
. Jess 114
. Jesse 100
. Lilla 148
. Lyda 152
. Martha 98,131,141
. Mary Ann 98
. Maude 98
. Neety 155
. R.A. 34,49
. R.G. 133
. Ransom 98
. Ret 100
. Robert 142
. Suella 98
. T.J. 98
. Thomas 98
. Vila 5,28
. Vilia 25
. W.H. 133
. W.M. 61
. W.S. 186
. Watson 28
. William 98,142
. Zeb 142
MASON,A.P. 25
. Amanda A. 3,9
. E.J. 188
. Floren 188
. I.B. 188

. J.B. 3,9
. James 9
. Joe 188
. Maggie 9
. Maggie J. 3
. Mary 25
. Pollard 188
. R.F. 9
. R.H. 18,64,188
. Sallie 9
. Sallie M. 3
. Thomas B. 188
. W.A. 3,9
. W.J. 3
. W.L. 3
MASSEY,
   Fannina P. Mrs. 163
MASSIE,Fidelia 28-29
. Frank Mrs. 77
. Jennie P. 177
. Malisse 153
. Merritt 177
. W.S. 28
MATHERLY,Hartford 120
   Martha L. 120
MATHEWS,C.W. 4,19
. John 141
. Mary Louise 141
. Thomas 8
MATHEY,Bettie 85,101
MATHIS,M.G. 119
   W.H. 119
MATTINSON,A.J. 186
. Martha V. 186
. Ora 186
MAUZY,C.K. 75-76,81,95
. 98
. Charles 75-76,81,95
. 109
. Thomas 109,112,131
MAXWELL,W.M. 24
MAYFIELD,Delphia 141,146
. L.M. 141
. Stephen 141
. Steven 146
MAYO,Artildey 26
MEAD,Caroline R. 96,99

. E.G. 109,155,165
. George W. 95,99
. Mary A. 155,165
MEADE,E.G. 178
   Mary A. 178
MEADOWS,A.D. 109,132
. Emma J. 6
. F.M. 132
. J.J. 6,11,35,47,60,80
.   91,109,113,123,129
.   130,132,135,138,144
.   145,149,155-156,160
.   164
. Jane 109
. Marcus 109
. Minnie Lee 35
. W.D. 132
. W.H. 52
. William 132
. William M. 109
MEARS,B.D. 153
. Belldora 91
. G.B. 91,153
. M.E. 153
MEGGERSON,A.M. 5,25
. J. 10
. John 5,25
MELTON,Joseph 95
MERCER,F.H. 135,167
. Foss H. 97,127,174
. L.D. 12,14,19
MERRILL,Blanceh 127
   Blanche 105
MILLER,A.C. 51
. A.O. 158,162
. Alex 73
. Bettie 138,160
. C.S. 99
. D.H. 56,99,119,143
. D.S. 72,99,119,143
. D.T. 56
. Daniel 1
. David 1,87,117
. E. 51
. E.H. 51
. E.W. 56,72,143
. Ellen 114

```
=================================================================
```

==

===

PURCER,James	36,59	RANKIN,J.C.	48,64,69-70	RHODES,Bettie	113
. John	36,59		179	James H.	79
. Luke	36,59	RANSOM,E.G.	178	RICE,C.E.	84
PURSER,James	21,25,27,58	RAWLINGS,J.E.	79	Lillie	84
. Jim	21	RAY,J.H.	110	RICHMOND,Caroline	37
. John	21,25,58	READY,Laura	186	Cyrus	37,96-97,127
. Luke	21,25	. R.B.	186	RIDDLE,Charlie	163
. Malvina	21	. T.B.	187	. Fannin Mrs.	163
. Paralee	21,25	REAGOR,Mattie	183	. H.E.	176
QUICK,J.P.	13	REAMS,Jessie	63	. Henriette B.	163
Paralee	132,144	. R.H.	63	. John	163
RAINES,W.P.	53	. R.M.	64	. M.F.	176
RAINS,Ann	30	RECORD,A.M.	181	. Richard	163
. Crit	161	REDMAN,Monroe	5	. W.B.	163
. I.R.	161	REDMON,Henrietta	169	. W.M.	169,176
. Isaac	3,16,30	W.H.	169	RIGGS,George T.	138,140
. John	30	REED,Ava M.	84	.	144
. Oscar	161	REEDER,E.	111	. Sallie	145
. R.K.	30,37,48,54,161	. E.E.	59	RIGSBY,Delilia	8
. R.R.	3,16	. Edwin	111	. Henritta	129
. W.P.	30	. J.S.	59	. Nancy	129
RAMSEY,A.J.	42	. M.J. Mrs.	93	RITCHEY,A.S.	179-180
. A.R.	61	. Martha Jane	93	. Alfred	179
. Andrew	42	. N.A.	93,113	. Alfred Brown	180
. D.A.	42	. W.M.	93,113	. J.B.	179-180
. David	42	REILLY,Ninah H.	97	. Mary	179
. G.B.	158	William W.	97	. Mary Hill	180
. G.W.	80,89,101,110,158	REYNOLDS,Allie C.	15	. Myra	179-180
. H.B.	42,60	. Ann	41,83,138,159-160	ROACH,E.C.	69
. Hattie	60	. Charles	138	. E.J.	69
. I.C.	158	. Charles H.	15	. J.M.	3
. Isaac	158	. D.G.	159	. Jennie	126
. J.C.	63,166	. Dillard	138	. Lon	90
. J.C. Jr.	154	. Dillard C.	151	. Lou J.	116
. J.C. Sr.	133,136,154	. Dillard G.	15,160	. Mattie	108,159
. J.R.	88,101,110,128	. E.K.P.	30	. Mollie	69
.	130,137,151,154	. E.N.P.	41	. N.A.	14
. James	167	. E.R.P.	15-16	. S.E.	108,159
. Joe	158	. Edna S.	15	ROBERSON,C.F.	6,50
. Joseph	42	. George Francis	15	. G.W.D.	6,43
. Martha	41	. J.G.	160	. George	50
. Mary	3	. Jesse E.	15	. H.J.	50
. Rebeca	149	. Mamie	15,138,151	. Ida	43
. Susan Ann	172	.	159-160	. J.H.	6
. T.J.	158	. Sarah J.	15	. M.B.	74
. W.T.	154	. Susan Ann	15,151	. M.E. Mrs.	150
. William	50	RHEAY,J.H.	126	. P.A.	6,43-44

==

Name	Page	Name	Page	Name	Page
SMALLMAN,(cont)		. A.R.	98,177	. Tomie	87
. M.D.	30,167	. B.F.	172	. Tommy	67
SMARTT,A.W.	153	. Bettie	153	. Vera	87
. Alice	140	. Bob	158	. W.	15
. B.M.	153	. Bryon	1	. W.H.	1,22,30,33,49,61
. C.A.	154	. Butler	1,127,177	.	69,77,95
. Charles I.	180	. Byron	177	. W.O.	15
. D.C.	32	. C.W.	64	. W.R.	86
. E.W.	9,57-58,65,71-72	. Cindrilla	14	. William	177
.	78,91,95,97,100	. D.B.	113	. Wyatt	64
. F.C.	36	. Emma Hite	177	. Z.R.	15
. F.G.	10,43	. F.M.	72	SMITHSON,Bettie	63,179
. F.M.	142	. G.R.	36	SMOOT,C.M.	134
. F.M. Mrs.	139,142	. G.W.	15,36	. D.P.	3
. Frank	32	. George M.	108	. Doc	134
. Frank G.	27	. George Mead	96	. E.F. Mrs.	145
. Furman	153	. George W.	187	. E.L.	9
. G.D.	153	. H.	1,19,22	. George	134
. G.M.	10,154	. Harrison	22,30,33	. I.	134
. G.M. Mrs.	153	. J.A.	116	. J.C.	3,134,187
. Hannah	158	. J.A. Dr.	96	. J.H.	3
. Hervy	32	. J.M.	14,18,153	. Jess	134
. J.E.	58	. J.P.M.	92	. John C.	145
. J.P.	10,27,153-154	. J.U.	49	. Matilda	3
. Josie	27,43	. J.W.	22,83,98,167	. Nannie P.	3
. L.S.	54,74	. James	70	. T.M.	3
. Leucion	10	. Joseph	178	. Tom	134
. Lucien	27	. L.A. Mrs.	150	. W.H.	3,134,145
. Lucy	32,58,71,167	. Laura	87	. W.H.Mrs.	134
. Martha	180	. Lecil	72	SNADERS,James	23
. Myrick	142	. Louisa	36	. W.	23
. Nannie E.	95	. M.A.	42,81	SNIPES,Albert	69,125
. R.K.	182	. Margaret	187	. Amanda	122
. R.M.	156	. Mary	17	. Amanda J.	135
. R.W.	116,140,156,161	. Mattie	36	. Arthur	86
.	170,177,184,186	. Minnie	178	. B.W.	42,69
. Robert W.	99,116-117	. Mira	22	. Baxter	122
.	154	. Nannie	36	. C.W.	69
. S.H.	58,63,71	. O.	1	. G.W.	185
. Sadie	167	. Pete	1	. George	69,125
. T.C.	58,71,180,184	. R.F.	97	. J.A.	69,86
. Thomas C.	32	. Robert W.	90	. J.Albert	86
. W.C.	27,54,74	. S.M.	26	. J.W.	125,135
. W.D.	10	. Sallie	127	. John	125
. W.E.	75	. Sarah	70	. L.	125
. W.H.	43,51	. Tennie	156	. L..	69
SMITH,A.	1,22,30,33	. Thomas	70,133	. L.B.	86

==

```
WEBB,(cont)                      . J.W.                     30  WILKERSON,O.P.              50
. Elizabeth             167      . John                     37  . O.P. Mrs.                 80
. F.P.              116,146      . John R.                 150  . W.M.                      50
. H.B.                  128      . John W.              48,54  WILKINSON,B.C.             157
. I.G.      128,137,146,156      . Johnnie                 150  . C.L.                     157
. I.W.                  141      . L.E.                 92,117  . G.L.                     157
. J.B.                  167      . Luther E.                28  . T.A.                     157
. J.F.                   37      . Oscar                   150  WILLEY,J.H.          96-97,127
. J.H.                    5      . Pauline                 150  WILLIAMS,A.J.          156,164
. J.K.              137,156      WHEELER,A.C.               54  . Alfred H.                 97
. J.K.P.      2,35,116,146       . A.D.                39,42,64  . E.D.                      43
.                       185      . Della                    54  . E.H.                   21,29
. J.L.                   37      . Holly                   187  WILLIAMSON,B.A.            163
. J.M.                  167      . J.E.                     54  . H.C.                 160,163
. James 64,70,81,128,156        . James A.                     . H.J.                     163
. James Jr.           60,90      . Mary M.                  64  . Ida                      163
. James K.              128      . N.B.                    187  . Oscar                    163
. James K.P.            101      . S.H.          77,104,118  WILLIS,A.F.          79,117,134
. Jim               137,156      . Van                      54  . A.J.                      79
. John T.                 5      . Will                     54  . A.L.                     143
. L.B.                    2      WHITAKER,Dr.              133  . Charles E.               117
. Landis                128      E.                        116  . Farmer                   134
. M.E.                   90      WHITE,George T.           184  . H.                   134,143
. Maggie            126,137      . J.E.                     31  . John L.       138,142,148
. Mary L.               129      . Martha J.               185  .        150,152,154,169,187
. Mattie            122,128      . Mary                    119  . Sally                     79
. Nancy               14,37      . Sallie M.                59  WILLSON,Bula                25
. R.                     35      . Thomas                  119  . E.C.                      25
. R.A.              116,146      WHITEAKER,G.W.             68  . E.P.                      25
. R.D.                   37      WHITLOCK,J.H.          53,72  . J.H.                      25
. Riley                 128      Mabel                     185  . J.M.                      25
. Robert                  2      WHITSON,George M.          86  . John G.                   25
. S.C.                  167      . W.V.              8,65,115  . Kirk                      25
. S.E.                  137      . William V.              182  . Nora                      25
. S.E. Mrs.             156      WHITTY,E.L.C.              87  . W.G.                      25
. S.F.                    2      WILBER,E.F.                56  WILSON,Allen              4,12
. Sarah                 105      . Estella                  90  . Dora                     188
. Sindrilla               2      . J.M.                  56,90  . E.C.               1-2,4,20
WELDEN,Sarah C.         108      WILBUR,Alden H.            55  . E.P.                   1,20
WELDER,Sarah C.         108      . Estella F.               55  . Edward                    83
WEST,Adam               159      . Jeremiah M.              55  . Eleatha                   83
. Anna                  150      . Roy S.                   55  . Ensley D.                 12
. Audrey                150      WILCHER,A.P.              160  . Hugh                      53
. Della                 150      . Allie              138,160  . Hugh Jackson              53
. Elevis                150      . Jesse                   138  . Isaac L.                  12
. Harry                 150      . Jessie                  160  . J.B.                      12
. J.R.                  137      . R.H.                    160  . J.D.                      12
```

==

WOOD,(cont)		. Marion	170
. Vick	78	. Martha	170
WOODARD,Mary Ann	98	. Mary	170
WOODLEE,Abner	135	. Nannie J.	183
. Ada	45	. Seth	49
. Albert	3	YAGER,E.M.	87
. B.F.	106	Judith	5
. D.H.	75,91	YORK,B.H.	140
. D.W.	75	. Charlietta	126
. Dee	131	. E.B.	66
. E.H.	131	. E.M.	171
. Ed	131	. Ella	14
. Emma	95	. Lou	66,132,144
. F.E.	74-75,78,95	. Lue	73
. Frank	45,70,75,131	. Parlee	31,38,140
. Frank E.	131	. S.F.	140
. Franklee	73	. Sam Mrs.	140
. H.	135	. W.C.	126
. Harrison	131	. W.H.	31,38,63
. J.C.	75	YOUNG,Hop	186-187
. J.W.	74-75,78,95	. James	165,187
. James	3,25	. Joseph	165,186
. Lela	3	. State	182
. Levi	115	. Will	186-187
. Levi C.	115,129	ZEINGLE,C.C.	58
. Louisa	45	ZURNGLE,C.C.	54
. Lue	73	ZWINGLE,C.C.	66,73,75-76
. Mary	45		
. Polly	189		
. Sallie	135		
. Susan J.	175		
. U.C.	44		
. Zipporah	61		
WOOTEN,D.H.	75,95,97		
. David H.	80		
. Nannie E.	97		
. S.L.	22		
. Sallie	95,97		
. W.H.	95,97		
WOOTON,David	9		
WORFORD,J.F.	60		
WORLEY,Mrs.	161		
WRIGHT,Alford	170		
. C.C.	74		
. Chellie	183		
. Clarence	184		
. Ethel	183